SETTLERS IN CONTESTED LANDS

SETTLERS IN CONTESTED LANDS

Territorial Disputes and Ethnic Conflicts

Edited by Oded Haklai
and Neophytos Loizides

Stanford University Press
Stanford, California

Stanford University Press
Stanford, California

Library of Congress Cataloging-in-Publication Data

Settlers in contested lands : territorial disputes and ethnic conflicts / edited by Oded Haklai and Neophytos Loizides.
    pages cm
    Includes bibliographical references and index.
    ISBN 978-0-8047-9559-3 (cloth : alk. paper)
    ISBN 978-0-8047-9650-7 (pbk. : alk. paper)
    1. Colonization—Case studies. 2. Colonists—Case studies. 3. Boundary dis-
putes—Case studies. 4. Territory, National—Case studies. 5. Ethnic conflict—Case
studies. I. Haklai, Oded, 1972– editor. II. Loizides, Neophytos, 1974– editor.
JV185.S47 2015
325'.3—dc23

                                                            2015011263

ISBN 978-0-8047-9652-1 (electronic)

For Na'ama, Maya, and Tom
(Oded)

For Ayşe, Mira, and Teo
(Neo)

Contents

Illustrations

Maps

Figures

Tables

Acknowledgments

SINCE WE STARTED WORKING ON THIS PROJECT IN 2009, we have accumulated many debts. We are grateful for funding from the Social Sciences and Humanities Research Council (SSHRC) of Canada (Haklai) and from the Leverhulme Trust and the British Academy (Loizides). Queen's University in Kingston, Ontario, the Truman Institute for the Advancement of Peace at the Hebrew University of Jerusalem, George Washington University's Institute for Security and Conflict Studies at the Elliott School, the University of Kent, and Queen's University Belfast provided each of us with a supportive atmosphere where we could develop our ideas and advance the project. Opportunities to present numerous drafts at seminars and workshops in these institutions, as well as at various conferences, provided us with indispensable feedback. We thank the many individuals who participated in these events for their comments, suggestions, and support. At Queen's University in Kingston we are also grateful to Olga Talal for valuable research assistance.

At Stanford University Press, we are hugely indebted to Geoffrey Burn, our executive editor, for his firm confidence in this project. The inimitable positivity projected by Geoffrey provided us with vital encouragement throughout. We also thank Stacy Wagner, who encouraged us to submit the manuscript to Stanford when our ideas were only in their formative stage. James Holt guided us meticulously through the production process.

We are particularly indebted to our chapter authors for their contributions. We feel privileged to have worked with such a strong group of scholars, who without any qualms responded quickly to our many requests for revisions as we (and they) broke ground in new scholarly terrains. Without their contributions, this project would not have materialized.

Lastly, we thank our partners, Na'ama (Oded) and Ayşe (Neo), and children, Maya and Tom (Oded) and Mira and Teo (Neo). The sacrifices required of immediate family are well known to anyone who has ever worked on a scholarly book. No words can truly convey our gratitude to them for all their support over the long years it has taken to bring this project to fruition. This book is dedicated to them.

SETTLERS IN CONTESTED LANDS

1 Settlers and Conflict over Contested Territories

Oded Haklai and Neophytos Loizides

Now, Israel is going to have to take some difficult steps as well, and I shared with the [Israeli] prime minister the fact that under the roadmap and under Annapolis, there is a clear understanding that we have to make progress on settlements. Settlements have to be stopped in order for us to move forward. That's a difficult issue and I recognize that. But it's important and it has to be addressed.

—*Barack Obama, May 18, 2009*

LESS THAN TWO YEARS AFTER PRESSURING A RESIS-tant Israeli government to halt all settlement activities, the administration of the United States abandoned its demand.[1] Proponents of a halt to settlements were dismayed by this about-face and denounced the recalibrated policy. In retrospect, it appears that the newly elected Barack Obama may not have fully appreciated just how thorny the settlement issue was, despite recognizing its political significance.

Settlements in contested territories are by no means unique to the Israeli-Palestinian conflict. In fact, they have presented major challenges in many conflicts around the world in the contemporary era. To name only a few, the ramifications of settlers from Turkey in Cyprus remain a central concern in ongoing negotiations over the future governance of the island; Luzon settlers in the Mindanao islands of the Philippines are a profound source of contention; the future of French settlers in Algeria proved to be one of the toughest obstacles the French government had to overcome when it sought to withdraw from its North African colony; and Javanese settlers in Aceh, Arab settlers in Kurdish populated parts of Iraq, and Chinese settlers in Tibet have all been viewed as significant aspects of inter-communal and inter-nation conflicts.

That settlers and settlements will cause contention is not a given, however. Population movements from one part of the world to another have character-ized much of modern history. In many instances, especially in Anglo-Saxon settler societies, migration is celebrated as a source of cultural vibrancy and a desirable resource for a cosmopolitan society (Pearson 2001). Elsewhere, for instance, in the Baltic Republics, the presence of settlers has been initially contested by indigenous populations, but the latter have gradually, if reluc-tantly, come to accept Russian speakers as permanent inhabitants (Laitin 1998; Hogan-Brun et al. 2008). At the same time, there is little doubt that in many instances, population movements referred to as settlements, particu-larly those on a large scale, are accompanied by protracted, sometimes violent, ethnopolitical conflict.

Relationships between "old" and "new" populations have been examined from several angles, with immigration and "sons-of-the-soil" literatures often providing contrasting evaluations of relationships between "newcomers" and "indigenous" groups. On the one hand, immigration studies emphasize that newcomers, particularly migrants, almost never fight civil wars. Kym-licka (1995, 67–68) and, more recently, Laitin (2009) argue that international migrants are less likely to mobilize for self-government or other political rea-sons and are almost never implicated in civil war violence, even when they face security threats in their new communities. Ultimately, however, there is a significant analytical distinction between immigrants "effectively permitted" into a *non*-disputed territory and settlers introduced, as we argue in this vol-ume, purposefully, with the explicit aim of gradually transforming patterns of sovereignty in a disputed region.

Sons-of-the-soil studies, on the other hand, emphasize hostile relations between migrants and native populations.[2] Fearon (2004) and Fearon and Laitin (2011), for example, argue that sons-of-the-soil conflicts engender the most protracted civil wars worldwide. This literature typically focuses on domestic population movements involving the migration of members of one or more ethnic groups into a region inhabited by a different ethnic group in search of better material opportunities. Ensuing conflicts are, thus, generally understood to be primarily about scarce resources. To the extent that sons-of-the-soil conflicts invoke identity, it is usually only in an instrumental way, to serve the interests of self-utility maximizing (and mobilizing) elites.[3]

Thus far, the politics of settlers and settlements in contested territories has not been studied as a principal phenomenon in its own right. Considering that settlements have been a conspicuous feature of many protracted conflicts around the world, the scarcity of comparative and theoretical studies published on this topic is puzzling. Settlements, as this book shows, are a distinct phenomenon whereby demographic engineering is put into play in order to consolidate territorial control, and where identity questions often play a primary role.[4] Indeed, as Ron Hassner (2006/07) usefully demonstrates, in many protracted conflicts over territory, the disputed territory actually has little material value.

The remainder of this introductory chapter provides the comparative framework of analysis for the rest of this volume. Our overarching purpose in this book is to provide a comparative investigation of how settler-related conflicts have unfolded in different parts of the world, identify common patterns and case-specific peculiarities, and generate insights into this highly important phenomenon. There is much to be learned by comparing and contrasting the ways settler-related conflicts emerge, evolve, and resolve (or not). Why and how are settlement endeavors initiated and pursued? How do sending states and settler populations respond to ensuing conflicts in the settled contested territories? How do the relations between sending states and their settler populations transform over time, particularly if their preferences diverge and the sending state reassesses its settlement policies? Bringing together cases from around the world with many similar characteristics as well as revealing differences, this book's various chapters address these interrelated questions. Ultimately, settlers may not be the only factor fueling protracted conflicts over territories—but their influence is certainly powerful.

Settlers and Settlements

We define *settlement* as political action involving the organized movement of a population belonging to one national group into a territory in order to create a permanent presence and influence patterns of sovereignty in the settled territory. It is largely because of their political and ideological attributes that settlements are distinct from other forms of population migration and have become such an intensely contentious issue worldwide. Simply stated, in the modern era of nationalism, settlers and settlements have served as mechanisms of control and territorial expansion over disputed territories.

Settlement endeavors can take many shapes and forms. Settlements can take place in scarcely or already densely populated territories. Settlers can arrive in relatively early stages of state-building processes, like the Anglo-Saxon settlers in the United States, Canada, and Australia, or during advanced stages of expansion of existing states, including empires, like the French and British settlers in their respective empires. Settlement projects can take place in internationally disputed territories, like Western Sahara or the West Bank, or in territories contested between ethnic groups within the borders of a recognized state, like Kirkuk in Iraq. Settlers can remain linked to their sending states, but they can also gradually disengage from them and build a post-settlement state, like Rhodesia, Canada, and New Zealand (Pearson 2001). Settlers can be mostly civilians, like Turks in Cyprus, or primarily military personnel, as in the case of Polish soldiers in territories that Ukrainians claimed as their own following World War I.

One thing our definition of settlements immediately reveals is the close relationship between the demographic makeup of a population in a given territory and the processes of state formation and the shaping and reshaping of territorial boundaries. Unlike conventional immigration, settlement projects are closely tied to the physical expansion of a core state into contested lands. Indeed, the processes of modern state formation and state expansion, including imperial states, have typically relied heavily on this close relationship. The boundaries of the contemporary Chinese state, for example, were largely shaped by the movement of the Han population to outlying areas starting in the 15th century (Shin 2006). Bureaucratic institutions followed the population movements, allowing the Ming Empire to expand the territory under its control. The story of state-construction in North America is comparable. Population movements westward in both Canada and the United States shaped the boundaries of these two polities (Weinberg 1935; Frymer 2014). So significant was settler presence in the U.S. state-building project that the 1787 Northwest Ordinance decreed that 60,000 inhabitants constituted the minimum population required for a new state to be admitted to the Union. The presence of this number of residents must have seemed to the authors of the Ordinance as necessary for ensuring a permanent American hold on the settled territories. Likewise, as touched on above, Poland sought to expand to Galicia following World War I through settlements of military personnel in the territories, while some Israeli governments have sought to influence the position of Israel's eastern border through the instrument of settlements in the territories captured from Jordan in the war of 1967.

What has always been important for shaping the patterns of sovereignty is for the settler population to be identified as belonging to the racial, ethnic, or national community to which the sending state belongs, thus boosting the prospect of settler loyalty to the settlement project. The purpose of settlers, therefore, has typically been to perform the function that Brendan O'Leary (2001, 101) calls "right-peopling" the territory. Thus, to return to our earlier example, for the Ming Empire's expansion endeavor to be successful, its settler population had to be Han. Several centuries later, on the other side of the Pacific, most U.S. state-builders sought settlers who were white Anglo-Saxons. Incorporating territories that were not dominated by white Anglo-Saxon Americans was undesirable (Weinberg 1935, 160–189; Onea 2009; Frymer 2014). Hence, when the non-Anglo-Saxon Dominican Republic sought accession to the Union in 1869, it was rejected. Similarly, the settlement projects studied in this volume typically identify settlers as belonging to the "core group" or "titular nation" that dominates the sending state, such as Jews in Israel, Arabs in Iraq, or Javanese in Indonesia.

Yet although states have a definite objective in right-peopling, it ought to be noted that settlers can fail to form an ethnically or politically homogeneous group. French settlers in Algeria were not exclusively "French" but included Spaniards, Italians, Maltese, and Greeks (Lustick 1985). British settlers in Northern Ireland included both Anglicans and Scottish Presbyterians, a distinction that has shaped modern Irish history and remains prevalent in Ulster politics. Similarly, settlers in modern U.S. history have been diverse, as indicated by the introduction of "othering" terms, such as "hillbillies" to refer to those of Ulster-Scottish background in the Appalachian mountains, "butternut settlers" for southerners competing for land with northern Yankee settlers, and "carpetbaggers," a pejorative term for Yankee colonists moving south after the American Civil War. The chapter by Mundy and Zunes on Morocco's settlers in Western Sahara identifies how the plans of the sending state can be derailed when the settlers do not belong to the "right" group. According to Mundy and Zunes, Morocco had to reconsider its planned referendum on the future of the contested lands—a referendum about which it had made international commitments—when it realized the settlers might not vote in accordance with the desires of state elites.

The demographic imperative underpinning settlement projects also suggests population movement in the other direction (O'Leary 2001, 33–37). In some cases, the infusion of settlers from the "right" ethnicity or national group is accompanied by the forcible removal of the "wrong" people in attempts to alter the demographic balance (McGarry 1998; Ron 2003). For example, Greek Cypriots were forced out of Northern Cyprus following the Turkish invasion in 1974. Likewise, Kurds were forced out of ancestral lands in Iraq. And as Stefan Wolff (2004) reminds us, 20th-century Europe witnessed millions of people forcibly moved in population transfers related to redrawing territorial boundaries, including relocations during a number of Balkan wars and the expulsion of Germans from several central and eastern European countries following World War II. In his work on ethnic cleansing, James Ron (2003) concludes that since the second part of the 20th century, the forcible removal of unwanted populations has been more common in areas not yet incorporated into the legal sphere of the expanding state (e.g., Serbia in Bosnia). In contrast, strong states sensitive to strengthening international norms will avoid outright expulsion of unwanted populations in areas already included in their legal sphere of influence (e.g., Israel in the West Bank).

Settlers have been more than an instrument for creating demographic facts on the ground and improving the sending state's claim to sovereignty over the contested territory. They have also been incorporated into the governance structures of acquired territories (Lustick 1985, 81). Examples include Japanese settlers in Korea and Russian-speaking populations moved by the Soviet Union, effectively a Russian empire, to the Soviet republics. Arabs in the Kurdish area of Iraq too, as discussed in the chapter by Natali, played a significant role in staffing local administrations, and of course, French direct rule throughout its empire was characterized by French officeholders settling in the acquired territories.

In many cases, in fact, settlers have assumed a "higher status" in a disputed territory, effectively "transforming natives into serfs," as in Algeria, South Africa, or Smith's Rhodesia; the latter is one of the last cases of a polity to be explicitly ruled by a settler minority (Guelke 2012, 231). But the opposite can be observed, as well. The chapter by Loizides discusses instances of settlers forming an underprivileged group among natives, as for instance, Anatolian Turkish settlers did among Turkish Cypriots in the northern part of Cyprus. In this case, settlers provided demographic reinforcement as they settled among their "own people" (i.e., fellow "Turks") rather than the rival ethnic group (i.e., Greek Cypriots) and into an already established institutional order created by their group, namely, a Northern Cyprus state.

In any event, settler experiences are not uniform. Different categories of settlers in different contexts play different roles and relate to their settled territories and sending states differently. At least one important distinction exists between ideologically driven settlers who are politicized and justify their actions in identity terms, on the one hand, and underprivileged populations who are less interested in territorial politics and have migrated for economic reasons, especially if they have been promised an easy life and access to "empty land," on the other hand. The former category, comprised of settlers who are ideologically driven agents of settlement activity, like some Jewish settlers in the West Bank, tend to view their activity through an identity prism and are more likely to politicize. In his chapter, Haklai explains that Jewish Israeli settlements cannot be fully understood by focusing only on Israeli-Palestinian relations. Rather, in a triad relationship, settlers comprise one distinct actor whose independent actions, sometimes in defiance of the central government of the sending state, are consequential for shaping the settlement endeavor and the overarching territorial conflict. Their actions largely derive from a fundamental understanding of themselves as belonging to the settled territory; they view the land as an integral part of their Jewish being.

But not all settlers are ideologically driven agents. In several cases covered in this volume, populations are provided material incentives by sending states to settle in remote regions, like the Javanese in Indonesia, as discussed in the chapter by Eiran. In sociological terms, such non-ideological settlers can occasionally be compared with immigrant populations more interested in their personal and family advancement and much less concerned with the confrontational politics of the core state. Some settlers are passive instruments in the hands of the state, as Italians in Libya were during the first half of the 20th century. But as Pergher argues in her chapter, even under Fascist rule, there were limits to settlers' compliance, as disagreements between settlers and state authorities became endemic to the Libyan (and South Tyrolean) settlement program.

Several chapters identify heterogeneity as a factor in settler experiences. In his discussion of post-1974 Turkish settlers in Cyprus, for example, Loizides relates the low levels of settler politicization to heterogeneity in their ethnic and regional backgrounds, as well as their original status of entry, a point also made by Liaras about Sri Lanka in his chapter. Turkish governments have encouraged the settlement of Laz speakers from the Black Sea and Arabic speakers from the Hatay Province, while more recently, a sizeable Kurdish community has developed in Northern Cyprus. Settlers are differentiated not only along linguistic lines but also in terms of time and conditions of arrival in Cyprus, degree of assimilation, and political affiliation (particularly Kemalist versus Islamist parties in Turkey).

Similarly relevant is the case of Moroccan settlers in Western Sahara. The chapter by Mundi and Zunes observes that Morocco has not been "cautious" about the ethnic identity of its settler population in the region, and as a result, the state cannot be sure of settlers' commitment to Morocco's claim to the territory. Some of them may support independence. Jewish settlers, too, as discussed in the chapter by Haklai, are far from Homogenous sociologically (in terms of religious piety) or uniformly ideologically committed and politicized. In short, settlers are not a monolithic category, and they can be internally divided along multiple dimensions.

Notwithstanding variation among settlers, we caution that despite some resemblance between the immigrant experience and that of non-ideological settlers, it would be inaccurate to conflate these two phenomena or equate settlers with immigrants. First and foremost, conventional immigrants typically acknowledge and accept the existing sovereignty pattern in the place to which they are moving; their movement is not a facet in contestation over the land of destination. Settlement projects, in contrast, are political by definition (even when the settlers themselves are not politicized) and frequently rely on presenting another population's homeland as "empty land." Such an approach, of course, can have significant problematic implications for the claims and rights of pre-existing populations. This aspect, as we argue in the next section, has led to conflict in many cases around the world.

To sum up, settlers, whether politicized or passive, have typically facilitated territorial claims by creating socio-demographic and organizational "facts on the ground." Loyal settlers have been used as "a physical barrier that intersected the occupied region and made it easier to control" (Eiran 2010, 110). Settlers have typically been accompanied by state institutions, both civil and military, which they have normally been the ones to staff, thus strengthening transformation in the sovereignty patterns of the expanded boundaries. The intent of transforming the political landscape, in turn, engenders ethnopolitical conflict.

Conflict in Contested Lands

Although there have been instances where settled lands have been scarcely populated, in many cases settlement endeavors have taken place in lands to which other states and populations make claims. In some of these cases, native populations were repressed, dispossessed, and forcibly relocated, including in states now regarded as liberal democracies, such as Canada, Australia, and New Zealand. The indigenous populations were so politically and demographically overwhelmed, in fact, that no destabilizing, protracted conflict evolved (although these cases pose a set of interesting questions for native rights and reparations). In many other cases, however, native populations proved more resilient and contested changes to the sovereignty patterns occasioned by the infusion of settlers. Arabs in the West Bank; Kurds in the northern part of Iraq; Greek Cypriots; Angolans, Guineans, and Mozambicans under the Portuguese empire; and many others have disputed and fought against settlement drives.

Conflicts over contested territories have frequently taken on inter-nation or inter-ethnic characteristics. On the one hand, in the century following World War I, native populations justified their struggles in the name of national self-determination. Indeed, most of the states in existence today were established in the last century as empires disintegrated, at least partly because of pressure by local national movements (Wimmer 2013, 1–28; Migdal 2009, 169). These movements found international legal foundations for their demands for self-determination (in the form of independent statehood) in Woodrow Wilson's "Fourteen Points" speech as well as the United Nations' founding charter.

At the same time, in many instances, settlements have also been framed as a national right; the settling nation is portrayed as the territory's rightful owner. Sometimes rightful ownership can be based on a claim to an ancestral homeland, and sometimes on a claim to a promised land of destination (Anthony Smith distinguishes between two kinds of "sacred homelands: one is the promised land, the land of destination; the other the ancestral homeland, the land of birth" [2003, 137]). Indonesian elites, as explained in the chapter by Eiran, adopted a vision of a "Greater Indonesia" that heavily relied on the territorial boundaries of past empires, mainly the Majapahit. Likewise, the West Bank is frequently referred to in Israeli discourse as "Judea and Samaria," a central part of the Jewish biblical homeland and the location of the ancient kingdom of Judea (Lustick 1993b, 7–25; Haklai 2003, 796–798). And in the

19th century, the Manifest Destiny idea expressed the belief that the United States had a mission to expand (Brown 1948; Hietala 1985). Whether driven by the idea of a "return" to a land of origin or a land of destination, the process that settlements were meant to set in motion is the formation of what Anthony Smith calls "ethnoscapes," whereby landscapes and an identifiable people "merged subjectively over time" (Smith 2003, 136).

To be sure, national and ethno-religious ideologies have not always been the engine propelling the drive to secure a state hold on outlying territories through settlement. Economic considerations have also been significant. Silbey (2005, 7) argues American settlers in Mexican Texas in the early part of the 19th century were motivated by economic opportunities. Fearon and Laitin (2011, 200) attribute sons-of-the-soil conflict to tangible scarce resources (although their focus is a priori on civil wars revolving around material resources). Similarly, the chapter on Iraq by Natali in this volume suggests that Kirkuk in particular became "the center of the state's territorial expansionist and Arabization programs because of its strategic location as a source of petroleum reserves." Of course, the drive of European empires had a paramount economic imperative, or at the very least, merged economic and ideological motivations, as suggested by the comparative analysis of Mussolini's colonization program in Libya and in South Tyrol in Pergher's chapter.

Nevertheless, national and ethno-religious motivations and claims are both common and consequential. Several scholars observe that territorial claims blending national and religious principles tend to yield conflicts that are more difficult to resolve (Toft 2002; Hassner 2009). Monica Toft (2002, 84) convincingly shows that when a territory is connected to group identity, control over the territory in question becomes far more significant because it is perceived as connected to group security and survival. Goddard (2009), meanwhile, puts the emphasis on framing and how leaders justify their actions. Core states and settler populations commonly justify their actions in ideological terms, such as "keeping Ulster British," "building a Jewish state in Judea and Samaria" (the West Bank), or "turning Algeria into a New France." Ultimately, settler-related conflicts involving group identity questions do not lend themselves to a simple economic cost-benefit analysis when deciding if and how to deal with the conflict.

In this type of territorial conflict, the time factor constitutes a significant dimension. According to an interesting finding by Hassner (2006/07), the longer a territorial dispute lasts, the more entrenched it becomes. Is there a point at which the changing pattern of sovereignty in the disputed settled territory becomes irreversible? Lustick (1993b, 41–46) posits a "threshold" model. According to his theory, when the domestic politics of the sending state pertaining to possible disengagement from the disputed territory shift from the domain of regular political bargaining within the rules of the game to struggles over the integrity of the regime and the very authority of the state to determine the fate of the disputed territory, a threshold has been crossed toward irreversibility.

The dynamics identified by Hassner and Lustick should be all the more relevant for cases where settler populations make the disputed territory their new home (and where new generations of settler descendants are born). Examples from French Algeria and Dutch Indonesia demonstrate the importance of settler actors in the transition on the continuum identified by Lustick, although in both of these cases, sending states eventually retreated, and settlers withdrew along with the sending state.[5] Yet several of the most intractable contemporary territorial conflicts, including the Israeli-Palestinian, China-Tibet, and Greek-Turkish Cypriot conflicts, involve settlers as a key feature, and peaceful resolution has been elusive for decades. Thus, native nationalists have cause to be apprehensive about evolving ethnoscapes. They fear irreversible settler infringement on their putative national entitlement and often press for the settler population to be removed before the passage of time makes its presence permanent.

Furthermore, many populations resort to a sons-of-the-soil discourse to enhance their claims, even against inhabitants who are not recent arrivals (Weiner 1978; Fearon and Laitin 2011). According to Guelke (2012, 234–235), greater political legitimacy tends to be accorded to groups able to make a convincing claim for their historical presence in a territory. Asserting rights by virtue of prior presence (including earlier arrival, as many groups claiming indigeneity are themselves migrants who arrived earlier than the more recent settlers) has proven to be a useful means to enhance group legitimacy and support claims for privileges and rights over a territory and its resources in the face of demographic change (Horowitz 2000, 207–213; Lynch 2011). In such instances, the conflict can shift its focus from territory *per se* to the resources accessible via the territory, including land for agriculture, job opportunities, natural resources, or government services (Fearon and Laitin 2011, 200).

The temporal dimension can play an important role in settler claims as well. Settlers who cannot make a credible claim for return or do not have return as part of their national story may try to emphasize the longevity of their presence, a claim which in the Northern Ireland example can be traced to the 16th century (Guelke 2012, 231). When there is much to be gained from claiming early presence, relevant myths are sometimes injected into the narrative. For example, South African whites propagated a myth to legitimize their rule, arguing that Bantu speakers arrived almost simultaneously with Dutch settlers in the area of the Cape. In the end, this myth was refuted by archaeological evidence suggesting a much earlier Bantu-speaking presence (Guelke 2012, 231), yet the formulation of the myth in the first place attests to the significance attributed to time in settler-related conflicts: even settlers sometimes acknowledge the legitimacy bestowed by prior presence.

At what point does settler presence become permanent, and when is it no longer possible, or even permissible, to uproot settlers and their descendants? There is no agreed-upon answer (Carens 2000). Andreasson (2010) observes that the passage of time has transformed the image of the "settler" both domestically and internationally for South Africa and Zimbabwe. In South Africa, the term "settler" in reference to a particular part of the population has been gradually rejected as inappropriate and eliminated from public discourse. A comparable dynamic has been observed in Cyprus, according to Loizides (2011). Furthermore, the forcible removal of a population is increasingly seen as problematic today, increasing the probability that the longer a settlement project is sustained the more difficult it will be to undo it. But because new demographic facts on the ground come to define a community's entitlement to a contested geographical space, native nationalists often convey the urgency of preventing the colonization of a disputed territory and aim to uproot settlers at an early stage, before changing demographic balances undermine native claims to exclusive national sovereignty.

In the post–World War II era, or more accurately, during the era of decolonization, the settler dimension of conflict has received some (arguably insufficient) international acknowledgment. Besides Cyprus, Loizides's chapter looks at the dynamic in the Baltics, where the European Union (EU) has encouraged the naturalization of Russian speakers and even made the amendment of citizenship laws a precondition for EU membership (Ozolins 1999; Haklai 2013). The EU approach, it has been noted, does not derive from deep concern for the rights of the Russian-speaking population, but primarily from security considerations and the desire to avert domestic unrest in the European neighborhood (Csergo 2009). Regardless, the EU approach toward the

Russian speakers has been to view them as linguistic minorities rather than settlers.

For the most part, the focus over the past sixty-five years has been on the prevention of, rather than the remedy for, conflicts. Article 49 of the Fourth Geneva Convention Relative to the Protection of Civilian Persons in Time of War (1949), which lumps conflict together with occupation, stipulates, "the Occupying Power shall not deport or transfer parts of its own civilian population into the territory it occupies" (International Committee of the Red Cross 1949).[6] At its foundation, this article aims to protect a militarily weaker indigene against the actions of a more powerful state and is relevant only to international conflicts. It does not apply to settler-related conflicts within states, a problem explored in Liaras's chapter. Liaras discusses the absence of a comparable legal framework to prevent colonization of national minority territories, a problem relevant for Sri Lanka, where thousands of Sinhalese farmers were settled in the predominantly Tamil Eastern Province (elsewhere, Article 27 of the UN International Covenant on Civil and Political Rights has also been criticized for failing to cover cases of domestic colonization of national minority lands; see Kymlicka 2007a, 201–202).

Even in territories recognized by the international community as disputed, the relevance of the legal framework provided by the Fourth Geneva Convention is frequently contested. Determining whether a settled territory should be defined as occupied is not a simple matter. First, because in so many of these conflicts, the claim to the territory is made on national grounds, sending states argue that they are retrieving what is rightfully theirs. Indeed, because the dispute is about ownership, the description of the territory as occupied is likely to be rejected by settlement sympathizers. Consider, for example, the many supporters of Jewish settlers who define the disputed territories as "liberated" (Newman 2005, 194).

Second, can a territory be considered occupied if it lacked an internationally recognized owner or was governed by a foreign empire before being taken over by the sending state? This question is particularly relevant for regions gaining independence following decolonization where there is much territorial contestation. Morocco, for example, makes the case that Western Sahara never had an independent government. When Spain retreated in 1975, it handed administrative authority to Morocco and Mauritania. The latter withdrew in 1979 because of a war with the Polisario Front (Sahrawi independence movement), and Morocco took over the whole region. Thus, it can deny that it occupies territories rightfully belonging to the Sahrawis. Likewise, Israel can argue that since the British withdrawal from Mandatory Palestine, there has not been an internationally recognized sovereign in the West Bank. There has never been a Palestinian state, and the 1948–1967 annexation by Jordan, from which Israel conquered the disputed territories and which has since relinquished its territorial claim, has not received international recognition.[7] Moreover, the initial Mandate granted by the League of Nations to Britain for Palestine was to build a national homeland for Jews, not Palestinians. In both cases, the sending state makes the argument that, at the very least, it has a credible claim to the territory, one no less valid than the claim of any other party, and thus the disputed territory does not fall under the category of "occupation" as specified in the Geneva Convention. Noticeably, in 2014, it was reported that the Australian government decided to drop the label "occupied territory" from the part of Jerusalem conquered in the 1967 war (East Jerusalem) because such a label predetermines the status of the contested territory and essentially accepts the claim of the Palestinians (Ravid 2014).

Whereas international legal frameworks, despite the often-referenced Fourth Geneva Convention (and the Rome Statute of the International Criminal Court), have been largely ineffectual for the cases explored in this volume, the various chapters show that (1) conflict, (2) demographic balances, and in some contexts (3) the passage of time are consequential factors in the evolution of settlement endeavors and political outcomes. Of course, sending states can persist in their settlement efforts despite conflict, and the passage of time, as we have already stressed, makes the conflict more difficult to disentangle. By contrast, protracted conflict and limited capacity to influence the demographic balance may eventually lead a state to re-evaluate its settlement enterprise. The partitioning of the Irish island is instructive. The reasons why Britain withdrew from certain parts of the island but not others are largely related to the demographic situation and sectarian distribution created by population movements over a prolonged period (as well as the ability of those populations to mobilize support in their metropolitan centers). Similar considerations are apparent in proposals for Israel and the West Bank whereby Israel would withdraw from the majority of the territories but retain Jewish-populated settlement blocks.

History shows that when states reassess their settlement policies in light of conflict and demographic configurations, the possible scenarios are ample. If and when a sending state decides to withdraw from settled areas, settlers can acquiesce, as Italian settlers in Libya did, or resist, as French settlers in Algeria did. And when a sending state does manage to retreat, settlers can be removed forcibly, as, for example, Dutch settlers were in Indonesia; they can remain behind and be subjected to varying forms of discrimination, as happened with Russian speakers in Estonia and Latvia; or they can negotiate participation in new forms of governance, as in Northern Ireland at the end of the 20th century or in the present Cyprus peace talks. In some cases, settlers declare independent statehood in defiance of the withdrawing state, as in Rhodesia. Then there are cases where settler presence prevents full state withdrawal, for example, British settlers in Northern Ireland. Domestic politics sometimes come into play in this context as well, including the political power settlers and allies exert, an issue discussed extensively in Haklai's chapter on Israel and the West Bank. In short, there has been great variation in the contours and trajectories of the politics of settlements in contested territories throughout the world.

Overview

The era matters—a lot. What used to be a common practice during periods of imperial expansion is now highly contentious. Yet as the chapters in this volume discuss, and in contrast to conventional perceptions, organized movements of populations with the intent of influencing the patterns of sovereignty constitute a common feature of territorial conflict. Such protracted conflicts are frequently more difficult to resolve, presumably because policy options that were once available to empires to undo settlement projects by coercively removing settler populations have become increasingly less tenable. It should, therefore, be no surprise that many of the most intractable territorial conflicts in the world today, including Israel-Palestine, Northern Cyprus, and Western Sahara involve the presence of settlers.

This book brings together cases from a wide range of regions, including the Middle East, Europe, South and Southeastern Asia, and North Africa. Certain patterns appear across regions: changes to sovereignty configurations are sought after, with settlers becoming the means. Territorial conflict ensues, usually adopting a national facet, when pre-existing populations resist changes to the political landscape. Sending states then sometimes evaluate their territorial aspirations (and can decide to persist or recalibrate), taking into consideration, among other things, issues such as intensity of conflict and capacity to influence demographic trends, as well as the passage of time.

Sometimes, the conflict turns into a three-actor affair if the settlers gain independent agency apart from the sending state. A triangular relationship emerges: sending state–settlers, settlers-natives, and sending state–natives. The order of the chapters reflects the three sides of the relationship. The chapters on Israel, Morocco, and Italy focus mainly, albeit not exclusively, on the relationship between the sending state and the settlers. The chapters on Indonesia and Iraq pay more attention to the settlers-natives dimension, and the chapters on Sri Lanka and Cyprus highlight the sending state–natives relationship. This book transitions from the case with the most settler agency in the sending state–settlers side of the triangle (Israel) to the case with the least settler agency (Turkey/Cyprus). The conclusion develops some comparative insights emerging from these triangular relationships.

Notes

1. Secretary of State Hillary Rodham Clinton reportedly reinforced the president's message in an interview on al-Jazeera, stating: "We want to see a stop to settlement construction, additions, natural growth—any kind of settlement activity. That is what the president has called for" (reported in Kessler and Schneider 2009). Israel agreed to a temporary freeze of ten months but refused to extend it. In 2011, the United States vetoed a UN Security Council resolution condemning Israeli settlements.

2. Myron Weiner (1978) provides the work considered foundational in this area.

3. For an excellent analysis of this dynamic in Kenya, see Lynch (2011). Another good discussion, focusing on the Sudan and the Democratic Republic of Congo, can be found in Green (2012).

4. In some cases, demographic engineering through settlements has been combined with the forced removal of indigenous populations (McGarry 1998, 613–638).

5. For a good discussion of the role played by settlers in contesting the right of sending states to withdraw from disputed territories, see Spruyt (2005).

6. Although some might argue that the Convention applies only to war, occupation after war appears to be included. Article 49 treats occupation as a phenomenon in its own right, stipulating that "persons protected by the Convention are those who, at a given moment and in any manner whatsoever, find themselves, in case of a conflict or occupation, in the hands of a Party to the conflict or Occupying Power of which they are not nationals."

7. One recent effort to find legal grounds for the Israeli claim is a report compiled by former Supreme Court Judge Edmond Levi at the request of the Israeli prime minister (Levi Committee 2012).

2 The Decisive Path of State Indecisiveness: Israeli Settlers in the West Bank in Comparative Perspective

Oded Haklai

M ANY ANALYSTS IDENTIFY ISRAELI SETTLEMENTS IN the territories Israel conquered in the 1967 war as one of the key issues that needs to be resolved in the Israeli-Palestinian conflict (Lustick 1993b; Pressman 2003; Eiran 2010; Dowty 2012, 226–232; Elman, Haklai, and Spruyt 2014b). The significance of settlers in the context of this conflict derives from the conventional perception that partition of the territory into two sovereign states is the preferred and most feasible conflict resolution mechanism.[1] More generally, partition solutions to ethnonational conflict rely on the assumption that the intensity of hostilities between the warring ethnic groups makes it impossible for them to live peacefully together in a single state (Kaufmann 1996, 1998).[2] The underpinning, usually implicit, premise is that ethnic sorting is required for such conflict management (Kaufmann 1996, 1998; Bloom and Licklinder 2004; Johnson 2008);[3] Israeli settlements in the territories designated for a Palestinian state are seen as an impediment in this quest.

Contrary to common perceptions that view this case as sui generis, Israeli settlements in the West Bank exhibit familiar patterns observed in the introductory chapter and in several of the cases explored in this volume. First, settlement activity is a means to influence Israel's territorial boundaries by creating demographic "facts on the ground." Accompanied by bureaucratic institutions (civil and military), the presence of Israeli settlers serves to institutionalize Israeli sovereignty over parts of the putative Jewish homeland.[4]

Moreover, because the ethno-social boundaries of the nation are *Jewish*, rather than *Israeli* (see Haklai 2011, 36–48), it is Jews only who settle in the contested territories. Israeli non-Jewish settlers would defeat the purpose of retrieving the homeland.[5] Thus, the relationship among demography (or "right-peopling"), territory, and sovereignty is a main feature of this case, just as in the other cases covered in this volume. And as in the Moroccan case, discussed in the chapter by Mundy and Zunes, the international community views the indigenous population as having a right to national self-determination on the contested territory, even though the departure of European colonial powers from this territory was not followed by a state that manifested indigenous sovereignty (Israel conquered the territory from Jordan, whose own attempts at annexation were deemed unlawful by the international community).

At the same time, the Israeli experience also possesses distinctive characteristics. First, Israeli governments have not adopted a unified and consistent policy pertaining to settlements since the conquest of the West Bank and Gaza in 1967. As elaborated upon below, this lack of coherence stems partly from the dynamic interplay of variable international and regional conditions, the attributes of Israeli domestic politics, and contested notions of the relationship between territorial and socionational boundaries. Furthermore, in the Israeli case, settlers have proven to be a consequential agent of change that influences practices and outcomes beyond what is observed in most of the other cases discussed in this volume, particularly in the nondemocratic contexts. Political outcomes have been influenced by the dynamic and mutually constitutive interaction between state (and central government) and settlers.

The ensuing discussion pays particular attention to these multiple facets. Following a brief overview of the current settlements and settler characteristics, the discussion proceeds to intra-Jewish Israeli debates about the appropriate territorial boundaries of the putative Jewish homeland on which the settler enterprise is premised. The focus then shifts to the inconsistencies in state and central government approaches and diachronic changes in the settlement endeavor. The final section focuses on the settlers as consequential actors and explains how their independent agency complicates the politics of the conflict, making territorial compromise more difficult. Settlers have become an additional consequential actor, beyond the Israeli state, in the conflict as a whole.

Israeli Settlers in the West Bank

According to Israel's Central Bureau of Statistics (2011), at the beginning of 2010 there were about 297,000 Israeli settlers residing in over 100 settlements spread over the West Bank, excluding East Jerusalem. At the same time, the size of the Palestinian population, although contested, was estimated at around 2 million to 2.5 million (Lustick 2013). Whereas the bulk of the Palestinian population resides in the mountainous areas of the West Bank, about three-quarters of the Israeli settlers live in what are known in Israeli discourse as "settlement blocs." These concentrated settlements are located in relative proximity to the Green Line of 1967, on roughly 5 percent of the West Bank territory (although any determination of the exact number of settlers and the percentage of territory is dependent on where, precisely, the blocs' boundaries are delineated). In 2010, about 75,000 Israeli settlers resided in small communities in the more outlying areas, including in close proximity to Palestinian-populated areas. It needs to be stressed, however, that in contrast to many other settlement projects, such as the Iraqi one in Kirkuk, described in Natali's chapter, the Israeli settlers reside almost solely in exclusively Jewish communities (one exception is a small enclave within the city of Hebron/ al-Khalil).

Delineated in broad brushstrokes, three population types currently reside in Israeli settlements in the West Bank: *haredi* (ultra-Orthodox religious), national-religious, and secular Jews. Some live in sociologically distinct communities, such as ultra-Orthodox towns (about 30 percent of the settler population), national-religious communities (about one-quarter), or secular settlements (about 15 percent), while some live in sociologically mixed communities (about 30 percent). Furthermore, some settlements have developed into substantive urban localities while others have a more countryside character. Some are strikingly proximate to the Green Line (only several hundred meters away) and are extremely well connected to the center of Israel through highways, while others are more remote and situated in greater proximity to Palestinian-populated areas. Finally, while some of the settlers are ideological, driven by the belief that they are advancing a national mission by inhabiting the territory, and choose to reside in outlying areas, many others are motivated by considerations of quality of life, lower cost of living, or a suburban lifestyle. The latter are more likely to be found in those settlements that are proximate to the Green Line.

The ultra-Orthodox population is mostly concentrated in three towns: Modi'in Ilit, Beitar Ilit, and Immanuel. In 2010, the first two were the largest settler towns (the population of Modi'in Ilit was close to 50,000 and Beitar Ilit's was over 37,000), and they are about half a kilometer east of the Green Line. Significantly smaller than the other two, Immanuel (about 3,000 residents) lies deeper in the contested territories, over 13 kilometers from the Green Line. It is also one of the most impoverished Jewish communities.

The national-religious and secular settlers' communities are more diverse, with the former typically considered to be more ideologically committed and more politicized. How settlers have mobilized to obtain their objectives is discussed in the "Settlers as Consequential Actors" section of this chapter. It is important to stress, however, that it would be wrong to consider the secular population to be wholly non-ideological. At least one important political party waving the banner of "the Whole Land of Israel" in the 1980s cast itself as secular, namely Ha'Tehiya (the Revival). Moreover, two of the chairpersons of the Yesha Council—an umbrella organization that brings together all the local councils of West Bank settlements to represent the collective interests of the settlers—have been secular, including Danny Dayan, who served between 2007 and 2013.

Right-Sizing the Boundaries of the Putative Homeland

As the introduction to this volume discusses, settler projects in contested territories are often accompanied by national homeland claims that can have far-reaching implications for the trajectory of the territorial conflict. What is often overlooked, however, is that the precise boundaries of the putative homeland can be subject to intragroup disagreements. Sizing the desirable boundaries of the homeland may be influenced by a number of considerations, including the demographic composition of the disputed territory and the extent to which the demographic balance can be shaped by population movements. In the Israeli case, as will be analyzed in this section, several competing considerations have been at play in relation to claims to the lands in dispute with the Palestinians.

The territories contested between Israel and the Palestinians are the ones Israel conquered from Jordan in the 1967 war, including those commonly referred to as the West Bank and East Jerusalem (Israel unilaterally withdrew from the Gaza Strip in 2005 and makes no ownership claim to this territory).

Many Jewish Israelis, religious and secular, view these territories as part of their ancient homeland, *Eretz Israel* (Land of Israel). Therefore, incorporating these territories into Israel was debated as a plausible policy option in the aftermath of the war to ensure the "completeness" of the homeland territory. In this regard, the Israeli case resembles Indonesia's desire to incorporate territories ruled by the historical Majapahit empire, as described in Eiran's chapter, as well as Mundy and Zunes's description of Morocco's claim to the territory historically administered by the Moroccan Sultan ("Greater Morocco").

At the same time, Israel did not formally annex the West Bank or extend its civil law into these territories. This policy decision, which has generally been accepted as a matter of course, is far from trivial. It stands out in comparison with the other cases studied in this volume, including Indonesian policy in East Timor, Morocco's endeavor in Western Sahara, and the Italian case in Libya. Significantly, it also differs from Israel's approach toward East Jerusalem, which although it fell short of de jure annexation, included a significant expansion of municipal boundaries and jurisdiction coupled by extension of Israeli civil laws (Lustick 1997). Why was the West Bank treated differently? Explaining the atypical treatment of the West Bank can help to illuminate the overarching diachronic inconsistency in central government settlement policies.

Ehud Eiran's research (2014) points to the important impact of international constraints on the decision making of Israeli leaders. It is plausible that United Nations Security Council Resolution 242 of November 22, 1967, which called for an Israeli withdrawal from conquered territories in return for peace, was consequential for the absence of the West Bank's annexation. And yet, Resolution 242 was equally applicable to the newly acquired territory in and around Jerusalem.

Another potential explanation for the different approach toward the West Bank relates to the extent of the sanctity attributed to Jerusalem. Ron Hassner (2003, 2009) argues that sacred space is typically perceived as indivisible and is therefore a major cause of protracted conflict. Jerusalem's old city contains what the Jewish religion sees as its holiest site and is therefore considered nonnegotiable. However, it should be remembered that the non-annexed territories also contain sacred sites, including tombs and places of worship.

Monica Toft (2002) stresses the importance of territory to group identity as a source of conflict. She postulates that "for ethnic groups, territory is invariably tied to the group's identity. Control over territory means a secure identity. For states, control over territory is directly linked to their physical survival" (Toft 2002, 84). Toft's argument would lead us to expect Israel to take measures to protect its hold on all the territory it captured from Jordan, because this territory is central to its homeland and so tightly tied to Jewish national identity. Indeed, all major streams within the Jewish national movement (the Zionist movement) saw the West Bank as integral to the national homeland before Israel announced its independence. While the precise geographical boundaries of the homeland were negotiable among Zionists themselves, even the least territorially ambitious Labor Zionists, who set the tone in the Zionist movement from its early days, viewed Judea and Samaria (the historical Jewish name for the territories captured in the 1967 war) as part of *Eretz Israel* at the time.[6]

In light of this, the fact that the Israeli government has refrained from annexing the West Bank is puzzling. To be sure, as the other cases in this volume vividly demonstrate, annexation by no means guarantees successful change in the status of the territory, nor does it ensure international acceptance. Yet the absence of an unequivocal pronouncement about incorporating the West Bank into Israel signals a somewhat low degree of decisiveness about the appropriate territorial boundaries of the state, an issue that would have likely contributed to the inconsistent settlement practices since 1967.

Zionist inconsistency on the geographical position of the appropriate borders is not new. Already in the prestate period, territory had competed with other factors and values, including the pragmatism of achieving sovereign statehood (Galnor 2009). These trade-offs were never made lightheartedly and took into consideration diplomatic, regional, and geostrategic constraints (Biger 2008, 70; Galnor 2009, 76). For example, the 1937 Peel Commission's recommendation to partition Mandatory Palestine forced the Zionists to confront a very concrete choice between territorial aspirations, on the one hand, and sovereignty expressed in an independent Jewish state on only part of the putative homeland, on the other hand. In the aftermath of World War II, there was even greater willingness to prioritize Jewish statehood on only some of the territory over the seemingly unattainable goal of redeeming all of *Eretz Israel* (Shindler 2009). The acceptance of the United Nations partition plan of November 29, 1947 (UN Resolution 181), manifested the culmination of Zionist reconciliation with the necessity of forgoing access to (let alone sovereignty over) the whole of the putative national homeland in favor of the more urgent, tangible, and obtainable objective of establishing a sovereign Jewish state on only part of the territory. Ultimately, the armistice lines of 1949 did not leave Israel with control over all parts of *Eretz Israel* west of the Jordan River, and by that point, Labor Zionists had already relinquished aspirations for control of putative national homeland territories on the eastern side of the Jordan River (Shelef 2010, 34).

In the eighteen years that followed the 1949 ceasefire agreement, the relationship between Jewish national homeland boundaries and Israeli state boundaries was a moot question. Jordan annexed the West Bank, which comprised most of the territory designated by the UN partition plan for the Arab state (including the eastern part of Jerusalem). Israeli state leaders accepted the boundaries created by the 1949 armistice lines, the so-called Green Line, as the de facto borders of the state, even though they contained only about three-quarters of the territory west of the Jordan River. Shelef (2010, 43–46) has observed the routinization of Israel's 1949 borders in things such as the ruling Labor Party's educational material, map images, and leaders' statements. Even the more maximalist Zionist streams did not engage in challenging the territorial status quo (Shafir and Peled 2002, 160).

The results of the 1967 war not only reignited the homeland boundaries debate, but also made it more concrete than ever, because the Israeli state now controlled parts of *Eretz Israel* that it previously did not. As in the prestate years, the value of holding onto the national homeland did not stand isolated from other considerations, including international constraints, demographics and social boundaries, peacemaking prospects, and security questions.

Different leaders and segments of the population did not have a uniform vision, and differed in their calculus and their evaluation of the significance of the territory in question relative to other values and objectives. On the one hand, most of the Israeli Right, including religious Zionists and Likud-affiliated Zionists, held the West Bank/Judea and Samaria as fundamental to the national homeland, and therefore to their identity, even though they too forwent claims to national homeland territory east of the Jordan River. Although differing in the level of their piety, both religious and secular Rightists viewed the ancient, biblical Land of Israel as inseparable from the Jewish state now that the state had gained hold of it. Religious Zionists viewed it in religious redemptive terms: reuniting with the land was interpreted as the beginning of messianic redemption (Sprinzak 1985).

Laborites and others on the left, on the other hand, developed new conceptions of national identity that viewed narrower borders as the most suitable.

Among other things, they argued that incorporating all the newly acquired territories would create a demographic challenge to Jewish sovereignty. The occupied territories were inhabited by a Palestinian Arab population that was clearly outside the social boundaries of the Jewish nation. Granting the Arab inhabitants equal civil and political rights would endanger the Jewish hold on the state, hence undermining the Jewish state enterprise as a whole. But denying them these rights would undermine the desired democratic character of the polity. Moreover, annexation of all the conquered territories would diminish prospects for peacemaking with surrounding Arab countries (Shelef 2010, 47–48). Eventually, Labor Zionists and the dovish Left prioritized Jewish socionational boundaries, democracy, and peace treaties with neighboring Arab states over territorial expansion, and they conceived of these objectives as being more important to Jewish Israeli identity than the land of Judea and Samaria/the West Bank.

Thus, in the aftermath of the 1967 war, sizing the appropriate boundaries of the state was far from being readily decided upon in intra-Jewish Israeli debates. Various consequential actors valued rival priorities differently at different points in time. As the next section discusses, this indecisiveness was consequential for incoherence in policy and practice in the decades that followed the 1967 conquest.

Central Government Policies: A Diachronic Overview

As conceptions of the appropriate territorial boundaries remained undecided, settlement policies and practices remained contested too. Over the decades, different government ministers and state officials have had different visions and weighed diverse priorities differently.

Researchers disagree about the extent to which even the launch of the settlement activity in the first place was a product of strategic design. Eiran (2014) argues that in the decade following the 1967 war, the Labor-led Israeli government initiated a settlement enterprise in an attempt to influence the permanent status of the captured territories. According to Eiran's research of government sources, cabinet ministers believed that the fuzzy legal status of the West Bank—which unlike the conquered Golan Heights and the Sinai Desert did not have an internationally recognized sovereign before 1967 (Jordan's annexation was recognized only by the United Kingdom and Pakistan)—provided opportunities to incorporate it into Israel.[7] At the same time, the ministers understood that unilateral annexation by Israel would not gain international recognition nor determine the permanent status of the territories. Furthermore, given the precedent of the 1956 Suez crisis, they also anticipated immense international pressure to withdraw from the newly acquired territories. Their evaluations were corroborated by United Nations Security Council Resolution 242 in November 1967, approximately five months after the war, which introduced the "land-for-peace" formula and called on Israel to withdraw "from territories occupied in the recent conflict," leaving the extent of withdrawal open to rival interpretations (Dowty 2012, 122–123).

An additional factor that entered into the calculus, as discussed in the previous section, was the presence of a large, indigenous Palestinian population that was outside the social boundaries of the Jewish Israeli nation. At the end of the 1967 war, the number of Palestinians residing in the West Bank was estimated at close to 585,000, while the Palestinian population in Gaza was estimated at just over 350,000 and that in East Jerusalem at slightly over 65,000 (Ennab 1994, 64). Much of the West Bank population was in the mountainous area that separated the Jordan Valley Rift—relatively unpopulated notwithstanding the Jericho region—on the east from the Green Line on the west.

Factoring all these issues into the government's calculus, Eiran (2014) concludes that the Labor-led Israeli government, guided by the assumption that population movements are more difficult to reverse than unilateral declarations, sought to launch a settlement project in lands that were relatively unpopulated by Palestinians and could influence the position of the future border. Given this intent, Israeli leaders were in no hurry to enter into negotiations with neighboring Arab states over the future of the West Bank. On the contrary, delays increased territorial aggrandizement opportunities. The belief that time was on Israel's side and that, therefore, the Arabs had to make the first move for peace is well captured in the famous statement by Minister of Defense Moshe Dayan, "I'm waiting for the phone to ring" (cited in Oren 2002, 315).

In contrast to Eiran, Gershom Gorenberg (2006) highlights the lack of intentionality in, or (to use his word) the "accidental" character of, the settlement drive in the first ten years. First, he points out that the government never formally adopted any particular plan. According to Gorenberg, in the first few years, many in the governing party were "confused: They had accepted the need for partition, yet the music of biblical names such as Hebron and

Jericho aroused them as well" (Gorenberg 2006, 49). The lack of a clear and unified government vision is well illustrated in the first part of a statement by the security-minded Deputy Prime Minister Yigal Allon before the Labor Party Convention in 1969: "While the government decided not to decide on the future borders of Israel, it made a number of decisions about security-based settlement activity" (cited in Eiran 2014, 215).

Shafir and Peled (2002, 160) concur that some of the very first settlements "were established . . . in spite of the government's inability to decide on the fate of the West Bank." According to Shafir and Peled (2002) and Gorenberg (2006), as a result of internal cabinet disagreements in the first years, it was the actions of individual influential ministers pushing in different directions, rather than the central government as a whole, that ultimately proved most consequential. Some of these ministers were primarily motivated by the homeland redemption sentiment, and some were primarily concerned with security; others reasoned that Israel could not grant citizenship to a large number of Palestinians, or alternatively rule over them, and thus had to use the territories as a bargaining chip in future negotiations for peace (Shafir and Peled 2002, 160–165; Gorenberg 2006, 48–71). Internal and personal rivalries were also at play and influenced the behavior of politicians. For example, Defense Minister Shimon Peres used his position to provide military protection for settler ideologues who built illegal outposts, in defiance of his bitter rival Prime Minister Yitzhak Rabin and Foreign Minister Yigal Allon, both of whom disapproved of this settlement activity and planned to concede the settled land to Jordan in return for a peace agreement. Meanwhile, Allon, who in addition to serving as foreign minister from 1974 to 1977 was also deputy prime minister for many years, sponsored settlements in the Golan Heights, even though the government had decided to trade these territories for peace with Syria (Shafir and Peled 2002, 160). And Moshe Dayan, who served as minister of defense from 1967–1974, opposed settling the Golan Heights but sponsored settlements in the Gaza Strip (which had been captured from Egypt).

By the time Labor was deposed from power in 1977, there were approximately 4,500 settlers in the territories of the West Bank (Central Bureau of Statistics 1978, 35). Of these, about 2,000 resided in the Jordan Valley Rift, which is where Allon—who formulated a plan that carries his name but was never formally adopted by the government—envisioned the desirable eastern border, for security considerations rather than homeland redemption. The Allon

Plan eschewed settlements in the Arab-populated, mountainous areas of the West Bank and envisioned ceding these territories to Jordan in a peace agreement. Some settlers resided in vicinities surrounding Jerusalem, also included in the Allon Plan. The rest of the settlers were ideologues who settled at their own initiative in places of historical and religious significance. It is important to stress that many of the settler-led initiatives were in regions the government sought to avoid settling because they were populated by Palestinians. In fact, many scholars have identified that such settlements were forced on the Labor government (albeit with the assistance of some sympathetic ministers, as mentioned earlier in relation to Defense Minister Peres), which ultimately decided against confronting settler activists in many instances (Newman 1985, 2005, 194–195; Haklai 2007, 722–723).

The fact that the number of settlers was small after ten years of occupation lends some credence to Gorenberg's (2006) skepticism. Had the government adopted a comprehensive and coherent grand design, it could not have seriously anticipated that 4,500 settlers would suffice to alter the demographic composition of the occupied territories in a consequential way. The fact of the matter was that in the area the Labor government was resolved to retain, East Jerusalem, it took far more resolute steps, redrawing the municipal boundaries, extending Israeli civil law, and significantly, building many more new neighborhoods for Jewish citizens. Furthermore, because the number of settlers living in the Jordan Valley Rift by 1977 reached only 2,000, Shafir and Peled (2002, 161) conclude that even this component of Allon's settlements plan was "implemented only half-heartedly by Labor governments."

When the more hawkish Likud came to power in 1977, the settlement project gained a significant boost, as the homeland redemption motivation came to the forefront and had considerable practical consequences. With Likud finding its ideological roots in Revisionist Zionism, its vision of the putative homeland was always geographically greater than that of Labor. Furthermore, the Revisionists always gave homeland territory far greater weight in their calculus. Thus, the Revisionists, in contrast to Labor, objected to the UN partition plan of 1947 on ideological grounds (Naor 2001). In fact, the Revisionists saw all of the territory under the original British Mandate for Palestine, including the East Bank of the Jordan River, which was part of the Jordanian state between 1949 and 1967, as part of the historical homeland. Accordingly, as far as Likud was concerned in 1977, by accepting an Israeli state only on the territory west of the Jordan River, it had already made a significant territorial compromise.

In contrast to common criticism, Likud was not oblivious to the decisive impact of demography. On the contrary, its settlement drive was premised on a recognition that changing the demographic composition of the territory was paramount for its future incorporation into the state (formal annexation was therefore premature and not an immediate priority). One prominent and ambitious vision sought to settle 100,000 Jews by 1985 and 1.3 million Jews by 2010.[8] Lustick points out that the planners did not expect the settlement drive to yield a Jewish majority (they projected 1.8 million Arab inhabitants in the territory in 2010), nor did they identify a tipping point whereby demographic change would prevent any outcome other than incorporating the territories into Israel. Rather, one of their main objectives was "to transform the image of the territories in the psyche of Israelis" (Lustick 1993b, 32–33) and cultivate an attitude toward Judea and Samaria as inseparable from Israel, partly through the permanent settlement of Israeli Jews.

To this end, it is worth noting that the Hebrew term used for settlements in Judea and Samaria/the West Bank is *hitnachalut*, as opposed to *hityashvut*. The latter is used in reference to conventional settlements. The former is a derivative of *nahalah*, which refers literally to land inheritance that transfers through generations. Judea and Samaria are regarded as *nahalat avot*, meaning land inheritance of the nation's fathers. The settlement endeavor is thus portrayed as redemptive, dealing with the retrieval of land believed to be the nation's rightful historical inheritance.

Close to 100,000 settlers moved into almost 100 new settlements in the West Bank/Judea and Samaria from 1977 through 1990. All types of settlements were built for diverse populations in different parts of the disputed territory, including urban and rural; suburban and remote; and ultra-Orthodox, religious-Zionist, secular, and mixed populations. Significantly, many of these settlements were constructed in areas of the West Bank/Judea and Samaria that previous Labor governments were keen to leave unsettled, namely the mountainous areas heavily populated by Palestinians.

To enhance the *hitnachaluyot* enterprise and given the limited pool of ideologues, the central government provided incentives for constructors to build in the West Bank and for homebuyers to cross the Green Line (Benvenisty 1984, 1986). Among other things, "the government charged construction companies only 5 percent of the value of the land, while in nearby areas on the Israeli side of the border they were obliged to pay 80 percent" (Shafir and Peled 2002, 173). Not only was the cost of housing much cheaper, but the government also offered considerable subsidies, grants, and concessional loans to buyers relocating across the Green Line. Many resources were dedicated to infrastructural projects and road construction to make the settlements more appealing to those looking to enhance their quality of life (Lustick 1993b, 33–34). The dynamic of providing economic incentives for relocation during this period is strikingly similar to that observed in many of the other cases in this volume.

Ultimately, the settlements built during this period were to shape the geographical map of Jewish presence in the territories conquered in the 1967 war. Although the number of settlers grew dramatically throughout the 1990s and 2000s, much of the growth occurred in already existing settlements and settlement blocs, altering primarily the demographics of the West Bank; however, it is important to remember that the geography of population distribution hardly changed.

To be sure, between 1984 and 1990, Labor was complicit in the growth of settlements, as it participated with Likud in national unity governments during these six years and even held the premiership from 1984 to 1986. And yet, as long as Likud did not annex these territories, Labor could conceive of reaching a land-for-peace treaty with Jordan over some of the territories captured in the 1967 war.

However, Labor's calculus was forced to change dramatically following King Hussein's declaration in May 1988 that Jordan was withdrawing its claim to the West Bank and was supporting the Palestinian claim to statehood. Under the new circumstances, settlements and Israeli annexation of East Jerusalem gained a whole new meaning that, although it took time to process, could not be ignored by the Laborites. To put it in simple terms, Jordan already had a capital city in Amman, and at roughly 89,340 sq km (excluding the disputed territory), Jordan was relatively large in regional terms. The West Bank and East Jerusalem (roughly 5,640 sq km) were at its outskirts, and, rightly or wrongly, it was more conceivable to Labor leaders that Jordan could be swayed to compromise on parts of the territories in dispute. The Palestinians as a national and political entity independent of Jordan, in contrast, were in a significantly different situation. The Palestinians had no territories other than the occupied West Bank and the Gaza Strip. In this new context, the implications of the settlements were substantively different, particularly settlements that were in the midst of the Palestinian population and at the heart of the would-be Palestinian polity.

Thus, after Labor regained power in 1992 and the government signed the Declaration of Principles on Interim Self-Government Arrangements (Oslo Accords) with the Palestine Liberation Organization (PLO), the government took a tougher stance on settlements. Prime Minister Rabin differentiated between what he referred to as "security settlements," which included those in the areas of the Allon Plan as well as the suburban ones in proximity to the Green Line, and the "political settlements" of the ideologues in the midst of Palestinian population centers (Haklai 2007, 723). The term "drying the settlements" infiltrated the discourse, and subsidies and grants were reduced significantly (although they were restored when Likud came back to power in 1996). Furthermore, Rabin used derogatory language in reference to protesting settler activists, such as the often-referenced "propellers" (Haklai 2003, 801). That said, the Labor government did build the ultra-Orthodox city settlement of Modi'in Ilit, about half a kilometer east of the Green Line, which has grown to be the largest Jewish settlement in the West Bank. With a population of about 50,000 people in 2010, this town accounts for a large portion of the total settler population growth since the early 1990s. Nevertheless, to the extent that preceding Likud governments sought to promote an understanding in the minds of Israelis that Judea and Samaria are integral to Israel, the Labor government in effect looked to do the opposite by depicting the ideological settlers as others and as undermining the state.

The new Labor-led government approach resulted in a raucous political atmosphere, reflecting the intense dispute over the link between the appropriate boundaries of the territorial homeland and the very identity of the nation (Waxman 2014). Israeli hardliners in the 1990s saw the very pillars of their national identity undermined and thus resisted the Oslo process with vigor (Haklai 2003).

The longer-term impact of the Oslo peace process on settlements has been dual. On the one hand, government construction of new settlements has slowed down, even after Likud regained power in 1996. Ultimately, even right-wing governments were forced to consider the changing regional environment and international constraints in their calculus. Among other things, commitments made in 1995 in what is known as "Oslo 2"; the internationally backed Roadmap to Peace, introduced in 2002–2003; and pressure by the Obama administration in 2009 for a settlement freeze, have all constrained Israeli governments of different ideological stripes.

Furthermore, in the two decades that followed the signing of the Oslo Accords, and despite the elusiveness of peace, Israelis at large have gradually adjusted to the idea that further partition of the territory is necessary for managing their dispute with the Palestinians. With most international proposals—including the 2000 Clinton Parameters and the American-initiated Roadmap to Peace—being premised on partition, the debate turned far less divisive in the 2000s, as Israelis overwhelmingly shifted their support toward a two-state solution (Elman, Haklai, and Spruyt 2014b). Even the Likud Prime Minister Binyamin Netanyahu publicly pronounced his endorsement of this conflict resolution mechanism in his famous Bar Ilan speech (Elman, Haklai, and Spruyt 2014b, 11), a declaration that would have been unthinkable among Likudniks only two decades earlier.

The route of the security/separation barrier that was unilaterally built by Israel following the second *Intifada* is also informative; many of the settlements that are proximate to the Green Line are on the Israeli side of the barrier, whereas many of the more outlying and ideological settlements were left on the Palestinian side. Thus, according to Waxman (2014), most Israelis, including many among the political hawks, have come to accept that the presence of an indigenous Palestinian population in the contested territories requires adjusting the appropriate boundaries of the Israeli state along borders narrower than those envisioned by the Revisionist and religious Zionists. Waxman suggests that the question of withdrawal from homeland territory has become one largely of extent rather than of principle.

At the same time, the number of settlers in the West Bank (as opposed to officially built new settlements) had almost tripled since the Oslo process began. As noted earlier, by the beginning of 2010, close to 300,000 Jewish settlers resided in over 100 settlements in the West Bank territories (Central Bureau of Statistics 2011, 92) and about 350,000 in 2013 (Central Bureau of Statistics 2014, 126). The very high growth of the number of settlers since Oslo can be attributed mostly to expansion of existing settlements, mainly on the Israeli side of the barrier. However, there is greater complexity involved. Over 100 new unauthorized settlements, often referred to as "illegal outposts," have been built by settler ideologues since Oslo, either in defiance of the central government or with the tacit consent of powerful allies in the cabinet, depending on who was in the government at the time (Haklai 2007, 2014). Whatever the attitude and approach of the central cabinet and individual ministers to dealing with these settlements, the unauthorized outposts would not have been constructed without the activism of settler ideologues.

Ultimately, the presence of Jewish Israeli settlers in the contested territories, and their political activism, has turned into a significant intervening variable in the calculus of governments evaluating territorial sizing. The presence of a population could complicate territorial redesigns, in that it makes the ethnic sorting that is presumed with partition more difficult to implement. Hence, in addition to explaining formal government policies, understanding settler activism is also essential for evaluating the contours of Jewish settlements in the territories captured in the 1967 war.

Settlers as Consequential Actors

One of the more distinctive features of the Jewish Israeli case is the consequential role of the Jewish settlers. In many of the other cases discussed in this volume, settlers have constituted a mere instrument manipulated in the hands of a sending state. The case of Fascist Italy's settlers in Libya is a case in point; no analyst seriously believes that the Israeli state could relocate its settlers with the same ease as the Italian regime. But even in comparison to more similar cases, such as Turkish settlers in Cyprus or Moroccan settlers in Western Sahara, the extent to which Jewish settlers politically mobilize and exhibit influence is relatively distinct.

Jewish settler activism did not begin with opposition to the Oslo peace process, of course. A lot has been already written about the religious-Zionist settler movement Gush Emunim (Bloc of Faithful) and its ideological tenets and political mobilization (Newman 1985, 2005; Lustick 1988; Zertal and Eldar 2007; Feige 2009; Taub 2011). The movement—established in 1974 and largely guided by the teachings of Rabbi Abraham Isaac Kook, the founder of the religious-Zionist stream, and his son Rabbi Zvi Yehuda Kook—attributed religious significance to the reunification of the Jewish people with the Promised Land. In a nutshell, this perspective views reunification with the land as a religious mission of utmost importance. The outcome of the 1967 war is viewed in messianic terms as an additional step toward redemption.

Whether religious law has supremacy over state law is a contested question among religious Zionists (Sprinzak 1985; Newman 2005, 196–198). Many religious Zionists believe that maintaining the integrity of the state and remaining within its framework is a mission of no less importance than maintaining hold over the Promised Land.[9] Indeed, the objective of land redemption is seen as a collective Jewish good, and to this end, persuasion of the rest of Jewish Israeli society is a high priority mission. Michael Feige (2009) has documented the settlement activists' strategy of trying to "settle in the hearts and minds" of Israelis with campaigns such as "Yesha is here," which aim to enhance a collective mindset among Israelis that Judea and Samaria and the rest of Israel are a single unit.[10]

Religious Zionist settlers have been at the forefront of settlement efforts, and many have defied central government formal policies. In the late 1960s and early 1970s, they rejected the Allon Plan, which not only restricted Jewish settlements but also opposed settlements in ancient biblical sites in the mountainous areas. Gush Emunim set out to settle in places like Ofra and Sebastia, forcing the hand of the government, which looked to avoid confrontation with the settlers (Newman 2005, 194–195; Haklai 2007, 722). According to Yoram Peri, Prime Minister Rabin later admitted that allowing the first unauthorized Gush Emunim settlements to remain—thereby setting a precedent—was an error for which "he never forgave himself" (Peri 2006, 169).

The rise to power of Likud made Gush Emunim somewhat redundant because they shared territorial objectives. The government and the religious settlers were now allies, seeking to settle as much of Judea and Samaria/the West Bank as possible and prevent the possibility of future territorial partition. Thus, not only did the government build much more, as discussed in the previous section, but it also gave the religious settler ideologues practically a free hand to settle and frequently provided ex post facto authorization to their settlements. Many of the legal challenges presented by such settlements were resolved thanks to ideological allies in the Ministry of Justice (Zertal and Eldar 2007, 333–401).

Thus, Labor's 1992 electoral victory and the signing of the Oslo Accords provided a serious challenge to the settler movement. Rabin's government (and subsequent governments) was no longer willing to give a green light to settler activism nor to provide retroactive approval to settler-initiated settlements. In turn, settler defiance was manifested in a number of ways. First, several nonparliamentary movements embarked on a raucous civil disobedience campaign. Thousands of protestors took part in large sit-in demonstrations and blocked intersections. Significantly, the leaders of the protest movement challenged not only the legitimacy of the policy decision to make territorial compromises but also and more fundamentally the very legitimacy of the government itself and of a regime that enabled an elected government to withdraw from territory "granted to the Jewish people by the Divine Authority" (Haklai 2003, 796–799).

A second prong of defiant activity was to continue building settlements irrespective of central government policy. Over 100 unauthorized outposts have been established since 1992 in violation of Israeli law (Sasson 2005). These outposts exhibit variations in their degree of development. For example, some are populated by a handful of young people in mobile homes whereas others contain dozens of inhabitants, including families, residing in permanent structures. Some resemble neighborhoods of existing settlements while others are more remote and clearly separate from existing settlements. Many are connected to electricity and water and have paved roads.[11] Their main strength is in their spatial distribution. Many were built on hilltops on the eastern side of the separation/security barrier. Their purpose is to create facts on the ground that will make partitioning of the territory difficult.

The unauthorized outposts have been so worrying for international mediators that the Roadmap to Peace makes explicit reference to them and calls for the dismantling of all the outposts built since 2001. The outposts have also been a bothersome issue for the central government, so much so that Prime Minister Ariel Sharon, perhaps seeking to demonstrate his trustworthiness to the U.S. administration, appointed attorney Talia Sasson, previously a member of the State Prosecutor's Office and known for her unsympathetic view of the settlements, to investigate the development of the phenomenon, its legal facets, and the involvement of state agencies in illegal actions involved in its growth (Sasson discussed this appointment with the author in an interview in Jerusalem in 2006). The conclusions of her report were revealing and scathing on many fronts regarding the rampant illegal activity (Sasson 2005).

Yet, it would be wrong to think of settler politics solely in terms of a nonstandardized organization. Much of the settlers' power has derived from concomitant operation through institutional channels. Two particularly consequential organizations have been the Yesha Council and Amana. The former was formed in 1980 as an umbrella organization to represent the twenty-four local councils in the non-annexed territories. Its website claims that the settlements in these territories have particularistic needs, such as special security concerns, "recognition of state land," and the construction of bypassing roads (Yesha Council 2013). The Yesha Council has been at the forefront of settler nonparliamentary political mobilization, and of lobbying the government and the state on settlement issues and construction and in opposition to diplomatic initiatives that involve ceding land (Haklai 2014, 81–82).

Formed in 1978 as the settlement arm of Gush Emunim, Amana is registered as a co-operative, land-settling agency (it has an associate company, Binyanei Bar Amana, which undertakes the actual construction). Recognized by the state as a legal construction and settlement agency, it can compete in state tenders and has received land for construction from the Settlement Division of the World Zionist Organization. The organization's website boasts dozens of Amana-constructed settlements, almost all in the West Bank/Judea and Samaria (Amana 2013). Over the years, the state hired the construction services of Amana, including on the Israeli side of the Green Line. For example, Amana won tenders to build in southern Israel for settler evacuees from the Gaza Strip. This revenue-generating entrepreneurial activity has been indispensable for settler activism. Given its ideological roots, Amana has also been accused of facilitating unauthorized construction in the West Bank, projects that most construction companies consider high risk, thus contributing to the growth of the unauthorized settlements. According to one investigative journalist's report, Amana collects a small fee from each settler residing in one of its settlements (separate from municipal tax), which also helps to finance the organization and its unauthorized construction (Levinson 2013).

Notwithstanding important exceptions, it should be stressed that settler leaders do not invariably reject the authority of the state, even when government policies are inconsistent with their priorities. On many occasions, they have found ways to advance their objectives from within the state. Indeed, settlers have been actively seeking to integrate into positions of influence within the state apparatus and other public realms and to occupy positions in the administration that can advance their cause, a strategy that Haklai (2007, 2014) calls "state penetration." Useful targets include the Ministry of Housing and Construction and the Civil Administration, which is responsible for the territories conquered in the 1967 war (Haklai 2007, 2014, 80–84).

Considerable growth in the presence of national-religious youth in the military has also been particularly conspicuous. This growth has been facilitated by the institutional arrangement of Yeshivot Hesder, which allows national-religious youth to combine studies in the yeshiva with military service. This arrangement has considerably increased the input of national-religious rabbis into the military (Levi 2012). Furthermore, the large number of national-religious settlers among the officer ranks and in combat units, particularly those stationed in the West Bank, has caused concerns that military units will provide assistance to illegal settlements—a problem that has been documented—and that orders to evacuate unauthorized settlements will be disobeyed (Haklai 2007, 2014, 85–87). Indeed, when the government conducted the disengagement from the Gaza Strip in 2005, it minimized the involvement of soldiers who were more likely to dissent. To be sure, the face of the Israeli military does not resemble that of the French military in Algeria, where sympathy for French settlers led to mutiny against the de Gaulle regime.[12] And yet, as Yagil Levi (2012) has observed, the military's autonomy from the religious nationalists, and its ability to deploy a growing number of soldiers from this background in politically sensitive missions, has been increasingly constrained as the proportion of religious soldiers in infantry brigades has increased dramatically, from 2.5 percent in 1990 to over 25 percent in 2008.

Settler activists have mobilized in formal parliamentary politics as well. In the early 1980s, the Tehiya party explicitly championed the settlers' cause. Initially formed and led by secular advocates of the "Whole Land of Israel" ideology, the movement attracted many religious Gush Emunim activists, including Hanan Porat, one of Gush Emunim's founders. However, because the Tehiya party agenda was not religious, it did not address the holistic ideological vision of the religious settlers who viewed the settler enterprise as part of a broader national-religious agenda. Thus, throughout the 1980s and 1990s, Gush Emunim members and religious settlers had become increasingly attracted to the National Religious Party (NRP), for which settlements were more central. Since 1999, some religious settlers have chosen to join the Tkuma Party (as part of a larger National Union list), which takes an even more hawkish line than the NRP. Many others joined Likud in an attempt to influence its agenda from within. One conspicuous example is that of Moshe Feiglin, one of the main leaders of the civil disobedience campaign against the Rabin government in the 1990s, who formed a grouping within Likud, called Manhigut Yehudit (Jewish leadership), the declared intent of which was to register religious Zionist settlers and sympathizers as Likud members in order to take over the party's leadership (Haklai 2007, 733). While the activists have not taken over the party's leadership, Feiglin did manage to win about one-quarter of the votes in the internal election for party leadership when he challenged Prime Minister Netanyahu in 2012. In 2013, he was elected to the Knesset on behalf of Likud. Beyond the personal dimension, the impact of Manhigut Yehudit has been that Likud politicians, including government ministers, wishing to get elected on the party list to the Knesset need to take care not to alienate this organized constituency, so they display uncompromising territorial positions or make favorable appointments in their offices (Haklai 2007, 733–734).

The source of settler power in parliamentary politics has been well analyzed by Hendrik Spruyt (2005, 234–263; 2014, 42–58). According to Spruyt,
the proportional representation electoral system in Israel, with its very low
threshold, generates a fragmented political system by providing incentives for
single issue and niche clientele parties to form. The fragmented composition
of the Knesset then leads to coalition governments that include many smaller
political parties whose primary interest is to cater to their clientele. These parties do not have an incentive to moderate their positions because, if they are
not appeased, they can withdraw from the government, leading to its weakness and potential collapse. As a result, they are in a position to pressure the
prime minister on the issues most salient to them. Parties supportive of the
settlers, thus, often have veto power on settlement-related issues. For example,
Prime Minister Ehud Barak lost his majority in the Knesset when the NRP
quit the coalition because of the Camp David negotiations in 2000. By 2001,
Barak was no longer Prime Minister.

It is important to add to Spruyt's analysis that central governments have
few incentives to confront settler nonparliamentary activity, even if illegal,
if they stand to lose coalition partners; this explains why governments, with
some exceptions, have tended not to invest in confrontation over the illegal
outposts. Furthermore, on many occasions, the price paid to settler-friendly
coalition partners comes in the form of cabinet portfolios that are useful to
their interests. One contemporary example is the appointment of Uri Ariel
as Minister of Housing and Construction in 2013. Ariel, a prominent settler
leader, was secretary-general of Amana in the 1980s and CEO of the Yesha
Council. He has made no secret of his desire to formally expand Israel's borders to the Jordan River. The post of Minister of Housing and Construction is
particularly well-positioned for this endeavor.

In addition to veto power, the settlers' cause has also derived power from
the outbidding dynamic that has developed in Israel as multiple parties compete for the settlers' votes. Analysis of voter behavior in the West Bank in
the 2000s reveals that a plurality of votes goes to national-religious parties in
their various incarnations (NRP, National Union, and Jewish Home, which
in 2013 and 2015 brought the NRP and Tkuma together), while a significant
chunk also goes to Likud. The secular, hawkish Yisrael Beitenu also received a
share of the secular vote in the 2009 elections. This competition has provided
incentives for parties appealing to this pool of voters to harden their line on
territorial issues, an outbidding dynamic that further strengthens the settlers

and makes negotiations over the contested territories with the Palestinians more complicated (Elman, Haklai, and Spruyt 2014b, 14–15).

In sum, the settlers have emerged in Israel as a consequential actor. Through a mixture of parliamentary and nonparliamentary mobilization, lobbying efforts, public relations campaigns, and active settlement construction (often unauthorized), they have been able to advance their objectives and make central government maneuverability in relation to the disputed territories more limited than in the other cases studied in this volume.

Conclusion

Jewish Israeli settlers in the West Bank constitute one of multiple actors with competing visions and priorities. Interestingly, the lack of a unified vision and consistent policy has not prevented the settlement endeavor from growing. On the contrary, political fragmentation and incoherence may have facilitated it by empowering settler advocates. This case is thus an example where conflict over contested territories cannot be fully understood in terms of relations between a sending state and an indigenous population. Rather, settlers configure as a third consequential actor within this relationship, as the settlement endeavor has been influenced by the mutually constitutive sending state–settlers relationship in a way that distinguishes this case from many of the other cases discussed in this volume. Proposed conflict resolution strategies for this dispute will be well advised to pay particular attention to this facet.

Notes

1. The so-called "two-state solution" has been the centerpiece of the peace proposals presented by President Bill Clinton during the Camp David Summit and Taba talks of 2000, the Roadmap to Peace that was introduced in 2003 by President George W. Bush and endorsed by the "Quartet" (the United States, the United Nations, the European Union, and Russia), and UN Security Council Resolution 1397 (March 12, 2002) and Resolution 1515 (November 19, 2003). The Arab Peace Initiative, endorsed by the Arab League in 2002 and re-endorsed in 2007, is also premised on Israel's withdrawal to its pre-1967 borders and establishment of a Palestinian state alongside Israel.

2. Chapman and Roeder (2007) further argue that partition's success hinges on the creation of nothing short of fully independent states.

3. Many scholars disagree with the idea that ethnic intermingling exacerbates conflict, including Laitin (2004) and Sambanis and Schulhofer-Wohl (2009, 84–85). Sambanis (2000) also questions the effectiveness of partition as a solution.

4. Ron Hassner (2006/07) has argued that even conquered territories that are of little material value can produce intractable conflict if over time they come to be perceived as an integral part of a state's territory.

5. According to the Central Bureau of Statistics (2013), about 75 percent of Israeli citizens were Jewish and approximately 20 percent were Arabs at the beginning of 2013.

6. In the midst of the debate about the precise boundaries of the national homeland, it should be remembered that the modern territorial boundaries of *Eretz Israel* were influenced by numerous international, regional, and local actors with interests in the area and the ability to influence political and administrative boundaries that had little to do with how Zionists imagined their homeland. For example, the administrative unit carved by the Ottomans shaped what later became Israel's southern border with Egypt. The British then redelineated the eastern boundary through the establishment of Transjordan, and the northern boundary following an agreement with France (the Sykes-Picot Agreement), see Biger (2008).

7. For a good discussion of the dilemmas involved in considering the settlements and international law, including implications of Article 49 of the Fourth Geneva Convention and the 1998 Rome Statute that created the International Criminal Court, see Galchinsky (2004).

8. This was known as the Drobless Plan or the One Hundred Thousand Plan, formulated by the head of a newly established settlement division in the Jewish Agency (Drobless 1978, 1981).

9. A leading settler rabbi, Shlomo Aviner of the Beit El settlement, for example, has consistently maintained a statist approach and typically opposed organized disobedience of state laws by settlers and disobedience by military personnel.

10. Yesha is the acronym for Judea, Samaria, and Gaza.

11. For more on the characteristics of the unauthorized outposts, see Haklai (2007, 724–726).

12. For the comparative perspective of the French military in Algeria, see Spruyt (2005, 88–116, 239–241).

3   Moroccan Settlers in Western Sahara: Colonists or Fifth Column?

Jacob Mundy and Stephen Zunes

SINCE ASSUMING CONTROL OF THE SPANISH SAHARA in 1975, Morocco has encouraged more than 200,000 of its citizens to work and live inside the territory now known as Western Sahara. There is no explicitly stated Moroccan policy for what amounts to a considerable change in Western Sahara's demography. The mass transfer of Moroccan citizens into Western Sahara is undoubtedly an effort to affect "facts on the ground" in Rabat's decades-old conflict with the Algerian-backed Western Saharan independence movement, the Frente POLISARIO (Frente Popular para la Liberación de Saguia el-Hamra y Río de Oro; hereafter, Polisario). From Rabat's point of view, the movement and presence of these settlers in Western Sahara is a non-issue. Morocco insists that it has sovereignty over Western Sahara and so it is Morocco's sovereign right to encourage or allow settlement in its "Southern Provinces" (also referred to as "Saharan Provinces") whether permanent or temporary. From Polisario's point of view, Morocco's state-sponsored settlement activity in Western Sahara is just one aspect of a decades-old effort to *Moroccanize* Western Sahara. Moroccan development efforts in Western Sahara—from administrative structures to the built environment—have attempted to erase any sense of difference between the occupied areas and the rest of Morocco. What looks, from the perspective of international law, like an illegal aggrandizement scheme is, from Morocco's point of view, nothing more than a development scheme aimed at addressing the underdevelopment of its "Saharan Provinces," in the same way that Morocco seeks to address development challenges in its other peripheral regions (e.g., the Rif Mountains or the Eastern High Atlas). This is far less than the *mission civilisatrice* discourse one finds explicitly in European settler–colonial discourse (as in the case of Libya discussed later in this collection) or latently in other examples (e.g., Israeli-occupied territories and Sri Lanka). The geopolitical logic behind Morocco's settlement activities in Western Sahara is clear enough: if Western Sahara becomes Moroccan—culturally, socially, politically, economically, spatially, and demographically—then what is the point of a referendum on self-determination? Self-determination is the key demand of Polisario and is still the basis of the United Nations' peace process there.[1]

From the perspective of the international community, Western Sahara remains in a strange state of legal limbo. It is still listed as a colony of Spain in UN documents. Morocco's historical claim to Western Sahara was soundly rejected by the International Court of Justice (ICJ) in 1975, an opinion that also informed the Court's 2004 opinion on Israel's separation barrier.[2] And like Israel's presence in the territories it occupied in 1967, Morocco's presence in Western Sahara has been denounced, albeit far less frequently, as an illegal occupation. Thus the presence of Morocco's settlers constitutes a violation of the Fourth Geneva Convention's Article 49.[3] Not only have these settlers contributed to Morocco's efforts to delegitimize the territory's fifty-year struggle for independence, they have buttressed the cultural, social, political, and economic networks now seamlessly interlinking occupied Western Sahara with Morocco proper. Needless to say, these settlers have also complicated international efforts to resolve the Morocco-Polisario dispute.

The growing number of Moroccan settlers in Western Sahara was largely ignored during the first decades of peacemaking after Spain's definitive departure from the territory in 1976. On paper, the 1991 UN Settlement Plan to resolve the conflict, formalized in the signing of the 1997 Houston Accords between Morocco and Polisario, said nothing about the presence of Moroccan settlers in the disputed territory. Western Saharan self-determination was widely understood to be the sole right of ethnic Sahrawis native to the territory, even if it was also understood, by the mid-1990s, that a significant portion of the population in the territory was actually of Moroccan territorial origin. Both the Settlement Plan and the Houston Accords seemed to assume that Moroccan settlers would leave with little fuss if native Western Saharans opted for independence. This assumption is easy to explain. In decolonization situations generally, settlers have normally not been included in referendums on independence. In the case of Western Sahara specifically, the 1991 Settlement Plan was copied almost verbatim from an earlier plan drafted by the Organization of African Unity (OAU) between 1978 and 1982, a period when Morocco's colonization efforts in occupied Western Sahara were just getting under way. In addition, Morocco's largest resettlement drive, the so-called Second Green March (see below), came in response to the 1991 Settlement Plan, the pending arrival of the UN mission, and the referendum that was to follow.

Only recently have observers and mediators recognized the growing importance of Moroccan settlers to the Western Sahara conflict. In terms of the peace process, a 2003 plan—tepidly supported by the UN Security Council—proposed a self-determination referendum that would poll both native Western Saharans and Moroccan settlers on the question of total independence for Western Sahara, full integration with Morocco, or autonomous status under Moroccan sovereignty. The inclusion of Moroccan settlers in the electorate was considered politically necessary to win Moroccan support for a referendum that offered the option of independence, though it flew in the face of traditional UN decolonization practice. The previous Moroccan monarch, Hassan II, had supported the idea of a referendum with an independence option. King Mohammed VI, however, rejected the independence option soon after coming to power. This change in position was adopted when it became clear that the UN Security Council would not allow the Moroccan government to compromise the fairness of the vote. Between 1994 and 1999, Rabat had attempted to stack the electorate with Moroccans posing as native Western Saharans, many of them Moroccan settlers inside Western Sahara. When presented with a referendum wherein its settlers were allowed to vote, as was the case in 2003, Morocco continued to reject the independence option as outdated and infeasible, and as an assault on its sovereignty.

After languishing for several years, the peace process was revived when Polisario and Morocco floated their own settlement proposals in 2007. These proposals addressed the issue of settlers in radically opposed ways. While Polisario expressed its willingness to offer Moroccan settlers residency and citizenship rights in an independent Western Sahara, Morocco's autonomy plan put aside a select number of parliamentary seats for Sahrawis in its proposed local assembly. This suggests that Rabat is well aware of the numerical disparity that favors Moroccan settlers over native Sahrawis. Other than this provision, Rabat has said little about how it will prevent a democratically elected autonomous government in Western Sahara from being overrun by non-native residents. According to the most recent reports of the UN Secretariat (April 2013), the negotiations over Western Sahara have not advanced beyond where they stood in 2007 when these proposals were first floated.

On the ground in Western Sahara, tensions between pro-independence Sahrawis and Moroccan settlers have been on the rise in the past decade. The first signs of this rift came in 1999, when massive protests were launched inside Moroccan-occupied Western Sahara. On the one hand, Sahrawi labor and student demonstrations were reportedly supported by a number of non-natives, albeit ethnic Sahrawis from southern Morocco. On the other hand, some accounts suggested that Moroccan loyalists had participated in subsequent attacks against the Sahrawi demonstrators (Damis 2001). Since then, Western Sahara has seen periodic but short-lived bouts of civil unrest, quickly suppressed by the state, particularly in 2002, 2005, and 2010 (Quarante 2012, 18). Indeed, the most disturbing reports of tensions between nationalists and settlers emerged in 2010. Sahrawi activists and international human rights groups accused the Moroccan administration of actively organizing or supporting loyalist mobs that have confrontationally, and sometimes violently, opposed the pro-independence activities.[4] These tensions culminated in the events of November 2010, when Moroccan security forces brutally suppressed a camp of Sahrawi demonstrators established outside Al-'Ayun (Laâyoune), provoking waves of protests and looting by both Sahrawi republicans and Moroccan loyalists (Mundy 2011).[5] At the same time, it has also become apparent over the course of the past decade that key figures in the Sahrawi human rights movement in Western Sahara are native to southern Morocco. While some of these Sahrawi activists remain resident in southern Morocco, others came to Western Sahara as a result of the Moroccan government's settlement policies, as we will see below.

Despite the important role that settlers have played, are playing, and will likely continue to play in this conflict's evolution, there has been no serious attempt to gauge the demographic scope and political significance of Moroccan settlement practices in Western Sahara. Using open-source data and building on our prior work (Zunes and Mundy 2010), we aim to address this lacuna as much as possible. After sketching the history of the Western Sahara conflict through its political geography, we will look at the human geography of the conflict, starting with an analysis of the native population and continuing with an attempt to come to grips with the qualitative and quantitative aspects of Morocco's settlement push in Western Sahara. This preliminary effort will get us closer to assessing the role of settlers in Western Sahara vis-à-vis Moroccan state interests. The third part of this chapter examines the evolving role of settlers within the conflict, from the margins of the peace process in the 1990s (when settlers were implicitly excluded) to the center of it in the 2003 UN peace plan (in which they were explicitly included). Morocco's rejection of this plan, while ostensibly based on a principled a priori opposition to any challenge to its claim of sovereignty over the territory, could also be based on an a posteriori demographic reality, one in which a significant percentage of Moroccan settlers are possibly ethnic Sahrawis. While native Western Saharans might be a minority in their own country, Morocco's settlement policies have possibly made ethnic Sahrawis a significant group demographically, if not politically as well.

The Political Geography of the Western Sahara Conflict

The Morocco-Polisario dispute over Western Sahara was triggered in November 1975 when Morocco invaded Madrid's largely neglected desert colony, Spanish Sahara (Mundy 2006). The conflict's deeper conditions were laid in the preceding decades. Emerging from Hispano-French colonialism in 1956, Morocco asserted a historical claim to large swathes of western Algeria, northern Mali, and all of Mauritania and Spanish/Western Sahara, an idea known as Greater Morocco. By 1970, Morocco had eventually come to renounce all claims to its neighbors' territories except Spanish Sahara. Initially colonized by Spain in 1885, the territory that would become Western Sahara was definitively plotted in a 1912 agreement with France that also formalized Spanish protectorates in northern and southern Morocco (see Map 3.1). Like French Morocco and Spanish Northern Morocco, Spanish Southern Morocco (also known as the Tekna or Draa Zone) was administered in the name of the Moroccan sultan. Spanish Sahara—Río de Oro and Saguia el-Hamra—was considered outside of Moroccan territorial influence when it was initially colonized, a pivotal fact underscored by the ICJ in its 1975 opinion on Morocco's claim to Western Sahara. Complicating matters, however, is the fact that the largest population of ethnic Sahrawis residing outside of Western Sahara could be found in the areas of Spanish Southern Morocco. Though ethnic Sahrawis had inhabited the south of Morocco prior to 1885, a significant percentage of ethnic Sahrawis migrated to southern Morocco

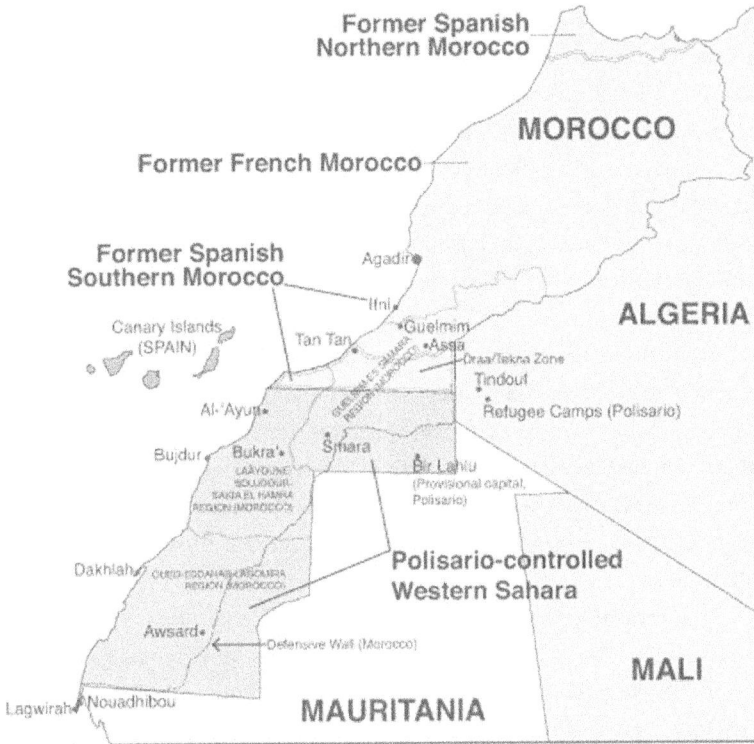

MAP 3.1 The political geography of Western Sahara conflict
SOURCE: Data from Economist Intelligence Unit 2003; United Nations, Cartographic Section 2007; Reyner 1963.

in the late 1950s and early 1960s because of drought and armed conflict. It is on the basis of the Moroccan monarchy's tenuous and contested ties of sovereignty to these Moroccan Sahrawis prior to Spanish colonization that Morocco today claims sovereignty over all of Western Sahara.

In 1974, Spain, conceding to growing indigenous nationalist resistance and foreign pressure to decolonize, announced plans to hold a referendum on independence. Morocco successfully stalled the vote by asking the ICJ to look into its territorial claim on Spanish Sahara. Mauritania, having also claimed Spanish Sahara, joined Morocco's request. The ICJ's landmark opinion rejected most of Morocco's and Mauritania's claims; it reaffirmed, above all, Western Sahara's right to self-determination, including the option of independence. Despite this outcome, King Hassan declared his intent—only hours after the ICJ released its opinion—to march 350,000 Moroccans into the

Spanish colony to reclaim the territory. Should Spain attempt to repulse this invasion, Morocco warned, war would ensue. For months, Moroccan troops had been massing along the Moroccan-Spanish Sahara border. Despite Spanish protests that Morocco's actions constituted a breach of international peace and security, the UN Security Council issued only a verbal disapproval of the Green March. Unwilling to be dragged into what would be depicted as a colonial war with Morocco and facing a potential succession crisis with Generalissimo Francisco Franco on his deathbed, Spain negotiated a transfer of power to Morocco and Mauritania in mid-November 1975. The last Spanish troops withdrew three months later, in February 1976.

The Morocco-Polisario war for Western Sahara lasted from that time until a UN-brokered cease-fire took hold in 1991. The initial Moroccan-Mauritanian takeover caused a sizeable proportion of the native population, upwards of 40 percent, to seek refuge in Algeria. Formed in 1973 to fight Spain, Polisario received a massive increase in material, diplomatic, and humanitarian aid from Algeria following Morocco's invasion. Mauritania experienced a number of embarrassing setbacks against Polisario forces and withdrew from the conflict in 1979, leaving Morocco as sole occupying power. During the first five years of the war, Polisario fared well against Morocco. Polisario's freedom of movement meant that its forces could strike Moroccan forces almost anywhere, even in southern Morocco. An influx of Saudi, French, and U.S. aid, coupled with increasingly effective counterinsurgency tactics by Morocco, turned the tide against Polisario in the early to mid-1980s. Beginning in the late 1970s, Morocco began constructing a series of heavily mined and defended barriers, either dug out of the ground or built along ridge tops; by 1987, these walls, known as "the berms," effectively divided Western Sahara into two unequal zones—a larger one under Moroccan control and a smaller one under de facto Polisario control (see Map 3.1).[6] This military stalemate and Morocco's 1981 commitment to a referendum helped spur renewed UN efforts to settle the dispute, which had been under OAU mediation since 1976. After ostensibly obtaining the parties' agreement to a cease-fire followed by a repatriation of refugees and a referendum, the Security Council approved the creation of the UN Mission for the Referendum in Western Sahara (MINURSO) in April 1991. A cease-fire followed five months later. The referendum has yet to take place, and the refugees continue to languish in Algeria.

The Human Geography of the Western Sahara Conflict

The Sahrawis and Their Diasporas

To understand Morocco's settlement activities in occupied Western Sahara, one must first come to a basic understanding of the native population of Western Sahara, the Sahrawis. In its most basic sense, the term *Sahrawi* is the Arabic adjective for "Saharan," and so hints at the origin of this collective identity. The people who were native to the area of Spanish Sahara were of course not themselves Spanish, so they called themselves simply Saharan or, in Arabic, Sahrawi (Mundy 2007). This situation is then complicated by three other factors. First, the larger population of those who would come to see themselves as Sahrawis inhabited a broader area than the territory of Spanish Sahara and maintained familial linkages with populations in the adjacent colonial territories of French Morocco and Spanish Southern Morocco; French West Africa (mainly Mauritania and Mali); and French Algeria. Attempts to map the geographical distribution of the social groups (sometimes called "confederations" or "tribes") whose historical range includes the territory of Western Sahara make this fact clear (see the tribal maps in Barbier 1982; Damis 1983, 8; Ibn 'Azuz Hakim 1981; Vilar 1977). Second, colonial repression and droughts in the 1950s and 1960s greatly disrupted established patterns of Sahrawi life in the Spanish-administered colony, driving many to seek refuge or opportunity in the neighboring French colonies and independent states.[7] Third, as the inhabitants of a UN-recognized, non-self-governing territory, the native people of Western Sahara have the right to independence; this right does not, however, extend to the entire ethnic group, only to Sahrawis born within the boundaries of the former Spanish Sahara. For this reason, a distinction must be made. On the one hand, Sahrawis can be thought of as an ethnic group inhabiting Western Sahara, southern Morocco, and western Algeria, as well as northern Mauritania and Mali. On the other hand, only some of these Sahrawis are native to Western Sahara. That is, all (native) Western Saharans are Sahrawis, but not all Sahrawis are native to Western Sahara. Identity, of course, does not always obey such clean distinctions, but such is the arbitrary yet sacrosanct norm of *uti possidetis* that, with few exceptions—notably West Papua, East Timor, and Western Sahara—guided the decolonization of a billion people during the 20th century (Franck 1987). Ironically, the major argument for maintaining colonial boundaries was to stave off the very kinds of irredentism that are at the heart of Morocco's claim to Western Sahara and the nearly four decades of conflict it has engendered.

Given the fact that Western Sahara's fate has been tied to a plebiscite on independence in which only native Sahrawis should vote, the size of indigenous population is intensely contested. Following the 1991 UN cease-fire, the "war" for Western Sahara became a demographic struggle. Control of the composition of the electorate for the proposed UN referendum would determine the final status of Western Sahara; ballots, not bullets, would decide the victor. When Polisario agreed to a UN-organized referendum in 1988, the liberation movement insisted on a plebiscite in which only native Western Saharans listed on the last Spanish census taken (1974), and perhaps their direct descendants, could cast a vote. Morocco, in contrast, argued that the 1974 Spanish census was incomplete. Many native Western Saharans had fled the territory late in the Spanish colonial period, Rabat argued. And indeed, the biographies of several members of Polisario's founding vanguard seemed to offer some support for Morocco's claim: having fled to southern Morocco in the 1950s and 1960s to escape drought and colonial repression, a sizeable number of Sahrawis, including some of Polisario's key leaders, had not been counted in the last Spanish census. Some members of Polisario's leadership had also taken part in the 1957–1958 uprising against Spanish and French colonialism, an uprising that mobilized guerrillas in southwestern Algeria, southern Morocco, and Mauritania. Brutally crushed by a joint French-Spanish counterinsurgency effort, this brief conflict is ostensibly tied to some of the demographic shifts registered in the native Sahrawi population at the time, particularly the flight of thousands of Western Sahara refugees to southern Morocco to live with Sahrawi kin.

From the beginning of the UN referendum process, the cynical politics behind the positions of Morocco and Polisario were clear enough. Polisario was convinced not only that strict fidelity to the 1974 census would guarantee an authentically native Western Saharan electorate but also that such an electorate would vote overwhelmingly in support of independence. While a small percentage of native Western Saharans might be excluded (including some of Polisario's leadership), it was considered more important to guard against the alternative proposed by Morocco: establishing new eligibility criteria to enfranchise Western Saharans not listed on the 1974 census, particularly those that had fled to Morocco in 1957–1958. To make matters worse, from Polisario's point of view, King Hassan's right-hand man, interior minister

Driss Basri, well known domestically and internationally for his electioneering skills, had been put in charge of Morocco's effort to win the Western Saharan referendum (Jensen 2005, 73–74). Polisario feared that Basri would try to flood the referendum with Moroccans, particularly ethnic Sahrawis from southern Morocco who were not of Western Saharan territorial origin but could be easily mistaken for such. Morocco would eventually try to expand the voter pool by over 300 percent from the 1974 census, which had counted only 73,497 Sahrawis in Spanish Sahara.

A major problem facing the UN mission in Western Sahara was the lack of a formal agreement to hold the parties to account. From 1991 to 1997, the UN mission operated without the parties' signature to a common plan to implement the referendum. In addition, the mission was enabled under Chapter VI of the UN Charter, which meant that the mission's administrators had few carrots and no sticks with which to entice or coerce cooperative behavior from the parties (Theofilopoulou 2006, 3–6). Under these conditions, the mission was forced to take Morocco's concerns seriously.

Central to Morocco's electoral strategy to win the referendum was the suggestion that as many native Western Saharans lived in southern Morocco as in Western Sahara. Some Spanish colonial officials disputed the Moroccan claim that tens of thousands of Western Saharans had fled to southern Morocco during the late colonial period, though other officials felt the 1974 census was indeed methodologically suspect. The most intensive demographic studies conducted by the colonial administration, those in 1942 and 1967, which measured the population before and after the disruption of the 1957–1958 Saharan uprising, revealed an insignificant change in the indigenous population (Chopra 1994, 78). Figure 3.1 shows the population trends reported by official documents from 1955 to 1974.

On the one hand, assuming the general accuracy of these numbers, there is a clear drop between 1955 and 1959, which corresponds to the years of the 1957–1958 insurgency and refugees. This drop could support Morocco's claims. On the other hand, the 100 percent jump in population from 1962 to 1964 suggests two possibilities: a more accurate count or a return of the refugees from the 1957–1958 war.[8]

Outside of the studies by the colonial authorities, there were almost no other significant efforts to gauge the size of Spanish Sahara's native population. The UN General Assembly sent a visiting mission to Spanish Sahara in the summer of 1975, which, among its various goals, tried to get solid figures

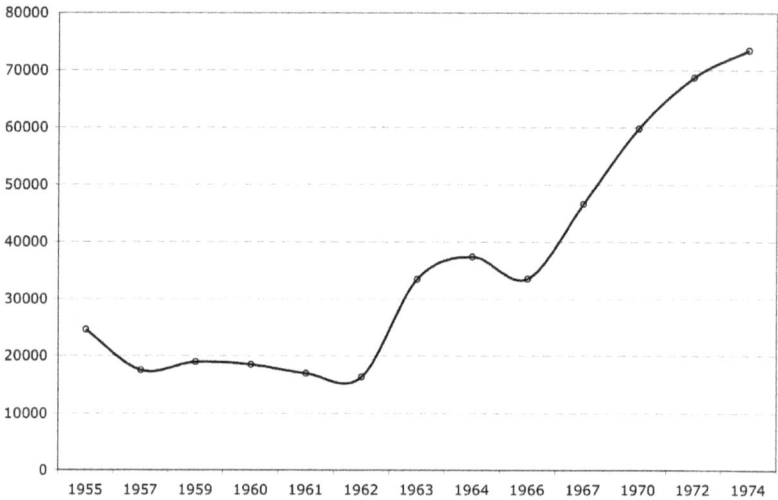

FIGURE 3.1 Population of the Spanish Sahara
SOURCE: Aguirre 1988, 603.

on the number of native Western Saharans residing outside the territory. This mission took place in the context of Spain's attempt to hold a referendum on independence and Moroccan-Mauritanian efforts to halt this referendum by requesting an opinion from the ICJ. At that time, the Spanish authorities believed there were equal numbers of native Western Saharans living in exile in southern Morocco and Mauritania, but no more than 9,000 in total. Morocco claimed a figure of 30,000–35,000 native Western Saharans on its soil. Algeria claimed 7,000. Polisario actually claimed the highest figure: 50,000 "political refugees and exiles" living in the neighboring states. Perhaps for the sake of political legitimacy during its nascent years, Polisario often exaggerated the potential population of Western Sahara. For example, Polisario told the 1975 UN mission that there were 750,000 Western Saharans by "historical association with the Territory," a figure ten times larger than the one Polisario supported in 1991 (A/10023/Add.5, 1977, paragraph 156).[9]

All in all, it took the United Nations six years to establish an electorate for the proposed referendum in Western Sahara that has yet to take place. The length of this process is partly due to the constant stalling tactics of Morocco and Polisario (Theofilopoulou 2006, 4). It is also the result of the UN mission being forced to interview every applicant in person so that Sahrawi tribal elders (shaykhs, or *shuyukh*), one nominated by Polisario and one nominated by Morocco, could evaluate the candidate's claim to Western Saharan-ness. More often than not, the political allegiance of the shaykhs resulted in split decisions, forcing MINURSO to fall back on documents (e.g., colonial identity cards or the 1974 census).

The UN mission arrived at a figure of 86,386 voters. Of the 244,643 applications the UN mission had received, the vast majority of applicants had come either from Morocco proper (99,225) or from Moroccan-occupied Western Sahara (83,971).[10] Together, this was more than double the 72,370 names on MINURSO's updated version of the 1974 Spanish census and more than four times the number of applications sponsored by Polisario from the refugee camps (42,337). In other words, Morocco's main claim—the existence of a significant Western Sahara diaspora living in southern Morocco—was not supported by this outcome. Only 5 percent of Moroccan candidates from Morocco (6,875) were qualified to vote. Fewer than half of Moroccan-sponsored candidates from occupied Western Sahara qualified to vote either (41,150).[11]

The outcome of the voter identification process not only revealed the lengths to which Morocco would go to keep the territory, it also revealed two interesting facts about the size of the indigenous population and the ethnic composition of Morocco's settlers in occupied Western Sahara. If we take eighteen as the median age in 1994 (the cut-off date for applications), then we arrive at a rough population figure of approximately 170,000 native Western Saharans in the mid-1990s.[12] While the provisional UN voter list also appeared to undermine Morocco's claim that a large number of native Western Saharans had fled to southern Morocco in the 1950s and 1960s, Morocco might also have inadvertently shot itself in the foot by moving many of those refugees back to Western Sahara in the early 1990s. In preparation for the referendum after the 1991 cease-fire was announced, Rabat moved roughly 100,000 people into the territory for the vote. This act, which the Moroccan government called the Second Green March, was the first major indication that Rabat would go to great lengths to ensure a victory (see below for more analysis). Assuming that the Second Green March was composed almost entirely of ethnic Sahrawis of Western Saharan origin, this would more than account for all of the refugees who had fled to southern Morocco some thirty to forty years earlier. It is otherwise difficult to account for MINURSO's final tally vis-à-vis the 95 percent failure rate of Moroccan applicants residing in Morocco.[13]

The provisional voter list also called into question the population figures attributed to the Sahrawi refugee camps in Algeria. In 1975 and 1976,
the violence of the invading Moroccan and Mauritanian forces, coupled with
the hasty retreat of the Spanish administration, helped generate a significant
population flight from Western Sahara. While this constitutes a de facto case
of ethnic cleansing, there is no evidence for a Moroccan program to purge
Western Sahara of its native inhabitants. Indeed, Moroccan propaganda frequently and falsely portrays the Western Saharan refugees as Moroccan citizens held against their will by Polisario and Algeria in concentration camps.
Unlike settlers in some other cases, Morocco's settlers have not been a part of
ethnic cleansing (as in the case of Israel) nor have they conveniently filled an
ostensible vacuum created by the 1975–1976 flight of nearly half the population. Whether or not Morocco could accommodate the sudden return of these
refugees, as Rabat insists, is an entirely different logistical and political question. The majority of the refugees in Algeria, as our research and that of others
has demonstrated, are vehement nationalists.

Since 1981, Polisario and Algeria—as the refugees' host country—have
claimed a population of roughly 150,000 (Hodges and Pazzanita 1994,
364–365). These figures are double those of the 1974 Spanish census, and so
they are difficult to take seriously. As Morocco often points out, and donor
countries sometimes underline, Algeria and Polisario have never allowed a
thorough UN High Commissioner for Refugees (UNHCR) or World Food
Program (WFP) census in the camps. Polisario and Algeria claim, first, that
they have their own census data for the camps and, second, that a UN census
should take place only in the context of a global resolution to the conflict. The
UNHCR conducted a repatriation survey between 1998 and 2000 in preparation for the then-expected referendum. This survey produced an estimate of
129,863 refugees in the camps, but the methodology—the survey interviewed
only heads of households—raised questions. Even assuming that Polisario
encouraged camp residents to exaggerate their household size, this figure is
still a far cry from the now routinely cited figures of 155,000–165,000 refugees. The 2000 MINURSO voter list also suggested that the refugee camps
accounted for roughly 40 percent of the native population. This raises two
questions. How did two-fifths of Western Sahara's 1974 population double to
150,000 in such a short period? And if there are 150,000 refugees in the camps,
why did only 34,000 qualify to vote? Either Polisario withheld applications to
vote in the referendum; there was an enormous baby boom after 1976; or, the

most likely explanation, Algeria and Polisario have inflated the camps' population figures to receive more international humanitarian aid.

Settlement Patterns in Moroccan-Occupied Western Sahara

Controversies over population statistics are often an important feature of territorial disputes involving population transfers and other demographic manipulations. The war for Western Sahara in the 1990s was largely a demographic war because the key question was *Who votes?* When the idea of expanding the vote to all residents in Western Sahara was floated in 2003, the *Who votes?* question lost its power. Here we see, as in the case of Kirkuk, which Denise Natali analyzes in this volume, that the power of numbers is a given only in certain contexts and contingent circumstances. The reason we give so much attention to these figures in the case of Western Sahara is to make the argument that the numbers do matter in Western Sahara if we are to understand Morocco's rejection of a proposed final status referendum to include all Western Saharan residents, including Morocco's settlers. One can imagine other situations where the numbers would not matter at all. Nothing is currently stopping Morocco and Polisario from reaching a negotiated political solution in which Polisario abandons Western Sahara's right to independence in favor of broad autonomy under Moroccan sovereignty. That said, the UN Security Council's engagement with the Western Sahara peace process since the late 1980s has been premised on the notion that there will be a referendum in Western Sahara in order to decolonize the territory officially. The most recent resolution on Western Sahara (UN Security Council Resolution 2218 of April 28, 2015) reiterated the council's willingness to support any mutually agreed political solution so long as it provides for self-determination. The question of self-determination presupposes knowledge of the self and the other. Above we described the Western Saharan self. Below we account for its Moroccan other.

Following Spain's final departure from Western Sahara in February 1976, it took Morocco several years to secure what became known as the *zone utile,* or the useful triangle, in the north of the territory—the largest city, Al-'Ayun; the second largest, Smara; and the phosphate mines at Bukra'. From this secure position, Morocco began constructing a series of heavily mined, monitored, and patrolled defensive barriers consecutively outward in the late 1970s, in what is perhaps one of the last century's greatest feats of military engineering. With significant aid from France, the United States, and Saudi Arabia, Morocco was able to implement this successful defensive strategy by slowly and methodically denying Polisario its precious freedom of movement. By 1987, Morocco's defensive walls—the berms—had reached their current extent, running from southern Morocco (near Tata) to the Atlantic coast near the Mauritanian border. Having secured the major population centers of Western Sahara (Al-'Ayun and Smara in the north and Bujdur and Dakhlah along the coast), Morocco began to increase its settlement activity.

Besides the division of Western Sahara between the Moroccan-occupied area and the nominally Polisario-controlled strips in the northeast and southeast (see Map 3.1), other factors make it difficult to understand the recent evolution of Western Sahara's demographics. One factor is Morocco's administrative zoning, which does not correspond with the internationally recognized borders of Western Sahara. At the largest scale, Morocco is organized into sixteen economic regions; each region contains a number of provinces or prefectures, which are further divided into communes and municipalities. The Moroccan administration in Western Sahara is divided into three regions, officially named Oued Eddahab–Lagouira,[14] Laâyoune–Boujdour–Sakia El Hamra, and Guelmim–Es Samara. While the southernmost Oued Eddahab–Lagouira region rests firmly inside Western Sahara, the other two regions overlap with southern Morocco (see Map 3.1). Moroccan statistics, therefore, need to be considered carefully. For example, the region of Guelmim–Es Samara boasted a population of 462,410 in the 2004 Moroccan census, yet 90 percent were registered in provinces or prefectures lying mostly or entirely outside Western Sahara. Inside Western Sahara, five major provinces accounted for the majority of the population in 2004: Al-'Ayun (210,023),[15] Dakhlah (78,854), Smara (60,426), Bujdur (46,129), and Awsard (Aousserd) (20,513). If we look at just these population centers, we arrive at a rough estimate of 415,945 people in the Moroccan-controlled parts of Western Sahara. Adding or subtracting any populations from the barren desert areas under Polisario control east of the Moroccan barrier would likely add or subtract only several thousand at most.[16]

A recent study of school enrollment rates by the sociologist Mohamed Cherkaoui provides some insight into the general patterns of settlement in Moroccan-occupied Western Sahara (Cherkaoui 2007).[17] According to data obtained from the Moroccan Education Ministry, the provinces of Al-'Ayun, Bujdur, and Sakia El Hamra (some of the first to be secured during the war) saw total enrollment grow from 3,061 in 1977 to 57,341 in 2007. While the greatest percentage gain was between 1977 and 1981, the largest numerical increases happened between 1981 and 1991 (11,535) and then between 1991 and 2000 (27,955). The increase between 2000 and 2007 was a mere 19 percent (9,316), which suggests that the settlement rate has significantly decreased. If nearly 40 percent of the native Western Saharan population still lives in exile (according to the 2000 MINURSO voter list), these figures present a picture of Moroccan settlement patterns in which the greatest numerical expansion took place between 1990 and 2000 (roughly corresponding to the period after the 1991 UN cease-fire). Settlement then leveled off after 2000. During the war (roughly 1977–1990), occupied Western Sahara appears to have witnessed a steeper rate of settlement, with school enrollment skyrocketing by 555 percent. Such figures are highly suggestive of a state-coordinated campaign to populate Western Sahara, since (1) they are far beyond natural population growth patterns and (2) they must be reconciled with the dramatic 40 percent decrease in the native population in the 1975–1976 Sahrawi exodus.

A close analysis of population growth inside Morocco's Western Saharan provinces between the 1994 census and the 2004 census is interesting for two reasons. First, Morocco has not provided detailed demographic information on its settlement patterns in Western Sahara directly. The restrictions Morocco places on foreigners within Western Sahara also make it extremely difficult—practically impossible—to gather reliable and impartial data on the population. Large-scale surveys are out of the question. Second, the period from 1994 to 2004 includes the peak years of the UN effort to identify and screen potential voters for the independence referendum (1994–2000). Even though the infamous Second Green March, during which Morocco deliberately moved more than 100,000 "Sahrawis" into Western Sahara for the referendum, occurred well before this period (c. 1991–1992), an analysis of the 1994–2004 period might suggest some of the political logics of Moroccan settlement activities in Western Sahara vis-à-vis the UN referendum.

Between 1994 and 2004, the three southern regions grew significantly in population, from 598,495 to 817,929. For those areas that lie mostly within Western Sahara, the figures are roughly half as large: from 252,146 in 1994 to 415,945 in 2004. The population growth seen in the major provinces of Moroccan-occupied Western Sahara is above and beyond natural human growth patterns, and thus is highly suggestive of a state campaign to populate the region. Al-'Ayun saw 36 percent growth, Bujdur saw 112 percent growth, Dakhlah saw 130 percent growth, and the tiny inland settlement of Awsard saw an astounding 718 percent growth.[18] Collectively, these provinces grew by almost 65 percent, while adjacent provinces in Morocco—Guelmim, Tan Tan, and Tata—grew by only 10 percent. The Assa-Zag province, which is predominantly on the Western Saharan side of the border but whose major population center, Assa, is in Morocco, grew to 43,535 by 2004, an almost 100 percent increase. Nationally, Morocco's population grew by 14 percent between these two censuses (see Haut Commissariat au Plan 2005).

Natives and Settlers in Occupied Western Sahara

The *qualitative* aspects of Morocco's settlement patterns in Western Sahara are as important as the quantitative ones examined above. That is to say, *Who are these settlers?* is as important a question as *How many?* Factors such as age, socioeconomic status, and gender identification might have some bearing on the conflict, but "ethnicity"—for lack of a better term—is perhaps the most important qualitative factor when it comes to the politics of settlement in Western Sahara and the politics of the settlers themselves. A distinction (as noted above) must be made between the indigenous Sahrawi population of Western Sahara and the ethnic Sahrawis whose origins lie in adjacent regions in Mauritania, Algeria, and especially southern Morocco. In practice, Sahrawis rarely make such distinctions between Western Saharans specifically and ethnic Sahrawis generally. To be Sahrawi largely means to descend from one of the major social groupings ("tribes") whose traditional range of habitation either was predominantly within Western Sahara or included parts of it. When the United Nations attempted to organize a referendum in Western Sahara in the 1990s, criteria of both blood (Sahrawi ethnicity) and *land* (Western Saharan origin) governed every Sahrawi's attempt to seek enfranchisement in the vote (see S/23299, Annex I, para. 23, 29–31; Jensen 2005, chap. 5).

Another important aspect of Sahrawi identity is the use of the Hassaniyyah dialect of Arabic, which Sahrawis share with Mauritanians. This distinguishes Sahrawis from those who speak the dominant North African Arabic dialect (Darijah) used in most of Morocco and the Tamazight dialect (Tashilhit) used just north of Western Sahara. Sahrawis often distinguish themselves from Moroccans (whether Amazigh or Arab) in various ways, from food and dress to religious practices and gender relations. The cultures now thought of as Moroccan and as Sahrawi evolved in radically different environments. Whereas Morocco is very much a Mediterranean country, the Sahrawi have tended to share the characteristics of their Saharan neighbors, namely the Moors, Tuaregs, and other nomadic pastoralists of the great desert. These simple distinctions, however, are easy to complicate and deconstruct. One might consider the presence of indigenous ethnic Sahrawi populations in southern Morocco or the origins of the current Moroccan dynasty, which are in the Saharan oases of the western Algerian desert rather than the medinas of Fez or Marrakech. Further complicating matters is the impact of different colonial regimes on Moroccans and Sahrawis. Whether one is considering ethnic or national identities, what it means to be Moroccan and to be Sahrawi today cannot be understood without taking into account the context and impact of colonialism. It is a great error to think of the Sahrawi identity as an ethnicity first and a polity second, when the exact opposite is the case (Mundy 2014).

Moroccan recognition of the Sahrawi identity as an ethnicity, even less as a polity, has been ambivalent. As is often the case when a regime or state is threatened by a secessionist or anti-occupation movement led by a minority, the rebellious or insurgent identity is denied. Thus Moroccan discourse on Western Sahara often recalls Israeli denials of the Palestinian people's existence. In a recent intellectual defense of Rabat's domestic and international policies vis-à-vis Western Sahara, Abdelhamid El Ouali, a Moroccan scholar of law and politics, charged that Spain created the "pseudo-Sahrawi nationalism" in 1973 and that the Sahrawis are a "so-called people"—finding it necessary to place "Sahrawi people" in quotation marks. In its extensive index, El Ouali's book contains no entry for the term "Sahrawi" (El Ouali 2008, 93). One will also frequently encounter in Moroccan political discourse the idea of Sahrawi as a geographical identity rather than a political or ethnic one: Sahrawi as literally "of the Sahara." By this definition, Moroccan settlers, regardless of their ethnic background, can actually *become* Sahrawi. Ethnic Sahrawis, by contrast, are instead often called *Hassani*, in reference to their dialect of Arabic, Hassaniyyah. And because of the imperative to construct a unified post-colonial national identity, as well as the sensitivities surrounding the issues of Western Sahara and the Amazigh (Berber) movement, the Moroccan government has apparently never recorded demographic data on the various linguistic groups in its sovereign territory and the territory under its occupation.

That said, we can arrive at a rough estimate of the non-native population in Western Sahara based on two crude sources: the Moroccan government's census data and MINURSO's voter list. Above we estimated from the UN voter list a total native Western Saharan population of roughly 170,000 in 1994; less than half of that population (i.e., about 75,000) ostensibly lived in the area of Western Sahara under Moroccan administration. Given a total population of 252,146 in Moroccan-occupied Western Sahara in 1994 (based on the 1994 Moroccan census), the indigenous Sahrawi population accounted for about 30 percent of the total. If we assume that the native Sahrawi population grew at a natural birthrate whereas the Moroccan population in Western Sahara grew at an artificial rate (owing to continuing state-sponsored settlement), natives likely accounted for an even smaller percentage of the total population. If the native population grew in tandem with the rest of the Moroccan population in occupied Western Sahara between 1994 and 2004 (an extraordinary rate of 65 percent), one would then expect almost half the population (roughly 123,000) to have consisted of native Western Saharans in the occupied terri- tory in 2004. The more logical option is the former: while the Moroccan set- tler population grew at a rate of over 60 percent, the native population in the occupied territory increased to just 90,000–100,000 in 2004. This suggests that Moroccan settlers, as of 2004, constituted roughly three-fourths to five-sixths of the population in occupied Western Sahara.

The next question is the extent to which these settlers are drawn from eth- nic Sahrawi groups in southern Morocco. It is widely assumed that a large percentage of the Moroccan settler population in Western Sahara consists of Darijah-speaking Moroccan Arabs who are there for military service, are employed in the government bureaucracy, or are taking advantage of eco- nomic enticements. It has been widely reported that Morocco maintains an army of 100,000 to 150,000 soldiers in Western Sahara, the vast majority sta- tioned along the berms. Whether these soldiers (and any other non-perma- nent accompanying family members) should be added to or subtracted from Moroccan census figures is not known, which is to say that the total figure for Moroccans in the Western Sahara could range from 150,000 to 450,000, depending on whether or not the military presence has been taken into account in the 1994 census and/or the 2004 census.

Personal visits to Al-'Ayun (in 2001, 2003, 2005, and 2007) suggest that Tashilhit-speaking Imazighen (Berbers) from the Sus valley, Anti-Atlas, and Nun-Dra'a regions of southern Morocco are well represented in the private service economy, particularly restaurants and small shops. In recent his- tory, Tashilhit-speaking Berbers from the Anti-Atlas have become one of the dominant merchant classes in Morocco in the major cities north of Mar- rakech (Waterbury 1972). There is considerable geographical overlap and even ethnic intermingling between Tashilhit-speaking populations and Sahrawis in southern Morocco. Other major Berber populations in Morocco (in the Rif, Middle, and Eastern High Atlas) do not appear to have as strong a presence in Moroccan-occupied Western Sahara.

An analysis of the politics of settlement in occupied Western Sahara should also take into account the drivers bringing new populations to the contested territory. While some settlers are being "pushed" by the Moroccan government (e.g., those in the Second Green March, government functionaries, and those in military service), others are being "pulled" by the reportedly generous state subsidies and significant infrastructure advantages (Thobhani 2002; El Ouali 2008). Morocco's Saharan regions, for example, boast some of the highest per capita rates of housing, electrification, and roads in Morocco.[19] While it is certainly the case that military personnel, teachers, and other administrators benefit most from government incentives (double wages, housing, lower taxes, and subsidized goods such as petrol), it is not clear how much this applies to workers in the private sector. The significant service economy in Western Sahara (e.g., hotels, shops, and restaurants) could have developed independently but in parallel to the economic opportunities generated by government enticements targeted mostly at attracting non-Sahrawis to serve in the public sector far from home. This "pull," or "piggyback," effect is especially worth considering vis-à-vis parallel and illegal economic activities, which, as in the rest of Morocco, are increasingly compensating for chronic youth unemployment in occupied Western Sahara. Moroccan settlers who were induced to settle throughout the 1980s and 1990s by means of government incentives (mostly administrators and those working in jobs related to military service) likely helped to jump-start and fuel the market-driven forces that pull new people to work in Western Sahara today. This, however, is merely a preliminary hypothesis-building effort to understand all the possible forces—in addition to state-sponsored coercion and incentives—driving Moroccan settlement in occupied Western Sahara. For now, it is enough simply to acknowledge that in order to arrive at a more robust understanding of the forces behind Moroccan settlement activity in Western Sahara, we need more specific demographic and economic data than are currently available. The Moroccan government's four decades old siege mentality does not bode well for obtaining such information.

The International Politics of Settlers in Western Sahara

We are now in a position to return to the original question behind this study: why did Morocco reject a 2003 proposal for a referendum in Western Sahara even though its settlers—who significantly outnumber the native population—would have been allowed to vote? There are three possible answers to that question. One, Mohammed VI remains committed to the principle that his state's claim of sovereignty over Western Sahara cannot be put to a vote. Two, even if Morocco would likely win the vote, any sign of support for independence is unacceptable. Three, there is good reason to think Morocco might lose the vote. This last option is the one we would like to explore. While it is clear that Sahrawis *native* to Western Sahara now constitute a minority in their own country, this observation should be tempered by the fact that a significant percentage of Morocco's settler population is likely composed of *ethnic* Sahrawis from southern Morocco. Recent developments in the Western Sahara conflict suggest that the political allegiance of these ethnic Sahrawis might not be determined simply by the fact that they were born in Morocco and were brought to Western Sahara by the Moroccan state. Do these colonists now constitute a fifth column of Sahrawi nationalists?

During the first decade of the UN mission in Western Sahara (1991–2001), Moroccan settlers of non-Western Saharan origin were not formally incorporated into the peace process, yet they played an important role. Following the creation of MINURSO in April 1991, the Moroccan government brought forth a list of more than 120,000 additional "Western Saharans" to be added to MINURSO's revised 1974 Spanish census. If accepted, this supplementary roster—ostensibly compiled by Morocco's Interior Ministry—would have expanded the electorate by over 150 percent. The Moroccan government demanded that the United Nations add these voters with no questions asked, a demand that Polisario vehemently rejected. Polisario's understanding of the 1988 settlement principles was that only *individuals*, not government-sponsored lists, could petition to be added to MINURSO's preliminary roster.

To create facts on the ground in support of its position, Morocco also organized the Second Green March. On September 15, 1991, a little more than a week after the cease-fire took hold, King Hassan informed UN Secretary-General Javier Pérez de Cuéllar that the Moroccan government would soon move 170,000 of its citizens "back" to Western Sahara for the referendum. These were allegedly Western Saharan refugees from the time of Spanish colonialism, but more recently, in interviews with Jacob Mundy in 2003 and 2005, local human rights activists have claimed that the vast majority are ethnic Sahrawis of Moroccan territorial origin. Rabat was clearly betting that the UN mission would not be able to distinguish between, on the one hand, ethnic Sahrawis from Morocco and, on the other, Sahrawis native to Western Sahara. Though far more sympathetic to Morocco than to Polisario, Pérez de Cuéllar implicitly recognized that Morocco was clearly trying to corrupt the fairness of the referendum (Pérez de Cuéllar 1997, 349), though he also blocked his deputies from raising the issue in the UN Security Council (Goulding 2002, 211). The first head of the UN mission in Western Sahara even resigned his post at the end of 1991, citing the United Nations' unwillingness to challenge the Second Green March as a factor motivating his departure (see Chopra 1999, 198).

Even with the arrival of the UN mission in late 1991 and early 1992, outside observers still had a very difficult time engaging with the local populations inside Western Sahara because of the Moroccan security presence. United Nations personnel also reported being blocked from communicating or interacting with Sahrawi and Moroccan civilians in the occupied territory (Ferguson and Kennedy 1992, 50–51). A *New York Times* reporter wrote from Al-'Ayun, "In truth, surveillance is so intense that it is hard to know what the 100,000 or so people in this desert outpost really think about the referendum" (Noble 1992). What information did come to light often exposed the extent to which Morocco was attempting to influence the referendum by flooding MINURSO's voter identification centers with thousands of applicants with dubious ties to Western Sahara (see Human Rights Watch 1995; Adebajo 2002; Dunbar 2000). Polisario officials widely believed that Rabat had even bribed UN officials in the Identification Commission, especially those who had final say on an applicant's authenticity. The fact that MINURSO's Legal Review Unit would later disqualify 4,000 Moroccan-sponsored candidates hints that Polisario's accusations had some merit.

As noted above, Morocco's efforts to control the outcome of the vote by registering thousands of Moroccans largely failed. As many expected, the 2000 UN voter list largely conformed to the 1974 Spanish census, with a small percentage of voters being added. Morocco's response to the provisional voter list, which was to appeal every rejected Moroccan applicant (all 135,431), was then cited by UN Secretary-General Kofi Annan as one of many reasons to suspend the referendum process in favor of a political solution. Annan also noted that the 1997 Houston Accords signed by Morocco and Polisario contained no mechanism for enforcement nor was the Security Council likely to enact one to compel Morocco to accept a vote for independence (S/2000/131). It is worth noting two important assumptions driving Morocco's strategy to win the referendum in the 1990s. Morocco assumed that, one, it had yet to win the hearts and minds of the native Western Saharans living under its occupation, and two, ethnic Sahrawis from Morocco could nonetheless be counted upon to vote for integration with Morocco. The next stage in the Western Sahara peace process demonstrated that the Moroccan regime was no longer certain the latter assumption was still a safe one to make.

As the UN Secretariat and Security Council began pushing for a political solution to the Western Sahara conflict, the task of devising an alternative to the 1997 Houston Accords was given to the very man who had negotiated them: James Baker. At first Baker encouraged Morocco to explicitly describe the kind of autonomy it was then willing to allow Western Sahara. Months of stalling by Rabat led Baker to put forward his own plan in 2001. At one page in length, the Draft Framework Agreement (DFA) was short on details. Its main goal was to spur dialogue. For Polisario, the DFA was a radical departure from the Houston Accords in one key respect: it did not explicitly offer a referendum on independence, *conditio sine qua non* of self-determination as far as most Sahrawi nationalists are concerned. The proposal addressed the issue of self-determination through an ambiguous "final status" referendum, to be held within five years of the plan's implementation. Though the first autonomous government of Western Sahara would be a balance of native Western Saharans and Moroccan settlers, the electorate stipulated for the final status vote seemed highly favorable to Morocco: "To be able to vote in such a [final status] referendum a voter must have been *a full time resident of the Western Sahara for the preceding one year*" (S/2001/613, Annex I, para. 5, emphasis added). With this opening, the Moroccan government could have easily moved any number of its citizens into the territory in the year prior to the referendum in order to sway the vote. As was to be expected, Morocco welcomed the proposal, while Polisario—backed by Algeria—rejected it.

After going back to the drawing board, Baker presented a revised plan to the parties in early 2003. This new plan would have to satisfy a specific constraint enacted by the UN Security Council in its Resolution 1492: any solution to the Western Sahara conflict would have to offer the people of the territory self-determination. This mandate was widely interpreted as a rebuke to Morocco's rejection of self-determination and as a way of tying Baker's hands so that he had to offer Western Sahara a shot at independence, even if it would be a long shot. The 2003 Peace Plan for the Self-Determination for the People of Western Sahara (hereafter, Peace Plan), like the DFA, offered a five-year period of autonomy culminating in a final status referendum on independence, integration, or a continuation of the autonomy regime.

With respect to the role of Moroccan settlers, the Peace Plan's voter pool was decidedly more balanced than that of the DFA. There was no possibility of Morocco flooding the roster at the last minute. The Peace Plan's electorate would consist of persons of voting age on MINURSO's list, the UNHCR's repatriation list for the refugees, and any persons "who have resided continuously in Western Sahara since December 30, 1999" (United Nations Security Council 2003b, S/565, Annex II, para. 5). It is easy to see why Morocco preferred Baker's first proposal: the DFA had proposed a final status referendum with no explicit option for independence and would have been a plebiscite of persons resident in Western Sahara a year before the vote, thus giving Morocco more control over the outcome. The Peace Plan, however, limited the size of the electorate, making it more balanced between natives and settlers, and explicitly offered Polisario a shot at independence. It also offered Western Sahara a more robust and independent autonomy, one in which the local government would be limited to natives. Moroccan settlers, even ethnic Sahrawis from southern Morocco, would face electoral disenfranchisement in the first local elections to choose an autonomous government. They would, however, have the opportunity to vote in the final status referendum five years later.

Excluding Moroccan settlers from participating in the Peace Plan's autonomous government, as they would have under the DFA, made it more likely that Polisario officials and their supporters would dominate the elected bodies. The most important economic aspects of Western Sahara would come under local control, including future petroleum prospects, fisheries, and raw phosphate exports. This would disrupt Morocco's economic control over Western Sahara and give local authorities the power and resources to influence Moroccan settlers' opinions regarding the final vote. Some Moroccan settlers might even opt for independence with the Western Saharans, it was suggested, if the autonomous government, likely led by Polisario, demonstrated enough competence. Though the ostensible raison d'être of the Peace Plan was to ignite the imaginations of the parties and lead them toward a sensible political solution within its parameters, the final status referendum also undermined the Peace Plan. Baker had reasoned that the only way Morocco would ever participate in an act of self-determination including the option of independence was if the vote seemed likely to be in Rabat's favor. Much to everyone's surprise, Morocco rejected the Peace Plan while Polisario and Algeria embraced it. Baker had likely miscalculated Morocco's faith in its own settlers.

On paper, the Peace Plan's referendum seemed highly favorable to Morocco. It would be safe to assume that a significant percentage of the voters on the 2000 MINURSO list would favor independence, particularly the refugees. Then subtract this percentage from our calculations regarding the size of the total population in occupied Western Sahara in 1994, and one arrives at a pool of some 85,000 additional voters.[20] That is to say, there would likely have been parity in the numbers of Western Saharan voters and non-Western Saharan voters in the Peace Plan's referendum. That parity, however, would have been tipped in Morocco's favor by the pace of settlement in the late 1990s. Given the stunning growth in the Moroccan settler population between the 1994 and 2004 censuses (a rate of 65 percent), Morocco would seemingly have gained an electoral advantage by the 1999 cut-off date proposed in the Peace Plan. This would be especially true if the population increase between 1994 and 2004 was front-loaded to the years immediately before the 1999 cut-off date. Any population growth in the refugee camps would be accounted for in the 2000 UNHCR repatriation list. Population growth among the native Western Saharans living under Moroccan occupation, as we have argued above, would likely keep pace with a more normal growth rate of 1 to 3 percent. Nevertheless, although there is evidence to believe that the Peace Plan offered Morocco a prima facie advantage in the referendum, there is also a credible case to be made that the electoral balance was much more problematic for Morocco.

What might have led Morocco to reject the Peace Plan is the ethnic composition of the settler population inside occupied Western Sahara. As we saw above, reports from 1991–1992 indicate that Morocco transferred some 100,000 to 170,000 of its citizens (reports vary) into Western Sahara for the referendum being organized by MINURSO in the 1990s. These settlers were reportedly ethnic Sahrawis from southern Morocco; some might even constitute the contested native population outflow Western Sahara experienced late in the Spanish colonial period (i.e., the 1950s and 1960s). Having derived a population figure of 252,146 in occupied Western Sahara from the 1994 census, even the low-end figure of 100,000 for the Second Green March would suggest that a significant portion of the settlers in Western Sahara were ethnic Sahrawis in 1999. Though it is true that there are loyalist factions among the native Western Saharans who would vote for integration with Morocco, the added option of autonomy would split the vote among moderate or undecided Sahrawis who feel ambivalent toward independence or integration. As long as most native Western Saharans voted for independence, Polisario would have to win over only 10,000 to 20,000 Moroccan settlers to win the referendum proposed in the 2003 Baker Plan. While it is difficult to assume that Moroccan Imazighen and Darijah-speaking Arabs would vote for independence, it has also become less easy to assume that all ethnic Sahrawis from southern Morocco would vote against independence.

Is there sufficient reason to believe that Morocco's ethnic Sahrawi settlers in Western Sahara have become more sympathetic—or always were sympathetic—to the nationalist ambitions of Polisario? On the one hand, there is evidence to suggest that the populations inside occupied Western Sahara are some of the most loyal in the country. In recent Moroccan elections, occupied Western Sahara has consistently reported the highest voter participation in all of Morocco, while the national average voter turnout has steadily declined, from 85 percent in 1970 to current levels below 40 percent (Storm 2008). In the 2002 parliamentary elections, voter turnout was 70 percent in Western Sahara, 18 percentage points above the national average. Local elections the following year show a similar outcome: 68 percent participation in Western Sahara, versus a national average of 54 percent. While Morocco's 2007 legislative elections saw the worst turnout in the country's history (37 percent), the government boasted a 67 percent turnout in the Saharan provinces (see U.S. Department of State, Bureau of Democracy, Human Rights, and Labor 2003, 2004, 2008). On the other hand, the rosy picture these figures paint warrants some skepticism. First, the Moroccan government clearly has good reason to present the international community with inflated voter turnout numbers from Western Sahara, as this suggests that the region is the most patriotic in the country. Second, given the large military presence in Western Sahara, the high turnout could be an effect of voting in the barracks—a notoriously opaque practice open to manipulation. If we assume that such figures can be trusted, however, what are we to make of them vis-à-vis the peace process and Morocco's rejection of the 2003 Baker Plan? Are they solely an effect of pro-Moroccan mobilization on the part of settlers in Western Sahara? Or are they also a sign of Sahrawi support for integration with Morocco?

Writing in defense of Morocco's claim to Western Sahara, Cherkaoui's (2007) unique study of Sahrawi marriage patterns between 1960 and 2007 attempts to show that Moroccan and Sahrawi populations are slowly melding. Cherkaoui admits that Moroccan marriage contracts "do not necessarily mention tribes" and that his "study bears only on marriage in [Western] Sahara, not on spouse choice among Sahrawis in general." Instead, he derives his primary information from "residence zones" for birth on 30,000 marriage contracts and then infers ethnic origin (Cherkaoui 2007, 139–140). Cherkaoui (2007, 142) distinguishes between Western Sahara, "other Saharan regions" (e.g., former Spanish Southern Morocco and the Tekna Zone or Tarfaya strip), and "Morocco's non Saharan regions." His results show that since 1975, people of Western Saharan origin have tended to choose spouses who reside outside of Western Sahara one out of every two times.[21] Yet the study's findings suggest that over 80 percent of such inter-regional marriages occur between individuals born in Western Sahara and in the Sahrawi-dominated areas of southern Morocco (Cherkaoui 2007, 148, table 144). What begins as an attempt to demonstrate "the gradual social integration of Sahrawis into Moroccan society as a whole" (Cherkaoui 2007, 152) degenerates into a partisan argument against self-determination on the grounds that Sahrawis are allegedly voting for Moroccan integration through marriage. If self-determination is pursued, Cherkaoui (2007 148–149) warns, Sahrawi "separatist impulses" will engender an insatiable ethno-irredentism until all of southern Morocco to the High Atlas is incorporated into an independent Western Sahara. These sentiments are ironic, given that the Western Sahara dispute is the direct result of Moroccan irredentism, while Polisario has refused to back claims for a broader ethnic Sahrawi republic that might include southern Morocco. More importantly, Cherkaoui seems to provide evidence that could help explain why Morocco rejected the 2003 Peace Plan. If ethnic Sahrawis in Morocco and Western Sahara represent a contiguous social community, who is to say that they do not represent a contiguous political community as well?

While the phenomenon of Western Saharan nationalism has been intensely studied in the refugee camps in Algeria (see, e.g., San Martín 2010), very little is known about the Sahrawi nationalists who live under Moroccan occupation (one notable exception is Shelley 2004). And almost nothing is known about the extent of Sahrawi nationalism among the ethnic Sahrawis of southern Morocco. Evidence that Moroccan Sahrawis, particularly settlers in Western Sahara, might be sympathetic to independence has slowly emerged since 1999. That year, Western Sahara saw a series of Sahrawi-led student and labor demonstrations turn into full-blown demonstrations for independence. These protests, and their aftermath, revealed the two different images of Morocco's settlers in Western Sahara. A U.S. State Department Bureau of Democracy, Human Rights, and Labor (2000) report claimed that Moroccan authorities "encouraged gangs of local thugs to break into and vandalize the homes and places of businesses of some of the city's Sahrawi residents." Yet there were also reports that other Moroccan settlers—ethnic Sahrawis—had joined the protestors. These ethnic Sahrawis had been participants in the Second Green March of 1991–1992, when Morocco settled them in several temporary encampments on the outskirts of major cities such as Al-'Ayun, Smara, and Dakhlah. As the referendum was originally designed with a nine-month timetable, it was expected that these new settlers would soon vote and leave. By 1999, the conditions in the *al-Wahdah* (unity) camps—which had largely morphed into shantytowns—had become intolerable. Given the figures of 100,000 to 170 000 participants in the Second Green March, the residents of the *al-Wahdah* camps (incrementally demolished and replaced with housing in Al-'Ayun after 2000) could represent a significant source of support for Western Saharan nationalism, which, after all, is tacitly *Sahrawi* nationalism. If this is the case, there is an obvious set of reasons why Morocco would attempt to obscure the demographic situation inside Western Sahara. More importantly, the prevalence of Sahrawis within Morocco's settler population could also be a decisive, if unspoken, factor behind Morocco's rejection of the 2003 Baker Plan, as well as Rabat's continued rejection of any form of referendum that offers independence.

An important piece of evidence that points toward a more complicated picture of Moroccan settler allegiances can be found in the political activists leading Sahrawi resistance under Moroccan occupation. Following the 1999 uprising, Western Sahara saw increasing reports of sporadic youth demonstrations and more organized nationalist opposition, especially during the 2002 royal visit of King Mohamed. The situation burst open again in May 2005, when police repression of a small human rights demonstration precipitated a week of unrest that spread from Western Sahara to Sahrawi student groups on Moroccan campuses. While Moroccan security forces were able to put a lid on the situation, a general feeling of permanent unrest settled into Western Sahara in the years that followed. Five years later, Western Sahara saw the creation of a Sahrawi protest camp near the capital city of Al-'Ayun in October 2010, and its violent suppression by Moroccan forces the following month. This event briefly brought significant international attention to the Western Sahara conflict, until the unfolding demonstrations in Tunisia and then Egypt eclipsed the aftermath of the October Gdaym Izik protest camps inside Western Sahara (Murphy and Omar 2013; Wilson 2013). With respect to this chapter's tentative hypothesis, the most significant development since the outbreak of the 1999 protests and the two major outbursts that followed in 2005 and 2010 has been the increasing participation of Moroccan Sahrawis in the nationalist movement. As is the case with key figures in Polisario's exiled leadership, some of the most internationally visible figures in the Sahrawi rights movement actually originate from southern Morocco, not Western Sahara.

This leaves us with two questions that will require more time and additional research to answer. An important social scientific question is the extent to which the mobilization of ethnic Moroccan Sahrawis in the cause of Morocco's occupation has played a role in their counter-mobilization as actors within Western Sahara nationalist movement. An important political question is the influence these settlers will have on the Western Saharan independence movement and the UN peace process in the years to come. For now, it seems safe to conclude that the politics of Morocco's settlers in Western Sahara cannot necessarily be derived from the politics of their settlement.

Conclusion: Comparative Analysis

The historical and legal parallels between the cases of the occupied Palestinian territories and Western Sahara would seem to offer a warrant to compare and contrast Morocco's and Israel's settlement policies. In both cases, we have states that have attempted to aggressively expand their territory by force, though Israel has been far more ambiguous than Morocco with respect to the final status it sees as optimal. The Moroccan government has always been very clear about its desire to annex Western Sahara completely. In both cases, the suite of applicable international humanitarian law, particularly the Geneva Conventions, is very similar, though the Western Sahara conflict has been predominantly interpreted as a problem of decolonization rather than occupation. As Western Sahara is the last territory in Africa yet to be decolonized, one would think that the presence of foreign settlers there would attract more attention than it has so far. In comparison to cases of European settlement in African colonies (e.g., the case of Libya, which Roberta Pergher examines in this collection), Moroccan settlement in Western Sahara has been far less obvious and far less contested by parties outside the conflict's main participants. One factor here is the strangeness of Western Sahara's international legal status: it is a Spanish colony occupied by Morocco. East Timor had a similar status (as Ehud Eiran notes in his contribution to this volume): it was—and remained until its independence in 1999—a Portuguese colony invaded by Indonesia. The parallel fates and seemingly divergent outcomes of the Western Saharan and East Timor disputes point to another factor that seems to affect the international visibility of settlers: identity. Western Sahara is an Afro-Arab colony that is being occupied and colonized by an adjacent Afro-Arab state. It is this "brown-on-brown" quality—visible in East Timor, Sri Lanka, and Iraq as well—that also helps to account for the invisibility of the settler issue in efforts to represent and manage the Western Sahara conflict. And unlike other cases where states had very pronounced or visible policies to settle occupied territories (as found in Israel and colonial Libya), Morocco, except for the Second Green March, has been far more circumspect in its settlement activities.

The kinds of strong international condemnation that Israel receives for violating the Geneva Convention's prohibition of settlement in occupied territories (Article 49) have never really been voiced in relation to Western Sahara, though the same prohibition applies. Settlers feature heavily in the discourse on the Israel and the Palestinians, and they are widely considered an essential component of any solution to that case. In the case of Western Sahara, settlers have rarely been acknowledged, though it is clear that Morocco has used settlers for the same basic end as Israel—to change facts on the ground. Where a major difference emerges in these two settlement policies is in the issue of demography. Demographic issues are an important factor in the case of Israel (e.g., settler age groups and country of origin in the case of recent émigrés) but for different reasons than in the case of Western Sahara.

Another contrast is the extent to which settlement processes in Western Sahara have been top-down, whereas settlement in the Israeli-occupied territories has been more a process of the state pushing some settlers and other settlers dragging in the state. In Western Sahara, available data suggest that Moroccan settlers seem to be largely responding to government incentive programs, whether as civilians seeking a subsidized living or government workers (including military personnel) seeking better employment via service in the Sahara. Only in the instance of the Second Green March in the early 1990s, and what appears to be these settlers' enforced residence in Western Sahara, do we see something that looks like a possible case of coerced settlement. The extent to which Moroccans have been voluntarily drawn to Western Sahara, independently of state incentive programs or government employment, seems minimal and largely takes the form of private enterprise, including both legal and black market activity as well as seasonal labor. As we have suggested in this study, the political sympathies of Moroccan settlers might not be as clear as one would initially think. Moroccan citizenship— which even nationalist Sahrawis native to Western Sahara obtain by birth in the occupied zones—does not necessarily mean loyalty to king and country. The same must also be said of all people who identify as Sahrawis, as the divisions between loyalist, nationalist, and neutral Sahrawis likewise constitute an important but largely unexamined schism in the Sahrawi population as it exists today and has evolved over decades of conflict, exile, and occupation. To what extent the settler-on-native violence recently witnessed in Western Sahara has included Sahrawi participants—and to what extent this has been independently or spontaneously organized—is an important question that has yet to be answered. While the Moroccan government often downplays such reports or represents these events as spontaneous manifestations of loyalism, Sahrawi rights activists tend to present them as non-Sahrawi mobs organized or encouraged by the Moroccan security apparatus.

Another important question the Western Sahara peace process has yet to address is the number of Moroccans of non-Sahrawi origin who might favor autonomy or independence. Polisario's 2007 settlement proposal indicates that the independence movement assumes many Moroccan settlers would rather stay in Western Sahara than leave with Morocco should independence somehow come about. Whether or not this is a safe assumption to make is difficult to determine. What is known is Morocco's lack of faith in its settlers, as can be inferred from its rejection of the 2003 Baker Plan and its ongoing reticence about offering Western Sahara true autonomy or implementing that autonomy unilaterally. Given the argument that we made above, there is strong reason to think that a significant proportion of Morocco's settlers—if not a majority when combined with the native population—are Sahrawi by origin. It is not a rare thing in the history of territorial disputes to encounter a case of state-sponsored settlement that has resulted in significant blowback from the settlers themselves. As Oded Haklai notes in this collection, it is often difficult to sort out who is the horse and who is the cart when it comes to the true drivers of Israeli settlement policy because the relationship is dialectically evolving. The emergence of "price tag" violence in the West Bank—where Israeli settlers attack instruments of the Israeli state as the "price" of any withdrawal from Judea and Samaria—is only one indication of the extent to which settlers often become a double-edged sword for states attempting to instrumentalize them in territorial disputes. The fact that Moroccan settlers did not openly protest the 1997 Houston Accords, which reaffirmed Morocco's commitment to a referendum on independence, suggests that Morocco's settlers are very much under control. Incidents of settler violence in Western Sahara, as well as protests in Morocco, seem to be consistently related to instances where Morocco's claim on Western Sahara is challenged.

While Morocco seems to have its settlers under control, this does not mean Morocco has not experienced the same blowback as other states that have used settlers in territorial conflicts. In Western Sahara, Morocco's policies have backfired largely in relation to the importation of Sahrawis in the early 1990s. A policy intended to win an independence referendum for Morocco has actually made it clear that Morocco will likely lose a referendum if independence is an option, given the ambiguous loyalty of the large non-native Sahrawi population that now lives there. The Moroccan regime seems to have miscalculated the power of Western Saharan nationalism and the Sahrawi identity vis-à-vis Morocco's indigenous Sahrawi populations in the south; the extent to which prolonged and forced settlement in Western Sahara might affect the sympathies of Sahrawis forced to relocate into Western Sahara in the early 1990s for a referendum; and the time it would take the United Nations to establish a voter list for the referendum it would eventually abandon in 2000. Here we see the ways in which settlers can intentionally and haphazardly affect the capacity of a referendum to settle a territorial dispute, even in cases like Western Sahara where it is demanded by international custom.

Notes

The authors thank Brahim Ansari for his insights. Some of the data and arguments presented here were first presented in our book *Western Sahara: War, Nationalism and Conflict Irresolution* (Syracuse University Press, 2010). An earlier version of Jacob Mundy's contribution to this chapter was published in *Arab World Geographer*.

1. The UN Secretariat became involved in the negotiations in 1985. The UN Security Council created the UN Mission for the Referendum in Western Sahara (MINURSO, Mission des Nations Unies pour l'organisation d'un référendum au Sahara occidental). Current UN Security Council resolutions now call for a political solution that will provide for self-determination (e.g., S/Res/2099). In this chapter, United Nations documents are cited by unique serial number.

2. While the ICJ determined that the native Sahrawi people of Western Sahara constituted the sovereign power in Western Sahara at the time of Spanish colonization (c. 1885), the Court was convinced that ties existed between the Moroccan sultan and Sahrawi groups inhabiting the area where southern Morocco meets northern Western Sahara. These ties, according to the Court, were not enough to trump Spanish/Western Sahara's right to a self-determination referendum (see Franck 1976, 1987). Morocco's invasion of Spanish Sahara in October–November 1975 was clearly aimed at preventing Madrid from holding the ICJ-mandated vote (see Mundy 2006).

3. A 1979 UN General Assembly resolution (34/37) deplored what it called Morocco's occupation of Western Sahara. In few other documents has the United Nations explicitly named Morocco's presence an occupation. More recently, a 2002 opinion from the UN Office of Legal Affairs (S/2002/161) strongly implied that Morocco's presence could only be considered an occupation because Spain retained the status of de jure administering power. In the authors' personal correspondence with Harvard University's International Humanitarian Law Research Initiative (April 5, 2006, on file with Jacob Mundy), the opinion was offered that the "UN has formally agreed that Western Sahara is an occupied territory; therefore all parties would be obligated to follow the mandates of the Geneva Convention IV."

4. Clashes involving Moroccans and Sahrawis have been reported in response to the Moroccan crackdown on a Sahrawi protest camp outside Al-'Ayun on November 8, 2010, which precipitated some of the largest pro-independence Sahrawi demonstrations yet seen in occupied Western Sahara (Amnesty International 2010b). Human Rights Watch (2010) later reported that "following the initial violent confrontations [on 8 November], Moroccan security forces participated with Moroccan civilians in retaliatory attacks on civilians and homes, and blocked wounded Sahrawis from seeking medical treatment" (see also Robert F. Kennedy Center for Justice and Human Rights 2011). Video soon emerged of what appears to be a loyalist group running through the streets of Al-'Ayun on November 9, waving the Moroccan flag and brandishing weapons (see http://www.youtube.com/watch?v=rXDsIj6aX_8). Videos also appeared showing what is reportedly a loyalist-republican clash inside a secondary school in Smara at the end of November 2010 (see http://www.youtube.com/watch?v=IGPTTXG-hVE). Several months earlier, disturbing episodes of Sahrawi-Moroccan confrontations had also been reported: "Last Wednesday [March 31, 2010], 11 other Sahrawi activists were assaulted by a crowd of people chanting slogans in support of Moroccan rule in Western Sahara when they arrived at Laayoune airport after visiting the Tindouf refugee camps" (Amnesty International 2010a). Sahrawi-Moroccan confrontations are also reportedly occurring in Morocco proper. In March

2010, a southern Moroccan city with a large Sahrawi population, Tan Tan, also saw Moroccan security forces and civilians confront a delegation of Sahrawi activists who had recently visited the Polisario-administered refugee camps in Algeria.

5. Polisario and Morocco use different Latin transliterations of the place names in Western Sahara, especially for the major city, Al-'Ayun. While we do not want to add to the confusion, we have attempted to remain as close as possible to the Arabic, using a modified version (without diacritics) of the standard for Arabic transliteration used by the *International Journal of Middle East Studies*. For place names in Morocco, we use the official Moroccan name; where possible, we have provided the most widely used Francophone or Hispanophone alternate transliterations in parentheses.

6. For a recent account of the Morocco-Polisario war, see Strategic Studies Institute (2013).

7. On the relationships among Sahrawi patterns of living, politics, and environments, see Gila, Zaratiegui, and De Maturana Diéguez (2011).

8. During this period, droughts and the increasing availability of housing motivated many nomadic Sahrawis to move to the cities, where they were much easier to count (Pazzanita 2006, 350). An earlier 1954 survey used a count of tents rather than a head count (Damis 1983, 8).

9. Considering the ethnic proximity of Sahrawis to Mauritanians (in language, culture, and natural geography), this claim is perhaps not as wild as it first seems. During a research trip in 2003, Jacob Mundy encountered a native Western Saharan in Al-'Ayun whose sibling serves in Polisario's government-in-exile. One of his cousins serves in the Mauritanian government. A figure of 750,000 native Sahrawis is nevertheless a far cry from the figure for MINURSO's initial electorate (75,000) that Polisario backed in 1991.

10. These figures are taken from various reports of the UN secretary-general concerning Western Sahara (see S/2003/565 for the aggregate figure).

11. See S/2000/131, para. 6.

12. This was the approximate median age in Mauritania, though the median age was higher in Morocco and Algeria.

13. From a population of approximately 75,000 in 1974, a growth rate of 4 percent—extremely high, but not unheard of in refugee populations—would have produced 160,000 Western Saharans two decades after the last Spanish census. More reasonable growth rates of 2 to 3 percent would have produced a population of 111,000 to 135,000. Yet if eighteen was the median age in 1974, the number of voters from the Spanish census would then range from 55,000 to 67,500, leaving a deficit of roughly 20,000 to 30,000 native Western Saharans. Given the estimates of the size of the Second Green March (at least 100,000), it seems highly plausible that Morocco's massive resettlement of populations in 1991–92 might account for this potential shortfall.

14. The southernmost town in Western Sahara, Lagwirah (Lagouira), which sits south of Nouadhibou near the bottom of the long spit shared with Mauritania, is largely uninhabited and has been under de facto Mauritanian control since the days of the war, even though Mauritania renounced all claims in the 1979 Algiers

Agreement with Polisario. Morocco's presence ends at the small border post of Guerguarate.

15. Al-'Ayun province also extends into Morocco to cover the small seaside town of Tarfaya, which could affect Al-'Ayun's numbers by several thousand.

16. In an effort to create its own facts on the ground, Polisario is currently considering plans to expand its civilian presence in the areas of Tifariti and Bir Lahlu (in the northern zone), which might include refugee resettlement in those areas. However, no major refugee resettlement has been announced.

17. Here we assume that these figures are not a function of available infrastructure. Given the correspondence to the census data (at least for the period 1994–2004), this seems a reliable assumption, and Cherkaoui's own figures for the number of schools (2007, 111) suggest that supply followed demand. Enrollment rates (110) would affect these figures but not the way in which they suggest settlement patterns.

18. While the tiny settlement of Awsard (Aousserd) is located inland, the province of Awsard includes in its jurisdiction the southernmost strip of Atlantic coast. The majority of its population is likely accounted for by the large octopus-fishing industry that has grown up along the coast of Western Sahara since the 1991 cease-fire. During the cephalopod fishing season, the population of itinerant fishermen can reportedly swell by tens of thousands of workers.

19. See the Moroccan government website http://www.sahara-developpement. com.

20. By taking eighteen as the median age for a population of 126,073 minus the 41,150 native Western Saharans already accounted for on the 2000 MINURSO list.

21. The only time variable disclosed in Cherkaoui's (2007) graphs is the first (1975). The other time points are labeled by number (2, 3, 4, and 5) rather than by date, and no key is provided for these numbers. It seems possible that Moroccan settlers could account for the dramatic 90 percent drop in endogamy that Cherkaoui records. His response to this charge is to assert that this is not possible because birthplace is taken into account (145), but this does not rule out the possibility that the children of early non-Sahrawi Moroccan settlers born in Western Sahara could be affecting the results (e.g., the 16% of Western Saharans marrying outside of either southern Morocco or Western Sahara).

4 Settlement, Sovereignty, and Social Engineering: Fascist Settlement Policy between Nation and Empire

Roberta Pergher

From Alpine Peaks to African Shores

In 1938, Italian senator Ettore Tolomei, a staunch nationalist, applauded "the splendid exodus" of nearly 20,000 settlers to the colony of Libya (Tolomei 1938, 23). Italy had invaded Libya some twenty-five years earlier, in 1911. After having brutally suppressed native resistance, the Fascist regime was now dispatching Italian settler families to the North African shore. The 20,000 settlers were supposed to represent just the first wave of a tidal flow of Italians, with further groups of 20,000 to follow in each of the subsequent four years. Tolomei's "splendid exodus" might well appear to be merely the latest installment in the history of European colonialism. Certainly, this was how many contemporary observers saw it at the time. A chorus of international commentators, among them the London Times and Pravda, reported on the Fascist settlement program as a bold expression of colonial domination: a massive project, path-breaking in its state patronage, that provided land to hard-working Italians who in the past had to emigrate in order to make a living.[1] The program attracted particular attention, not least because in the interwar period the imperial powerhouses of Great Britain and France were contending with rising demands for greater autonomy or even independence from not only colonized populations but even their very own settlers. In many quarters the acclaimed model of colonial settler societies dominating native populations and bound to their "mother country" was being challenged. But here was Italy, engaging in a new colonial settlement project with vim and vigor, and brazenly indifferent to the plight of native populations.

The Fascist program was certainly reminiscent of other examples of settler colonialism. In previous centuries, the establishment of settler societies had enabled European states to make a more plausible claim over distant territories: settlers bolstered the occupation of far-flung lands; they provided economic ties to the homeland and ensured a more extensive exploitation of resources; moreover, permanent settlements fended off competition from other colonial powers interested in the same territory, warranting regional hegemony and international standing. Settler societies differed greatly from one another with regard to the institutionalization of their privilege, their incorporation into governance, and their access to state protection and subsidy, as well as their allegiance to their home country (Elkins and Pedersen 2005; Paisley 2003; Good 1979). Yet an increasingly confrontational relationship with the mother country as well as extremely violent and manifestly racist relations with the native population tended to unfold in almost all settlement colonies (Veracini 2010; Gott 2007; Wolfe 2006). These characteristics were in part true of Fascist settlement as well: the settlers sent to Libya were supposed to secure the North African shore for Italy; Fascist settlement planners, cognizant of the strains that could develop between settlers and home country, were keen to tie settlers into a particularly close relationship with the national community; and the quandary of native interaction, with its excesses of racism and violence, was a recurrent element also in the Italian case.

Yet if the "exodus" alluded to by Tolomei has thus far seemed little more than an interwar iteration of European settler colonialism, the second half of his 1938 commentary urges us to survey it from a different vantage point. For there he turned his gaze to Italy itself. According to the senator, "some state initiative would be providential also on national soil within the peninsula—for at least a few dozen families in each municipality from Salorno upward" (Tolomei 1938, 23). Tolomei here referred to the Italian province of South Tyrol at the northern border of the Italian kingdom—no desert colony to be reclaimed but rather a mountainous, predominantly agricultural area inside state borders. In fact, settlement efforts were already under way there too, though not on the same scale as in Libya, and clearly not yet enough to impress the ardent nationalist Tolomei, who had devoted his life to professing South Tyrol's "Italianness."

Italy had annexed the southern part of Tyrol, comprising South Tyrol and the Trentino, from the dismantled Austro-Hungarian Empire after World

War I, together with the northeastern territories of the Venezia Giulia, including Trieste, parts of Friuli, and Istria. Italian nationalists considered these to be genuinely Italian territories, "redeemed" from foreign rule through the sacrifice of war (Hametz 2005; Ballinger 2003; Sluga 2001). The native population, however, did not readily conform to any of the prevalent notions of Italianness: in the case of South Tyrol, over 90 percent spoke a German dialect or the Ladin language and lived by distinctive customs and traditions. Moreover, this was not a populace that welcomed the prospect of turning Italian. In fact, during the course of Fascist rule, many South Tyroleans increasingly came to favor the integration of their homeland into a different nation then under aggressive construction, namely the expanding German Reich of Adolf Hitler. Thus it was that the region's "Italianness," so fiercely asserted in nationalist ideology and rhetoric, still had to be accomplished in practice (Di Michele 2003; Steininger 2003). Various nationalist agitators, Tolomei among them, believed that the assimilationist efforts of the Italian state had not been successful and that only the settlement of Italian families would finally and incontrovertibly Italianize the territory. For Tolomei, settlement organized on a grand scale and implemented in capillary fashion was the key to transforming the province. For him it was thus natural to speak of the two settlement projects—the one pursued in Libya and the one hoped for in South Tyrol—in a single breath.

Although its implications have largely escaped historians, Tolomei's vision of a state program that would render contested territories "Italian"—both on the African shoreline and along the Alpine ridge—should alert us to the fact that Fascist Italy did indeed pursue a very particular settlement policy in the 1930s, one that extended across Italy's colonial and national domains. In spite of their different administrative position within the Italian polity—one a colony, the other a national province—Libya and South Tyrol were both to be transformed via the settlement of carefully selected families. The parallels in planning and execution in the two regions can be seen too in the anxieties about image and interaction with the native population and in the difficult relations between settlers and state agents. This hybrid project, at once colonial and domestic, is the subject of the present chapter.

Unlike the preceding chapters in this volume, this present one deals with a settler situation in the past. While some echoes may still be audible in the present, this settlement drive is long since over. It no longer *un*settles the present. Nevertheless, the Fascist case is instructive in a number of ways. First, it

raises questions about the relationship between imperial and national settlement projects. One approach to the hybridity of the Fascist project might be
to retain the notion of colonial settlement and argue that the concept is useful to make sense of state policy *within* the motherland as well as across the
sea. A varied body of scholarship has analyzed relations of domination within
nation-states through the analytical lens of colonialism (Hechter 1999; Hind
1984; Verdery 1979). While Italian scholars have tended to employ the concept
of internal colonialism mainly in relation to Italy's violently annexed south
(Gramsci 1995; Palloni 1979), there were clearly colonial facets to the relationship between the Fascist metropole and its ethnically heterogeneous borderlands in the north. Yet this chapter argues that for all the obvious colonial
resonances, Fascist settlement policy differed from past colonial settlement
projects. As we will see, both inside and outside the existing national boundaries the regime sought to use settlement to extend and consolidate the Italian
nation. Rooting Italian farmers became the means to legitimate and secure
Italy's sovereignty over contested territory in perpetuity. The argument here
in fact is that the Fascist project marks an important moment of transition, as
an imperial age of settlement gave way to strictly nationalist projects.

In the aftermath of the First World War, Europe witnessed a crisis in governance where, in spite of Britain's and France's extended imperial reach, the
political model of internal differentiations and hierarchies was increasingly
challenged, not only by the colonized but also among the colonizers. Imperial rule was on the wane, presaged by the demise of the Habsburg, Ottoman,
Wilhelmine, and Russian empires, and the Paris Peace settlements clearly recognized national self-determination as the politically and morally superior
political form. In this context, settlement policies, justifications, and experiences started to change too. As the editors of this volume explain in the
"Overview" at the end of Chapter One: "The era matters—a lot. What used
to be a common practice during periods of imperial expansion is now highly
contentious." The end of the First World War marked the beginning of a crucial period of transition in the purpose and justification of state settlement
projects.

This is not to say that population settlements resting on national prerog-
atives are less problematic, or indeed more benevolent, than their imperial
counterparts—as the examples in this volume amply make clear. The point is
rather that national settlement projects rest on different claims to legitimacy
and operate through different political arrangements than imperial ones.

Empires thrive on differentiation and accommodation, on hierarchies and allegiances (Burbank and Cooper 2010; Stoler 2006). A nation-state, by contrast, presumes a correspondence between its territorial reach and its people, with the latter understood as sharing distinct and immanent commonalities. Today, none of the states (or activists) that lay claim to contested territories via settlement would portray their efforts as "imperial." To the contrary, it is because the state has (or claims) national sovereignty that it actively pursues or quietly tolerates settlement; and settlement in turn is meant to cement state sovereignty. Where there is a perceived mismatch between the territorial distribution of a "people" (defined by language or ethnicity), on the one hand, and the location of state boundaries, on the other, a nationalist leadership can attempt to "right-size" or "right-people" its domain, or even do both, as the examples in this chapter showcase (O'Leary, Lustick, and Callaghy 2001). With respect to the citizenry, the contention is thus one of communality and homogeneity; everyone belongs—except for those who for some reason do not, even if they are native to the claimed national territory. The indigenous population in fact does not necessarily fare better under national than under imperial rule. Indeed, if it is believed not to fit into the national community, no accommodation becomes possible.

To be sure, the Fascists were not the first to blur the difference between imperial and national settlement programs and settler societies. The most obvious precursors could be found in Ireland and Algeria (Kenny 2004; Prochaska 1990). But as historians have pointed out, the question of whether these British and French territorial possessions constituted a form of national or imperial rule can be answered only in relation to specific policies and relationships and to past understandings of nation and empire. As Kevin Kenny has aptly put it for the Irish case, "Ireland's relationship with its more powerful neighbouring island—and with the global Empire which that island eventually produced—developed and changed over time. So too did the form, extent, and meaning of the British Empire" (Kenny 2004, 1). That both the Irish and the Algerian cases were resolved in the course of the 20th century in favor of national independence, conversely, corresponds to the broader change in perception and legitimation of nation-states vis-à-vis empires over the course of the last century. If the goal is to explore some of the conundrums and ambiguities that marked this transition, the case of Fascist Italy has the advantage that it developed over a short period of twenty years immediately following the watershed moment of the First World War. The Second World

War brought the end of the Fascist imperial venture, and soon enough the other European imperial projects failed as well.

The views offered by Tolomei with which this chapter began alert us also to a second reason for engaging with the Italian case. For in addition to eliding distinctions between nation and empire, Tolomei also revealed the place of settlers as objects of social engineering. Of course, in the long history of settler colonialism, settlers had always shown quite varied degrees of initiative. In some cases, settlement was instigated by metropolitan governments, seeking to reap the economic or security benefits of settled overseas territory. At other times, it was settlers themselves who initially claimed a territory and then demanded protection and privileges from their home country. And just as the origins of settlement could differ, the relationship between the home country and settlers could vary enormously. Yet even if the existing continuum was already broad, the communal bonds, responsibilities, and obligations to which Tolomei was alluding represented something new.

For what really marked Fascist settlement policy compared with all of its predecessors was the vastly increased role of the state. With the state's aspiration to bring scientific knowledge to bear on the management of society, Fascist settlement goals were far more demographic than merely territorial. Far more than European colonial settlers of the prewar period, the Italian settlers were subject to the regime's interventionism and at the same time charged with great responsibilities—revealing the Fascists' particular understanding of citizenship. Above all, the settlers were expected to become the new Fascist vanguard, the embodiment of a new relationship between the Fascist state, the Italian people, and the national soil. While exploring their distinctive lack of political agency in relation to earlier colonial settlers, however, this chapter will argue that even under Fascist rule there remained limits to the settlers' compliance, so that misunderstanding, disagreement, and mutual disenchantment between settlers and regime were endemic in the both the Libyan and the South Tyrolean settlement program.

The cases in this volume display a range from partial state extrication (in the case of Israel) to heavy state involvement (in the case of Sri Lanka) in population settlement. But even the most heavy-handed of these cases falls well short of the radical expansion in state control that characterized the interwar authoritarian states' settlement projects—the emphasis here is on Fascist Italy, but the examples of Nazi Germany and Japan also come to mind. Their approach was recognizably modern, on one level, but few or no contemporary settlement policies since the Second World War have seen quite the same micromanagement or quite the same vision of settler society as the vanguard for a reenergized nation as a whole. While the Fascists' totalitarian approach had little future in an age of democratic rule, it shows the extremes to which a modern state might go in commanding its population and that population's allegiance.

Changing the "Facts on the Ground": Fascist Land Reclamation and Social Engineering across Nation and Empire

My assertion that the Fascist regime was fixated on demography, population management, and social engineering will come as no surprise (Quine 1996; Ipsen 1996; Horn 1994). These preoccupations corresponded to wider European anxieties about the quantity and quality of national populations, but because of the hyper-nationalism exhibited by the Fascists and their commitment to state intervention, the readiness to convert demographic desiderata into transformative social engineering was far greater than in most interwar states, even if delivery fell far short of expectations. Best known are the many efforts to boost the numbers of the Italian population, improve its quality, and, increasingly, strengthen its "race." But the authorities also attempted to control its whereabouts, monitor migration, and select candidates for agricultural settlement. These policies not only resulted from a fanatical belief in the transformative powers of Fascism but were also intimately connected to the anxiety that Italians—their language, culture, tradition, welfare, property—needed to be strengthened, protected, and cultivated.

The Fascist emphasis on population management was colored by often incoherent and contradictory ruralist ideals (Stampacchia 2000; Nützenadel 1997). Fascist ruralism claimed to be modernizing while emphasizing manual labor. It glorified the work of women while supporting a patriarchal system. It honored traditions in the creation of a "new man." It sought to control social upheaval while avoiding meeting the demands of the deprived masses. And it called for individual initiative while imposing restrictive controls.

The regime's policy of *bonifica* (amelioration) sought to realize these ambitions: land reclamation and agricultural development, followed by rural settlement, were meant to expand the class of small landholders, who would then act as the kernel of a future vital and healthy nation. Given its reluctance to expropriate big landowners in order to settle landless peasants, the regime focused its efforts on a few highly propagandistic *bonifiche*, first and foremost the reclamation of the Agro Pontino (Pontine Marshes) south of Rome (Stave Tvinnereim 2007). Initiated in the late 1920s, the project entailed the construction of five towns surrounded by smaller hamlets and individual farmsteads, providing a new home for nearly 4,000 families resettled from all over Italy.

Smaller projects were planned and implemented across the peninsula, including the newly annexed northern provinces. There, however, the paramount goal of the *bonifica* was different: Italian settlers were meant to outnumber and absorb the non-Italian native population and through their "Italianness" render Italian sovereignty uncontestable. The numbers involved in these projects, however, were initially far smaller than the thousands of settlers dispatched to the Agro Pontino.[2] The main problem was the lack of readily available land. There were no large swampy areas that could easily be confiscated and transformed. Nor had there been an open rebellion, as in Libya, that would have "justified" a harsher treatment of the native population, including the seizure of property. And given the European setting, the government was certainly more circumspect in its policies of expropriation. Nonetheless, it did initiate concrete programs aimed at settling Italian peasants in order to Italianize the new borderlands inhabited by German speakers in South Tyrol as well as Croat and Slovene speakers in the Venezia Giulia. In the late 1920s and throughout the 1930s, local, non-Italian agricultural associations were banned and local, non-Italian credit unions undercut, forcing most of them, as well as their clients, out of business. Italian financial institutes took their place, with the explicit mandate to buy up troubled farmsteads or businesses one by one. In the wake of the world financial crisis, instead of finding assistance, local non-Italian farmers found in the Italian credit institutes ready buyers, who then passed the properties on to relocated Italian families at greatly reduced prices (Wörsdörfer 2004). Moreover, plans for extensive reclamation of unproductive areas were discussed at the highest level, even if only small projects were actually undertaken. In the case of South Tyrol, the industrial development of the provincial capital of Bolzano in the mid-1930s lured thousands of Italian workers into the region. While greatly changing the face of the provincial capital, this influx did not bring about a sweeping reversal of South Tyrol's demographic makeup as a whole (Visintin 2004). For Tolomei, as for many others invested in Fascist ruralist ideology, the biggest shortcoming of the Bolzano project was that it did not involve the "conquest of the soil," hence Tolomei's insistence in the late 1930s on the need for rural settlement.

Compared with settlement projects in the Italian heartland, such as the Agro Pontino where the goals were to reclaim unproductive land and settle the unemployed, in the northern borderlands the state had the primary goal of changing the "facts on the ground" (Lustick 1993b) by acquiring one parcel of land at a time and passing it from the hands of German, Croat, and Slovene speakers into those of resettled Italian speakers. To participate in any state-financed settlement program—whether in the Agro Pontino, in the northern borderlands, or in Libya—settlers had to have lots of children, good health, an unblemished moral record, and no criminal record. Ideally, they had to be peasants, preferably belong to the Fascist Party, and at the very least have no anti-Fascist credentials. But in the case of the northern borderlands, they also had to come from one of the "old" Italian provinces (those that had belonged to the kingdom prior to World War I) and have served in the Italian army, above all to exclude those former Austrian citizens who had fought for the Austrian forces in the Great War. In other words, no land was given to the landless German-, Slovene- or Croat-speaking Italian citizens who resided in the borderlands.

Then, in 1939, the regime entered into an agreement with Nazi Germany that would have considerably quickened the pace of Italian settlement in one of the annexed provinces, South Tyrol. The agreement was intended to confirm the existing border between Italy and Germany and dash German irredentist aspirations in the region once and for all by giving the local German- and Ladin-speaking population a choice: they could adopt German citizenship and emigrate to Germany or affirm Italian allegiance and stay in their homeland (Lill 1991; Eisterer and Steininger 1989). The result of this so-called Option, unexpected even by the Fascists, with nearly 90 percent of South Tyroleans opting to leave, would have created—had it been fully implemented—a *tabula rasa* of sorts, a slate of empty land to be repopulated anew.

In all of these borderland efforts to the north, there was never a doubt that the Fascists considered the territory Italian. The question was not, as in the colonies, whether alien populations would quiescently accept a subordinate role and enable or abet Italy in exploiting native resources. Rather, the question was whether the native populations belonged in the nation or could be made to do so. Far from espousing a strictly biological conception of Italianness, the Fascists pursued the forced assimilation of the non-Italian populations in the borderlands. Results, however, were far from meeting expectations, and thus settlement increasingly came to be seen as the key policy that would ensure that only Italians inhabited Italian provinces. Because all this was happening within the boundaries of the nation-state, presided over by national institutions and administrative and policing bodies, there were also limits to how violently and arbitrarily the Fascists could act or legitimate their actions. Certainly there were colonial elements to Fascist policy in the northern borderlands of the nation, and population settlement as a policy certainly reminds us of settler societies in colonial contexts. But ultimately the regime was building a national community within a national framework.

How far was this true though of the Fascist approach in the colonies? In 1922, when Mussolini marched on Rome and was appointed prime minister, Italy was a relatively small colonial power. It held territories in the Horn of Africa (Eritrea and Somalia), on the Libyan coastline (Tripolitania and Cyrenaica), and on the Dodecanese islands. Though some Italians had moved to these colonies, none of these possessions could be defined as settler colonies. None were occupied by a large number of permanent Italian inhabitants forming a segregated and influential community that controlled vast expanses of native land. Moreover, there seemed to be little interest in creating such an arrangement on the part of either the Italian government or private persons.

Thus, in the late 1920s, only a few thousand Italians lived in Libya, mainly in the port cities of Tripoli and Benghazi, with Italian emigrants to Africa preferring to settle in the nearby French colonies of Tunisia and Algeria (Choate 2007). Italy's Fascist government, however, came to take a different stance. After the near genocidal war against the Libyan resistance in the late 1920s and early 1930s and after the mass displacement of the Libyan population, particularly in Cyrenaica (Ahmida 2005; Labanca 2002b; Salerno 1979), massive demographic colonization became a real possibility. In 1938, a state-funded and state-administered settlement program relocated the famed 20,000 settlers hailed by Tolomei. Another group of nearly 10,000 followed in 1939 (Cresti 2011; Del Boca 1988; Segrè 1974). By 1940, some 110,000 Italians lived in Libya. At this point, the percentage of Italians among the predominantly Arab and Berber population of Libya amounted to nearly 12 percent, similar to the percentage of Europeans living in Algeria at that time, who, however, numbered over one million. The ultimate goal of the Fascist authorities was eventually to resettle 500,000 people from the Italian peninsula onto the North African shore. But as we will see, with the settlers, a new set of administrative arrangements was introduced as well.

Demographic objectives were employed also to justify Italy's attack on Abyssinia in 1935 (Labanca 2002a; Sbacchi 1997; Del Boca 1996). Soon after Mussolini declared the war won in May 1936 (though Italy would never securely hold all of Ethiopia), a couple of villages were built and several hundred settlers dispatched (Podestà 2007). The vision was grand: two million Italians were supposed to be relocated to a territory consolidated and renamed *Italian* East Africa. Yet the outbreak of World War II and the loss of Ethiopia in 1941 put an end to these ambitious schemes. Indeed, given that Italy held East Africa for only five years and only precariously, it is perhaps surprising that even a few settlement experiments were launched. The Libyan case, though, is much more extensive and interesting. For what the regime established there was something new. It still looked like an imperial project to many, and it had many of those traits, even for the settlers themselves. It also had something in common with the agricultural reclamation projects in the Italian interior, which aimed to create a settled, healthy, and fecund class from the unemployed. The primary goal of Libyan settlement, however, was different: namely, to expand the nation.

Nationalist rhetoric had long claimed that Libya was a natural extension of the Italian peninsula, Italy's "fourth shore," complementing its Adriatic, Ionian, and Tyrrhenian coastlines.[3] The vision became policy when Italo Balbo, Mussolini's heir apparent, started his governorship of the two colonies of Tripolitania and Cyrenaica in 1934 and united them into one. It became reality when in January 1939 the Libyan coastline was declared part and parcel of the Italian nation. The northern—more fertile, more commercialized, and more accessible—part of Libya became Italy's nineteenth region, comprising the four provinces of Tripoli, Misrata, Benghazi, and Derna, while Libya's southern territory continued to be administered by the military. On Africa's Mediterranean coast, as in Alpine valleys, settlement became the vehicle to give life and substance to the territory's presumed Italianness. There is no doubt that the Fascists were dreaming of reviving Ancient Rome and its *imperial* domination across the Mediterranean, but in practice they opted to turn the settlement program in Libya into a *national* project, invoking the legitimacy of nation.

On the one hand, because until 1939 Libya was a colony rather than part of the nation, the authorities were able to pursue their settlement goals with greater violence and fewer legal constraints than at home. Land was acquired through violent displacement in the late 1920s, followed up by sale contracts in the 1930s. By accepting money for having been expelled, Libyans found that they lost the property rights to their land. Cynically, the Italian state also requisitioned some land from its Libyan owners by way of a self-serving reading of Islamic law, finding that land that had remained uncultivated for over three years belonged to God and thus to the authority that represented God on earth.

On the other hand, however, the Fascists sought to build a settler society for the same reason as in the northern borderlands. The long-term goal of the Fascist regime was to send the "right people" and forge a lasting link between the Italian settlers and what was considered Italian soil.

To create a rooted Italian society as quickly as possible, the Fascists sought to transfer entire families rather than individuals, as had been the norm in the colonial enterprises of other European powers. Families purportedly recreated the "Italianness" of their home villages instantaneously and thereby made the inclusion of contested territories into the Italian polity incontrovertible, or so the authorities hoped. The presence of intact families was also meant to render future relocation more difficult. In addition, the state included special provisions in the settlement contracts in order to ensure that the land entrusted to the settlers would stay in Italian hands. Settlers gained full ownership only after thirty years of committed work on the farmstead, by which time they would presumably have grown attached to the soil and would no longer be tempted to sell their property and return to their home villages. Return migration was a recurrent pattern in the history of Italian emigration, whereas the Fascist state wanted to make sure that these settlements were permanent. The various programs thus built on the institution of private property, which, however, was not to be sold under any circumstances. In this respect, the expectations of regime and settlers diverged considerably: on the one hand, many Italian settlers in the colonies and the borderlands tended to approach their relocation as a sort of labor migration—"an experiment or a temporary expedient [rather] than a firm commitment to take up life" far from home (Bruner 2009, 77). The regime, on the other hand, wanted to bolster newly drawn borders and transform recently conquered lands into "truly" Italian territories. By importing Italian peasants, the regime hoped to dilute and eventually nullify the presence of non-Italians in these regions.

Unsettling Realities: Settlement
and the Native Population

All Fascist *bonifica* projects aimed at the creation of an "ideal" society—Italian, Fascist, and rural—composed of small landowners who would cultivate the land with the help of their families and lay the basis for a healthy and stable society. Such a seemingly benign vision, however, ignored the settlements' impact on the native population. After all, whatever these territories were, *tabulae rasae* they were not. Even the Pontine Marshes had been inhabited by people who had to be displaced and their land appropriated. Belying the dreams of virgin territory, Italian authorities and settlers were thus confronted with the reality of substantial native populations and invariably faced the question of who these indigenous people were, whether they could belong, and if so, on what grounds.

In his famous 1927 Ascension Day speech to parliament, Mussolini declared: "Up there, there is nobody but an Italian minority who speaks a German dialect. . . . We regard them as Italian citizens who forgot themselves and who must find themselves anew" (Mussolini 1959, 368–369). This view of the South Tyroleans as stray Italians found its implementation in harsh policies of assimilation, such as the prohibition of German schools, the introduction of Italian names, and restrictions on the local German press. Native South Tyroleans, for their part, responded to such nationalist impositions with an analogous nationalist entrenchment, asserting their linguistic and cultural heritage and upholding a supposed "Germanness" against the imposed "Italianness."

With the 1939 Option agreement, however, the picture became more complicated and Italy's policy more ambivalent, indeed paradoxical. On the one hand, South Tyroleans were given the option to determine their national affiliation because both the Nazis and the Fascists believed them to be intrinsically German; only German and Ladin speakers, no Italian speakers, living in South Tyrol could opt. Nazi Germany was willing to take the South Tyroleans precisely because of their presumed racially, and thus indelibly, Germanic nature. On the other hand, the Fascist leadership was willing to keep those who opted to stay on the assumption that they could be assimilated into the Italian nation. To some extent, this hybrid position of the South Tyroleans—sufficiently different that they could be relinquished, yet assimilable if only they so chose—fit the newly espoused theory of a racial kinship between Italians and Germans. Necessitated by the alliance between the two dictators, the idea that Italians belonged to the "Aryan race" tied Italy closer to Nazi Germany, and thus to the European continent, contradicting earlier claims which classified Italians as members of a Mediterranean or Latin race. At the same time, the voluntarism inherent in the Option showed that Fascism had not entirely lost its ambivalence on questions of race, biology, and assimilation.

One would expect the Fascists' assessment of the Libyan population to be far less ambivalent. After all, here was an African territory with a more obviously "racially" different, non-European population. Yet also here we can observe ambiguities in Fascist notions of race, assimilation, and belonging. There were plenty of disparaging interpretations, which conveniently served as a justification for the Italian invasion in Libya and the subsequent "pacification" campaigns. But a number of theories of a common Mediterranean heritage and even race were also in circulation, and clear distinctions were made between the Mediterranean peoples of North Africa, Libyans in particular, and black Africans (Schneider 2000). One colonial scholar, Raffaele di Lauro, maintained in 1940 that "in northern Africa, the dominating European powers are in contact not only with negroids, but also and mainly with native (Berbers) or immigrant peoples (Arabs) with a high degree of civilization" (Foresti 1984, 134). Such ideas underwrote assimilationist and collaborative policies, which were taken furthest by Governor Balbo, who in October 1938 demanded Italian citizenship for all Libyan men. Unsurprisingly, Mussolini rejected Balbo's proposal, in keeping with the racial laws against Jews issued that same year and those issued a year earlier for Italian East Africa, which prohibited marriage and relationships between Africans and Italians and precluded the offspring of such relationships from being considered Italian.

Governor Balbo's position toward the legal status of the Libyan population, however, should not blind us to the totalitarian aspirations of the settlement program, which sought the wholesale Italian settlement of Libya's most fertile coastal areas. While promoting Italian citizenship for Libyans, Balbo also wanted to relocate 5,000 Italian families to the Jebel Akhdar, the western, most fertile highlands of Libya, "so that not a palm of the 'Green Mountain' [would] escape" the Italians.[4] He wanted to create a uniformly Italian territory. At the same time, it is worthwhile noting that the demand for Libyan citizenship corresponded to the new position that the Libyan coastline was to hold in the Italian polity. In the governor's view, the new administrative arrangement for Libya necessitated revisiting the position of the Libyan population vis-à-vis the Italian state as well.

What the Libyan example and the South Tyrolean example clearly show is that population settlement always involved taking a stance on the position of the native population in relation to the new community under construction. As has been observed for many colonial contexts, the choice of settlement as a particular technology of domination generated an intensification in the rhetoric of difference (Young 1997); it was settler politics that made racism "necessary" (Gott 2007). Commenting on the relationship between colonizer and colonized, Udo Krautwurst speaks of the "desire of the colonizers to make themselves local while refashioning the colonized as threatening potential colonizers" (2003, 58). What Krautwurst writes about the colonial experience seems even more pertinent to the Italian efforts to extend the nation: the desire, indeed the necessity, to wish the native population away as compromising the "Italianness" of the territory and the legitimacy of national rule. This was as true of Balbo as of more hardline advocates of the racial laws. Balbo was less rigid only in arguing for a mixture of approaches. On the one hand, he pursued a kind of territorial apartheid by delimiting areas for Italians only, but on the other he aspired to meliorate legal discrimination by absorbing Libyans into an Italian citizenry. He was in this respect operating with the idea of nation as a citizenry with equal "rights," even if under Fascist rule the meaning of citizenship and the extent of citizens' rights had been substantially debased.

In a broader European ideological climate conducive to racial classifications, Italy's own racial consciousness was becoming more pronounced as the regime sought to expand and establish a more powerful presence in the world. The invasion of Ethiopia with its brutal warfare and speedy empire-building undoubtedly influenced and deepened racist beliefs and practices (Barrera 2003; Del Boca 1995). In East Africa, the regime was planning an apartheid system, which entailed the displacement of the native population and its relegation to circumscribed areas of the countryside and the cities (Fuller 2007). Under the Fascists, this was supposed to be a massively managed project, but because it was never implemented, it is unclear whether it had the distinctive goal of reproducing, and perfecting, a national society and thereby extending the territorial limits of what was Italy, as in Libya and South Tyrol, or whether it was to be a colonial outpost with the few ruling over the many.

Citizens or Subjects? Settlers' Agency
and Settlement Policy

In terms of settler agency, this study, as it deals with a dictatorship, is the outlier among the case studies in this book. For lack of agency among poor and under-privileged settlers and for extensive state management, probably the Sri Lankan settlement of the Tamil dry zone and possibly the settlement of East Timor come closest. On another level, however, it is the Western Saharan example in this volume that is most reminiscent of the Italian case, because of the discrep-ancies between the goals of a strongly interventionist state, on the one hand, and the outlook and agenda of the settlers, on the other. What is interesting in the Fascist case is certainly the level of supervision but also the level of auton-omy that the settlers retained. What is also striking is the extent to which both settlers and Italian officials shared an uncertainty as to their exact claim to the territory they were occupying: was it part of the nation or part of the empire?

In 1938, settlement supervisor Stern complained bitterly about the atti-tudes and behavior of the settlers in the Libyan village he oversaw. Stern belonged to the hierarchy of village managers, overseers, and agricultural experts monitoring settlers' compliance and using admonitions, fines, and the threat of repatriation to keep them on track. He explained that he had to apply "severe fines" to settlers for drunkenness, but also for having "secretly, with-out telling the administration," allowed their daughters to move to Tripoli and work as domestic servants. He lamented that farmers were unwittingly damaging their own self-interest as they failed to "recognize that [the settler] is not an employee and cannot gain advantage from deception." He prom-ised his superiors in Rome that he would continue to punish every infraction "severely in accordance with the colonial contract."[5]

The colonial contract signed by settlers was detailed and elaborate, outlin-ing duties and responsibilities, not only for the male family head who had signed the contract but for his entire family. Settlers in Libya were given pre-cise instructions regarding their daily work routines. For instance, the entire family had to work on the farmstead, and no family member was allowed to seek external employment or leave the farm on a workday without written permission. The agency's directives in terms of land cultivation and livestock management had to be followed to the letter.

Stern's report makes it clear that strict rules and sanctions were not suf-ficient to keep settlers in line. Settlers at times sent their daughters into domestic service instead of employing them on the farm. Settlers also held on to their local traditions. Sicilian women, for instance, worked inside the house and did not help in the fields, as settlement agencies had expected them to do. Settlers employed native Libyans even though the contract forbade it. They grew vegetables, which guaranteed a quick income, instead of tending their olive and citrus groves, which would yield only in a distant future. And they eventually sold their property, even to Libyans. Complaining about these and other infractions, administrators speculated about the reasons, taking settlers' non-compliance alternatively as a sign of guile, stupidity, or negligence.

Farmers, however, had their own views on how to best run a farm and family. Time and again the plans of the dictatorship and the settlement agencies were thwarted by the economic and social decision-making processes within individual families. In addition, settlers protested their situation and pressured agencies to assist them in better ways, at times meeting the agencies' directives with defiance and insolence. And as we will see in the next example, they played one Fascist agency or state institution against another, placing never-ending requests, and when all else failed, they resorted to begging and pleading. In other words, the fact that Fascism was a dictatorship imposing all sorts of rules should not preclude us from recognizing the agency of settlers. Indeed, the state program hinged on their voluntary participation and cooperation.

Their awareness of their roles as state agents, of having entered into a new relationship vis-à-vis the state, of fulfilling a national mission, and of having not only taken on responsibilities but also gained privileges marked the attitudes of settlers in Libya as in South Tyrol. Domenico Roso, for instance, was an agricultural settler in South Tyrol who had fallen on hard times.[6] In his plea with the settlement agency to postpone the payment of his mortgage, he claimed to be performing a vital national task in that he was withstanding social, financial, and environmental hardship in order to Italianize the province through his presence and labor. Alluding to his South Tyrolean, German-speaking neighbors, he portrayed himself as an Italian struggling for his family's survival amid "Italians who did not want to be Italian and who would want him dead." In his view, such sacrifice made him deserving of state assistance. The settlement agency initially ignored his plea. Then the prefect, the highest representative of the central government, intervened, concerned about the negative effect of Roso's destitution on Italian prestige. It was only then that the settlement agency granted the farmer an allowance—terminating, however, his contract a year later.

Settlers in the northern borderlands and in Libya believed they were appropriating land that rightfully belonged to "them" because it was located within the perimeters of "their" nation-state. Yet at the same time, they were not quite sure about the "Italianness" of their new home. Roso made it clear that the people around him, though citizens of Italy, were not "Italian" in the same way as he was, nor did they desire to become Italian. And interviewee Luigi Montelli, who was among the 20,000 sent to Libya, remembered that he missed "Italy," even while he stressed that "Libya was becoming Italian," thereby echoing how Fascist propaganda presented the "fourth shore" to the settlers.[7]

The novel sense of entitlement that many settlers perceived was often coupled with the perception of having climbed the social ladder. Letters from Libyan settlers spoke of not only "having found America" but also "living like their former masters." When they described to those close to them how they saw their new lives, their self-descriptions often revealed that they were operating with a set of ideas and interests different from the regime's. True, they might have been convinced that they deserved the land at the fringes of the nation and that their mission entitled them to state assistance. Yet what emerges from the correspondence of farmers in Libya is their association of their move to Libya with the Italian experience of emigration, rather than with the regime's project of nationalization. Moreover, alluding to their experiences in an agrarian culture marked by hierarchies, dependencies, and master-servant relations, settlers now considered themselves as masters, though over whom they did not say.

The settlers' own sense of social improvement, indeed of upward class mobility, generally did not reflect the impression of local Fascist leaders, who fretted over settlers' low-class status and unseemly behavior in the new provinces. The authorities feared that settlers were undermining Italian prestige more than they were strengthening Italian presence. While the goal was to send scores of Italians to the borderlands, the local authorities in Libya and South Tyrol wanted only "the best elements." Some local Fascist leaders in South Tyrol even favored a halt to immigration, believing that the newcomers were endangering the advantageous position of the Italians who already resided in the province. Settlement managers, Fascist officials, and government representatives had, of course, desk jobs and considered themselves to be "experts" and thus above the settlers who worked the land. They were for the most part committed party members, while many of the settlers had only joined the party out of necessity. Moreover, the former were part and parcel of a dictatorial administration and, as such, even more divorced from the latter than bureaucrats in a democracy presumably would be.

The discrepancies between the regime's ideology and the mental universe of its settlers were a worry to administrators. A report from 1940 depicted the state-sponsored settlers in Libya as "makeshift settlers," attracted by adventure and mistaken promises.[8] What settlement agents despised were destitute adventurers exploiting the program to chase quick riches irrespective of the "higher" national purpose, and incompetent settlers relying on state subsidy and assistance to ameliorate their situation. Beyond incompetence and a get-rich-quick mentality, what the state objected to was the settlers' assumption that they were entering a colonial setup, in which rotating representatives of the home nation would rule over and rely on local labor to make a good living from the land. From the regime's perspective, this was simply incompatible with its national vision of an enduring, hard-working, and homogeneously Italian society. On some level, the settlers of course knew they were operating in a national environment. They demanded state support in the name of Italy, and presented themselves as representatives of the nation. They were pleased to discover that they could indeed continue to buy the same products they were used to at home. But they sought to make a go of things as "colonizers" based on entitlement and exploitation of local labor. And they remained unsure whether they should believe regime propaganda that they were in Italy, or whether they should feel that they were in a "foreign" land.

Beyond Fascist Settlement

While we are accustomed to think of nation and empire as two very distinct enterprises, their juxtaposition in this case shows that the Fascists came to employ and justify settlement as a policy of nationalization even in their colonial realm. With their presence and labor, settlers were supposed to make the claim to the "Italianness" of recently conquered lands real and irrefutable. Rather than simply exerting colonial control, they were in fact transforming contested colonial territories into national homelands. Settlers were thus first and foremost a *national* vanguard extending the national community of the homeland, rather than simply the bureaucrats, traders, or landowners of past settler societies.

Just as important is the fact that what the Fascists had in mind was a redefinition of the national community—in the colony as well as at home.

The specificities of new "homelands" that the Fascist settlement project was expected to create in Libya and the annexed northern provinces remind us that the state was enacting a particular kind of nation. Settlers were supposed to vaunt their Italianness; reclaim, with their hard labor, contested lands for the greatness of the nation; and procreate to guarantee an Italian future on both sides of the Mediterranean. In this respect, the bonds of national fraternity were expected to be closer than ever before, creating a super-nation that reached from the Alps to Africa. Fraternity, but at the expense of liberty: the extraordinary degree of state control over the minutiae of settlers' lives shows not only that the Fascist settlement projects were very different from the settler-driven land grabs we associate with earlier colonialisms but also that the Fascist vision of nation contained little of the active, sovereign citizenry associated with liberal ideas of nation.

With its demographic logic, intrusive state control, and national rather than imperial objective, Fascist settlement policy is more reminiscent of the interwar expansionism of the Germans and the Japanese than of the settler societies under French, British, or Dutch rule. Like Nazi Germany in its quest for eastward expansion (Mazower 2008; Harvey 2003), Fascist Italy promoted a similar quest for "living space" and a program of demographic restructuring. Both regimes challenged the postwar European order and pursued territorial expansion and consolidation via settlement programs to accommodate their supposedly burgeoning populations. For Japan as well, demographic expansion was a guiding principle in its Manchurian settlement program starting in the mid-1930s, with its mind-boggling goal of relocating five million Japanese farmers in a period of only twenty-five years; 300,000 of which were actually resettled (Duara 2003; Young 1998). All three powers were seeking to establish themselves as global players at a time when the bourgeois consensus on the legitimacy of imperial expansion was being eroded.

Tolomei's "splendid exodus" and his vision for an Italian South Tyrol were thus in the vanguard of a new politics of settlement that differed markedly from colonial precedents. This was a new kind of settlement policy, bent on nation-building and thus much closer than earlier colonial endeavors to the definition of settlement put forth in Chapter One of this volume: "political action involving the organized movement of a population belonging to one national group into a territory in order to create permanent presence and influence patterns of sovereignty in the settled territory." In many ways, the Fascist project set the tone for the 20th-century settlement projects discussed in this volume. Unlike earlier colonial settlements, which had been much less organized, settlement was now the task of a clearly defined and carefully selected body of men and women, given the mission of embodying and strengthening the nation. Settlement was viewed as a means of asserting national control and presence, with strong communal bonds between settlers and homeland—in this case enforced by the state—in order to obviate settler independence.

But if the Fascist project was in some ways anticipating the future, in others it had no future at all. For Mussolini, war with the Mediterranean powers became inevitable to secure Italy's standing and open space for further growth. Yet the outcome of this longed for but untimely war made all the Fascist dreams of settlement moot. For Italy as well as for its allies Germany and Japan, expansionist settlement policy came to an end with striking abruptness. With wartime defeat, any ambitions for national expansion disappeared and with them ideologies of living space and practices of mass social engineering.

Whereas Libya and South Tyrol had formerly been part of the same strategy of national expansion and consolidation, the war and its aftermath presented the remaining Italian settlers with very different kinds of challenges. Because Libya was no longer in Italian hands—it was briefly administered by the British and became independent in 1952—many of the Italian settlers would leave their land over the following decades, and the last remaining ones were expelled in 1970, following Muammar al-Gaddafi's 1969 military coup. Ironically, it was only now that the national unity so yearned for by the Fascists appeared among the former settlers. As they sought Italian aid to defend their claims against Libya, it became imperative for them to identify primarily as *Italiani della Libia* (Italians of Libya), rather than as relocated Neapolitans or Venetians as they had done under Fascist rule.

South Tyrol, by contrast, remained part of Italy, and thus the relocated Italians could be relatively secure on their property. True, some of them have come to believe that the Italian community has been marginalized as the province gained political autonomy. They bemoan the fact that everything has become more "German" and far less "Italian" than South Tyrol's incorporation in the Italian state should have warranted. Many Italian speakers, like many of their German-speaking neighbors, continue to base their identities and politics on the assumption that linguistic, cultural, and "ethnic" differences are defining and definite. Yet nationalist strife has largely been overcome today, even if that result is as much through cultural separation as through social integration.

Notes

1. A collection of foreign articles translated into Italian can be found in Archivio Storico Diplomatico del Ministero degli Affari Esteri (ASMAE), Archivio Storico Ministero Africa Italiana (ASMAI) affari politici 1934–55, el. 3, cart. 99, fasc. 367.

2. Numbers are hard to come by. The documentation of the state-controlled *Ente per la Rinascita delle Tre Venezie* (Agency for the Agrarian Rebirth of the Three Venetos) has not yet been catalogued. It is held at the *deposito enti disciolti* of the Central State Archive in Via Salaria in Rome.

3. The image of a fourth Italian shoreline was extolled by poet Gabriele D'Annunzio in the immediate aftermath of the invasion of 1911 in his "Canzoni delle gesta d'oltremare," in *Merope*, vol. 4 of *Laudi del cielo del mare della terra e degli eroi* (Milan: Fratelli Treves, 1912).

4. ASMAE, ASMAI, Gabinetto, b. 70, f. Colonizzazione demografica in Libia: Balbo report on the reclamation of eastern Libya, August 4, 1938.

5. Archivio Storico Istituto Nazionale Previdenza Sociale (ASINPS), Carte Colonizzazione Libia (CCL), f. 5: service order 8, village Bianchi, January 22, 1938.

6. Archivio Centrale dello Stato, Opera Nazionale per i Combattenti, Servizio Agrario—Aziende agrarie e bonifiche—Alto Adige—Castel di Nova, b. 10, 269 anticipazioni, March 2, 1930.

7. In 2004, I conducted several individual interviews with ten former Italian settlers in Libya who now reside in Italy. I have changed the interviewee's name here to protect his privacy. The interview was conducted on July 15, 2004.

8. ASINPS, CCL, f. 129: report, July 1940.

5 The Indonesian Settlement Project in East Timor

Ehud Eiran

ON DECEMBER 7, 1975, INDONESIAN ARMED FORCES invaded East Timor, a 5,400-square-mile territory that shared the island of Timor with the invading nation. Indonesia was to control the island for the next twenty-four years. While controlling it, Indonesia placed tens of thousands of settlers in the East Timor territory. In 1999, Indonesia, as well as most settlers, left the territory. Following a three-year period in which the territory was administered by the United Nations, East Timor declared its independence in 2002 and is now called the Democratic Republic of Timor-Leste.

This chapter analyzes the Indonesian settlement project in East Timor and proceeds as follows. First, it places the settlement project in the broader context of the Indonesian claim to East Timor by investigating why and how Indonesia gained control over the territory. The second section explores the fundamental aspects of the Indonesian settlement project, looking at the various groups of settlers as well as their numbers. The third section explains why the Indonesian settlement project was initiated and pursued. This section also includes a discussion of the manner in which Indonesia used the settlers as part of its effort to subdue local resistance and deflect international opposition to its rule in the region.

How and Why Indonesia Gained
Control over East Timor

The island of Timor is located at the eastern end of the Sunda Archipelago in the South Pacific, some 400 miles northwest of Darwin, Australia (see Map 5.1). It is divided between Indonesia's West Timor and a now independent East Timor. The latter also extends to two other small islands (Atauro and Jaco), as well as the enclave of Oecusse on the western side of the island. During colonial times, the island's western half (now part of Indonesia) was under Dutch rule (until 1949), and the eastern half (now Timor-Leste) under Portuguese rule. When the Dutch left in 1949, the western half became part of Indonesia while East Timor remained under Portuguese rule until 1975. These different colonial paths contributed to different ethnolinguistic makeups. While the east was diverse, with nineteen to thirty different languages and dialects, the west had only three to seven main language groupings (Fox 2007; Taylor-Leech 2009).

On December 7, 1975, Indonesian armed forces invaded East Timor. At the time of the invasion, East Timor was in the process of emerging from four centuries of Portuguese colonial control and was embroiled in a civil war that had begun a few months earlier. Indonesia's expansion into East Timor was the result of a fusion between the latent ideational framework of a "Greater Indonesia," prevalent since the 1940s among sectors of Indonesia's nationalist elites, and the strategic calculations that evolved in the mid-1970s among sectors of its military elites.

The vision of a Greater Indonesia that would include East Timor was articulated in the 1940s by the formative institution of the Indonesian national movement, the Committee Investigating the Preparations for Indonesian Independence (BPUPK), which was established by the Japanese during the last months of their rule over the archipelago toward the end of World War II (Chamberlin 2009, 5–6). During the committee's first assembly (May 29–June 1, 1945) Mohammad Yamin, a leading member, argued in a paper titled "The Territory of Indonesia" that "a future Indonesia should include also the regions of Sarawak, Sabah, and Malaya [all in current-day Malaysia], as well as Portuguese Timor" (Chamberlin 2009, 5–6). Yamin grounded his vision in ethnic, historical, and strategic arguments. Ethnically, he argued, all Malays should share the same sovereignty. Historically, he suggested, a modern Indonesia was the "heirloom" of the past empire of Majapahit (c. 1290–1520) and to a lesser extent, that of Shrivijaya (c. 600–1300). Both, at least for part of their reign, controlled East

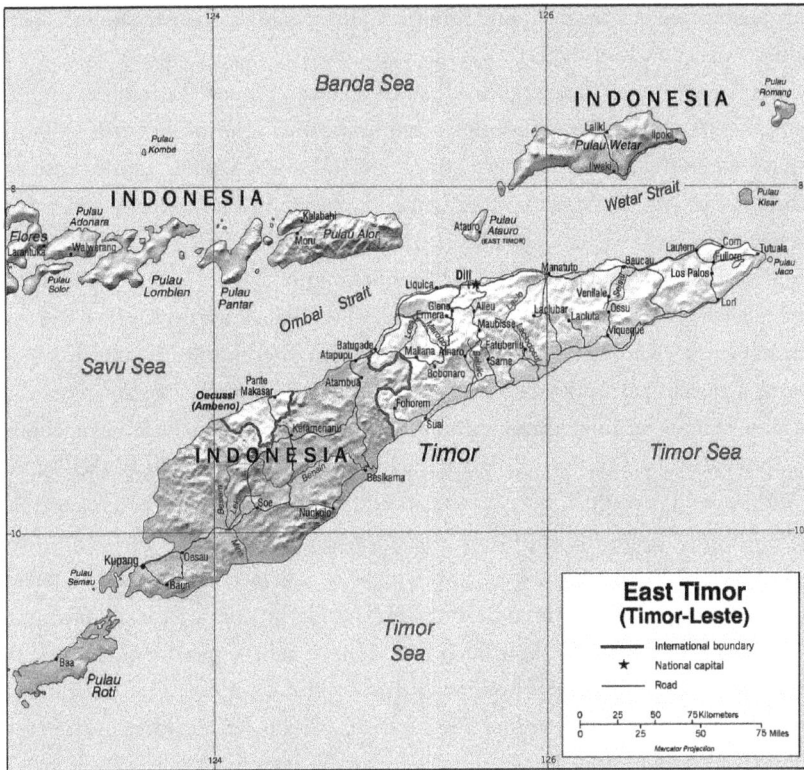

MAP 5.1 East Timor (Timor-Leste)
SOURCE: Central Intelligence Agency Library, 2003.

Timor (Smith 2000, 8; Kahin 2003, 37–38). By 1975, when Indonesia invaded East Timor, official Indonesian history focused on the empire of Majapahit, in part because it conveyed an image that was closer to Suharto's socioeconomic and cultural model of modern-day Indonesia (Wood 2005, 49–54). Strategically, Yamin argued, the future Indonesia should be a "republic . . . without enclaves" (Elson 2008, 108).

Sukarno, another influential member of the committee and later the first president of Indonesia, declared his support for Yamin's vision (Chamberlin 2009, 6). Both leaders were influenced by the realities that had unfolded during World War II: the defeat of European colonial forces and a belief that both the material and ideational aspects of colonialism, such as the division of the island of Timor between Portugal and Holland would not be restored (Elson 2008, 108). Once Indonesia gained independence, it did not, however, take any significant action to expand into East Timor until the 1970s, though it left some ambiguity over its territorial aspirations.

In the spring of 1974, regime change in Lisbon altered Portuguese preferences and led to a quick withdrawal from East Timor. The local population was unable to fill the institutional gap effectively. Indonesia was also encouraged by powerful international actors (the United States and Australia) to step in and prevent a potential pro-Communist competition. Even then, there was variation between different sectors of the Indonesian policymaking apparatus, with the president being cautious but the military intelligence apparatus (but not the military at large) pressing ahead for expansion. The Indonesian opportunity structure included weak competition in Timor. When the Portuguese colonial state withdrew in 1975, there were only limited expressions of an indigenous national identity. This was a result of the low level of development on the island, with some 90 percent of the population illiterate, as well as the heterogeneous ethnolinguistic makeup of the territory (Fitzpatrick 2002, 27).

Indonesian policies toward East Timor in the face of Portugal's retreat were not, initially, unanimous. On the one hand, the political class continued to send mixed messages about its future designs for the territory. Indonesia's military intelligence apparatus, on the other hand, supported expansion in order to prevent the creation of a left-leaning state on the borders of the now conservative Indonesia. Other military actors kept neutral.

These conflicted positions reflected the various possible interpretations of the country's colonial heritage. According to one approach, based in part on Yamin's writings, the division of Timor between two European nations, the Netherlands and Portugal, was a colonial act that should be erased. This approach also drew on some of the similarities between the two parts of the island, including ethnic, religious, and linguistic patterns, as well as on the weakness of the indigenous national liberation movement, the complete dearth of any past history of the territory as an independent entity, and the low level of socioeconomic development on the island. The other postcolonial Indonesian approach saw the East Timorese as an independent group, entitled to express their own will for self-determination.

Initially, Indonesian statements leaned toward the latter view and specifically to non-intervention in the situation. In June 1974, Indonesian foreign minister Adam Malik met the representative of the Timorese Social Democratic Association (which later evolved into the pro-independence party, FRETILIN), José Ramos-Horta, in Jakarta. Following the talks, Malik sent a letter to Ramos-Horta, in which he stated: "The independence of every country is the right of every nation, with no exception for the people of [East] Timor . . . whoever will govern in Timor in the future after independence can be assured that the government of Indonesia will always strive to maintain good relations, friendship and cooperation for the benefit of both countries" (Lloyd 2003, 76).

Yet, even at the meeting that led to this letter, Indonesia retained the possibility of expansion. Ali Alatas, who was a junior participant in the meeting, testified later that although during the meeting Foreign Secretary Malik stated, "We have no claims on East Timor. We will accept any outcome of a good decolonization," he also did not rule out expansion, if it was a result of a process in which all parties "got the same fair chance to compete," and he said that "whoever won in a clean and just decolonization process we would gladly accept" (Jenkins 1997).

In the fall of 1974, the statements of the political faction regarding the incorporation of East Timor became more pronounced, although Indonesian leaders still reflected the duality of earlier days. In a September 6, 1974, meeting with Australia's prime minister, Gough Whitlam, President Suharto said that while Indonesia hoped to incorporate East Timor, its anti-colonial ethos "would neither accept colonialism nor allow the Indonesian Government to seek to colonize others" (Parliament of the Commonwealth of Australia 2000, 122). In that meeting, Suharto reviewed one possibility for achieving both incorporation and adherence to "non colonization": an independent state of East Timor within a broader federation with Indonesia. This arrangement, however, would be impossible, said the president, due to the internal institutional constraints that emanated from Indonesia's unitary model. Finally, Suharto shared with his sympathetic Australian host Jakarta's preferred route for expansion into East Timor: "incorporation . . . on the basis of the freely expressed wishes of the people of Portuguese Timor" (Parliament of the Commonwealth of Australia 2000, 122).

A month later, on October 18, 1974, in a meeting with a Portuguese minister in Jakarta, President Suharto repeated his position when he told his guest that "Indonesia had no territorial ambitions in East Timor and was opposed to colonialism in all its forms as was clearly stipulated in its 1945 constitution." However, said the president, "Indonesia would accept Portuguese Timor's integration with Indonesia" under two conditions: (1) "if this was in line with the wishes of the people," and (2) if the "territory could become a part of the

Indonesian unitary state in accordance with the 1945 constitution" (Republic of Indonesia 1977, 18).

The second important actor in the transformation of the East Timor opportunity into a plan for territorial expansion was Indonesia's military intelligence. Beginning in the 1950s, that organization viewed East Timor as a potential threat to Indonesia's national security. The nature of the threat, however, changed over time, moving from concerns in the 1950s that the Portuguese-controlled territory would threaten non-aligned, Communist-leaning Indonesia to concerns in the 1970s that the decolonized region would become a hub of revolutionary left-wing activity against the now conservative, western-leaning Indonesia.

As tensions mounted among the three parties in the East Timor territory, the newly appointed commander of Indonesia's military intelligence, General Benny Murdani, was a vocal supporter of intervention. According to some sources, he initially ordered the secret deployment of special forces in the territory (Operation Komodo) in order to "destabilize the situation" (Singh 1994, 75), and when this goal was achieved in December 1975, Indonesia invaded the region. More favorable accounts of the Indonesian actions described Operation Komodo as geared "to prepare all necessary steps and contingencies in regard to an expected political change in Timor" (Pour 1993, 320). In July 1976, Jakarta formally annexed the territory and made it Indonesia's twenty-seventh province.

The Indonesian Settlement Project in East Timor

Types of Settlers

The Indonesian project included three groups of settlers. The first group was composed of Indonesian civil servants, such as military personnel, teachers, and bureaucrats, and their families. It is unclear what portion of this group relocated to East Timor on a permanent basis, and so some of these civil servants might not even qualify as settlers as defined by Haklai and Loizides in the first chapter of this volume.

The second group was made up of migrants, mostly farmers, who were transferred by the government from the main islands of Java and Bali as part of the population dispersal program, Trasmigrasi. The third group also consisted of migrants from other parts of Indonesia, but they arrived independently and are referred to as "spontaneous transmigrants" (Pedersen and Arneberg 1999).

The second group falls into Lustick's (1985) underprivileged class, as described in the introductory chapter by Haklai and Loizides. The two others groups fall, roughly, into his politically and economically connected category.

Civil Service Settlers

Following the formal incorporation of East Timor as Indonesia's twenty-seventh province, Jakarta deployed its state organs in the administrative void left after the withdrawal of the Portuguese colonial state. Indonesian civil servants manned the resulting new institutions. In 1983 there were 8,617 Indonesian civil servants in East Timor (Republic of Indonesia 1984, 10); by 1991 the number had grown to 11,036 (excluding armed forces). These civil servants were deployed in the newly imposed municipal government structure that included, as it did in other regions of Indonesia, a provincial authority led by a governor, thirteen subregions (*kabupatens*) led by heads of regions (*bupati*), that were further divided into sixty-four administrative units (*kecamatan*) led by subregional heads (*camat*). Each of the sixty-four *kecamatan* included a number of villages, which were governed by village heads (Republic of Indonesia 1984, 7). The body of Indonesian civil servants in the territory included most of the bureaucrats on each level, as well as representatives of national departments and agencies who operated in coordination with the governor.

Trasmigrasi

Some 25,000–50,000 transmigrants were placed in the territory (Pedersen and Arneberg 1999, 30; Parliament of the Commonwealth of Australia 2000, 80). Most transmigrants were deployed in East Timor's two western districts of Bobonaro and Covalima, while small transmigration projects were based in the northeastern district of Baucau and the southeastern district of Viqueque. The transmigrants were all farmers and were awarded land that was taken from Timorese farmers. The official reason for deploying the Indonesian farmers was local development, suggesting that the migrants would serve as "model farmers" in order to better utilize land cultivation (Pedersen and Arneberg 1999, 30; Aditjondro 1994, 63), mostly for wet rice crops. Government leadership in relocation was important in East Timor (and other locations) because land ownership models there made it difficult for individual migrants to secure legal rights to land.

Spontaneous Transmigrants

Finally, during the twenty-four years of Indonesian control in East Timor, the government allowed the movement of spontaneous transmigrants from other Indonesian islands to East Timor. These transmigrants did not enjoy government support, but they were permitted to settle wherever they chose, as opposed to the centralized relocation of population under the transmigration program. The largest groups that migrated were from the Bugis, Buton, and Makasar, three ethnic groups from Eastern Indonesia that had traditionally high rates of migration. Unlike formal transmigrants, migrants from these three groups moved into cities and filled the economic void left by the Chinese and Portuguese business owners when they departed with the Portuguese in 1975 (Tirtosudarmo 2000, 100).

Number of Settlers

To date, there is no agreement regarding the exact number of settlers Indonesia deployed in East Timor, with estimated figures ranging between 60,000 and 200,000 settlers (see Table 5.1).

The variation in estimates of the number of settlers is a result of data collection difficulties. Although the international authority that managed the territory in the years between Indonesia's departure and Timor-Leste's independence (1999–2002) conducted a number of surveys, difficulties remain. The analysis of existing population does not offer a good indication, as most Indonesians left in 1999 when Jakarta relinquished control over the territory. Simply counting the number of persons that left in 1999 would not provide an accurate figure either, not only because a portion of them were possibly only on temporary assignments in the region but also because tens of thousands of non-Indonesian Timorese who supported Indonesian control also left in 1999.

In addition, post-independence violence, displacement, and change of sovereignty all contributed to difficulties in ascertaining the number and specific location of settlers. The violence that surrounded those last days of Indonesia in East Timor led to the displacement of almost 75 percent of the territory's population. Although many of those displaced returned to East Timor, many of those who returned assumed control of property other than that which they had held prior to independence. One source estimated that possibly up to 50 percent of houses in the capital, Dili, were occupied in 2000 by people other than their 1999 owners.

TABLE 5.1 Competing estimates of Indonesian settlers in East Timor

Description	Source	Number	% of Total Population	Comments
Official transmigrants	Indonesian Board of Statistics (BPS) 1992, 49	4,453	0.5%	Reflects 1990 data.
1990 population not born in East Timor	Census 1990	46,682	6.2%	Reflects 1990 data.
1990 population not born in East Timor, including an estimated number of children (based on average number of children per family)	Census 1990	61,560	8.2%	Reflects 1990 data.
1990 population not born in East Timor, including children, adjusted to 1999 population	Census 1990	73,800	8.2%	Reflects 1990 data. Fixed proportion and new migrants.
1990 population not born in East Timor, including children	Indonesian Board of Statistics (BPS) 1990, 15	105,400	11.7%	Fixed proportion; assumes no new migrants 1990–1999; assumes immigration patterns in 1990–1995 were like those of 1986–1990.
Number of speakers of Indonesian	Indonesian Board of Statistics (BPS) 1990, 42	36,453	5.8%	Some settlers spoke other languages.
Figure mentioned in other places	Mentioned in the literature but official source unknown	150,000– 200,000	17%–27%	

SOURCE: Pedersen and Arneberg 1999, 54.

Competing land claims in the post-independence years created difficulties in determining ownership of land during pre-independence times, as many current occupants preferred not to admit any right of occupancy by others, including settlers. In turn, the targeted destruction of some 80 percent of the central land registry records (and the buildings that housed them) by pro-independence militias in 1999 limited the ability to determine past ownership in many areas (Fitzpatrick 2002, 6).

The official Indonesian census recorded non-Timorese who resided in the territory, but it did not distinguish between those who had relocated to the territory permanently and those who were there on a temporary basis. Moreover, the last Indonesian census was conducted in 1990, leaving researchers with no credible data regarding settlers for 40 percent of the time that Jakarta was in control of the territory (1990–1999). The massive displacement that year and the ensuing UN effort to repatriate some of the displaced persons and allocate abandoned properties to them created what a UN official in Timor described as the "uncertainty of competing claims to land" (Fitzpatrick 2002, 20).

The Indonesian Rationale for a Settlement Project and Local and International Resistance to Indonesian Occupation

The Indonesian settlement project in East Timor was driven by Jakarta's effort to develop its newly acquired territory. Jakarta invested significant effort in carrying out development projects, mostly in infrastructure and education. Sherlock (1996, 836) suggested that Indonesian investment for development in the region was the highest per capita nationwide. Jakarta's efforts included the development of a transportation infrastructure including roads and bridges, introduction of agricultural projects, and expansion of the education and health systems (Sherlock 1996, 836; Thu 2012, 201). Settlers played an important role in all of these: most of the teachers in the newly built schools were settlers, and settlers that came through the transmigration program led the wet rice commercial agricultural projects (Thu 2012, 201).

However, two other factors were critical in the launch of the settlement project. First, economic development was highly politicized. In Jakarta's view, social and economic advancement of the area would secure local and international legitimacy for its territorial designs in East Timor (Sherlock 1996, 835). Internally, development would further strengthen those elements of the Timorese population that supported integration with Indonesia, such as those associated with APODETI (the Portuguese acronym for the Popular Democratic Association of Timor), a party that existed prior to the invasion. The party's base drew on members of the Timorese elites that had ties to Jakarta, such as traditional leaders from the border areas as well as a group of former Indonesian officers who had emigrated to Portuguese Timor in the late 1950s (Parliament of the Commonwealth of Australia 2000, 114).

Externally, the Indonesians believed, demonstrating their ability to develop such an underdeveloped region would lend international legitimacy to their cause. Although Indonesia had secured physical control over East Timor, its sovereignty had not been recognized by the international community. The Indonesian government believed that it could affect the international community's position and that the community might eventually recognize Jakarta's expansion into the territory. However, the Indonesian government had only a partial view of how expansion would be legitimized. Indonesia's close western allies, the United States and Australia, recognized expansion but signaled their reservations about the manner by which it was achieved. For example, in testimony before the U.S. Congress, John H. Holdridge, U.S. Assistant Secretary of State for East Asian and Pacific Affairs, stated on September 14, 1982, that "U.S. policy regarding East Timor has been consistent through three administrations. We accept the incorporation of East Timor into Indonesia without recognizing that a valid act of self-determination has taken place there. Our efforts now are concentrated on doing what we can to improve the welfare of the Timorese people."

Australia held a similar position, as it had believed long before the Portuguese left that incorporation of Timor into Indonesia would be the final outcome. The Australian Cabinet summed up its assessment regarding Indonesia in Cabinet Decision 632 of February 5, 1963, which stated: "In relation to Portuguese Timor, the Cabinet accepted the view that in the current state of world opinion, no practicable alternative to eventual Indonesian sovereignty over Portuguese Timor presented itself" (Parliament of the Commonwealth of Australia 2000, 116–117).

The Indonesian central government further believed that the weak socioeconomic indicators in East Timor and Indonesia's ability to show that it was advancing the local population would allow it to secure international acceptance of annexation. For international consumption, the Indonesian government framed population removal in a way that supported the government's argument for sovereignty over the disputed region. Jakarta stressed the dire economic situation in the region in order to suggest that the area's incorporation into Indonesia was the only route to alleviating the desperate circumstances of the Timorese. For example, an official Indonesian document produced for external consumption suggested that "East Timor has not even reached the stage of underdevelopment" (Republic of Indonesia 1977, 10). In an informational document in 1984, Indonesia presented transmigration as intended to help the Timorese: "The increase in rice production in the Province of East Timor is . . . due to the increase in the skill of the people of East Timor in farming. In this context, mention must be made of the positive results from the effort made by the government to bring . . . expert farmers from Bali to East Timor. The exemplary farmers were placed alternately among the East Timorese farmers so that the Timorese farmers could learn from the Balinese farmers the right ways of farming" (Republic of Indonesia 1984, 51–52).

The settlement project and, more broadly, Indonesian control over East Timor were generally shielded by the United States. Washington supported territorial expansion of Indonesia, one of its allies, into an adjacent territory. In East Timor, as in Western Sahara, the Americans feared that the implementation of the right of self-determination would lead to the creation of a new state led by a pro-Soviet national liberation movement, and therefore they sought to block the competition. American support was especially crucial before the 1975 invasion. Indeed, Indonesia moved into East Timor only after it received what it understood to be a "green light" from Washington during the visit of President Ford and Secretary of State Kissinger to Jakarta in early December 1975. The two men already knew that Indonesia was considering an invasion, because Suharto had hinted about the possibility.

Ford and Kissinger made clear to Suharto that they would not object to an Indonesian invasion. Ford said: "We will understand and will not press you on the issue. We understand the problem and the intentions you have." Kissinger, however, stressed that "the use of U.S.-made arms could create problems," but then he added, "It depends on how we construe it; whether it is in self-defense or is a foreign operation." Kissinger also said, "It is important that whatever you do succeeds quickly" (Burr and Evans 2001).

U.S. support continued in earnest after the invasion. For example, the Indonesian armed forces were using American arms in their brutal operation in Timor (and thereby breaking U.S. law). The legal advisor of the State Department stated in a follow-up senior staff meeting on December 18, 1975, that the "Indonesians are violating an agreement with us" by using American arms in East Timor. However, Kissinger responded by stating that the United States should "do it [suspend arms deals with Indonesia] for a few weeks, and then open it up," because the Indonesian attack was a form of "self-defense" against the possibility of a "Communist government in the middle of Indonesia" (Isaacson 1992, 680).

Washington did not support the settlement project specifically. However, its broader support for the military occupation of the contested territory allowed the occupier to launch a settlement project while deflecting some of the international costs associated with occupation, expansion, and settlement. As noted, Washington continued the arms supply to Indonesia, despite the evidence that it was using them in a way that contradicted the terms of the arms deals. Moreover, U.S. Ambassador to the United Nations Daniel Patrick Moynihan admitted in his memoirs that his instructions regarding East Timor (and Western Sahara) were to make sure that the "United Nations would prove utterly inefficient in whatever measures it undertook." He then reported gleefully that he "carried it forward with no inconsiderable successes" (Moynihan 1978, 247).

The second factor that explains the pattern of population movement as part of a development strategy was the Indonesian institutional tradition of the transmigration population-relocation program. By the 1970s, Indonesia had a seven-decade old pattern of development through the relocation of population. A 1988 World Bank report defined transmigration in Indonesia as "the movement of people from overcrowded areas of the inner islands to less developed areas of the outer islands" (xvi). Transmigration reflected "a continuity of . . . goals throughout its long period—aims that have varied from time to time in focus but when analyzed present a basically consistent set of objectives" (MacAndrews 1978, 459). The Indonesian government defined the goals of the transmigration program as intending to "improve the lives of the poor and landless families and to develop Indonesia's many under populated islands by offering land and jobs to people who have neither" (Republic of Indonesia 1997).

Over the years, the program further advanced security-related goals, mostly pacifying areas that were not loyal to the central government and assisting in creating cultural homogeneity in the diverse country.

Dutch colonial authorities had initiated the permanent removal of farmers from the overly populated islands of Java, Bali, and (to a lesser extent) Madura. The Dutch Commission for Enquiring into the Declining Welfare in Java, which operated for much of the second decade of the 20th century, initially proposed removal of farmers as part of the "ethical policy" in Dutch colonial management. This new approach was driven by humanitarian sensibilities as well as a desire to develop a colonial market for industry in Holland (Tirtosudarmo 2001, 199).

The Commission produced a number of reports that both explained the reasons for the low levels in major welfare indicators (such as health and education) and made recommendations for their improvement (Blackburn 2004, 39).

The Commission also identified low agricultural production, caused by population pressures, as a major problem. The solution proposed: population removal. Indeed, transmigration became one of three cornerstones (alongside irrigation and education) of the ethical policy (Furnivall 1939, 232). By 1941, more than 300,000 people had been moved from Java to outer islands (Tirtosudarmo 2000, 89).

In 1956 Indonesia adopted the Dutch transmigration program. However, Indonesia expanded the program's goals into the realm of strategy. In its first five-year development plan (1956–1960), the government described transmigration as an "instrument to reduce population pressures in Java, provide labor in sparsely populated provinces, support military strategy and accelerate the process of assimilation" (Tirtosudarmo 2000, 90). In a 1985 speech at the National Defense Institute, General Murdani, who headed the 1975 invasion into East Timor, suggested that transmigration was the only economic policy that was directly tied to national security. He also justified the practice by which the military was consulted regarding the location of transmigration sites on the grounds that these locations were crucial elements of "territorial management" (Tirtosudarmo 2000, 95). As Table 5.2 shows, under Suharto the program was accelerated, in part because of World Bank support.

Effect of Settlers on Indonesian Control

Even if the Indonesian settlers played an important role in the social and economic development of East Timor, their introduction into the region had also fomented resentment against Indonesia. Although the Indonesian government expanded access to education, local school graduates faced, for most of the time under discussion, a labor market with limited opportunities. A dominant sentiment among the local population was that Indonesian settlers were awarded most of the jobs. Sherlock (1996) quotes Carlos Belo, then the Bishop of East Timor (and later Nobel laureate), as stating in 1991 to a reporter: "Those young people had long ago been complaining that there was no work for them after leaving school . . . all the teachers are from outside, all the civil servants are from outside. Go into any government office and all employees are from outside. For the simplest jobs in road building, they bring in people from the outside. And these workers bring their children and wives and sisters" (837).

TABLE 5.2 National transmigration figures, 1950–2000

	1950–1969	1969–1974	1974–1979	1979–1984	1984–1989	1989–1994	1994–1999	1999–2000
Target (families)	—	38,700	250,000	500,000	750,000	550,000	600,000	16,235
Families actually moved	100,000	36,483	118,000	535,000	230,000	n/a	300,000	4,409
Number of people	500,000	174,000	544,000	2,469,560	1,061,680	n/a	1,500,000	22,000

SOURCE: Adhiati and Bobsien 2001, 6.

A second layer of tensions emerged from racial stereotypes that arose among both locals and settlers, with the former, viewing the locals as "lazy," and the latter viewing certain settler populations as a "new group of extortioners who stand in the way of their [the locals] economic advancement" (Sherlock 1996, 839). Some of these tensions led to violent clashes between settlers and locals in 1994–1995 (Sherlock 1996, 839).

Final Observations

Indonesia's expansion into East Timor was a result of the fusion between the dormant expansionist ideology of Greater Indonesia and the opportunity that presented itself with the unexpected retreat of Portugal, the old colonial European power. Weak indigenous competition and U.S. support completed the opportunity structure. These opening conditions are similar to those in some of the other cases presented in this volume, perhaps most notably the Moroccan expansion into Western Sahara (see Chapter Four). In both cases, expansion occurred in the 1970s, deep into post-colonial times. In both cases, the weakness of the local population contributed both to the initial settler expansion and to the limited resistance by the indigenous population to the settlers.

As in other cases, this settlement project was intertwined with state-building and the assertion of sovereignty and territorial integrity. And as in other cases, such as the Moroccan and Israeli projects, these statist impulses collided with local claims for self-determination. The settlement projects, therefore, were a way for states to pursue expansion within the confines of the right of self-determination by "right-peopling" the territory, to use O'Leary's

(2001) term. Indonesia, like Morocco and Israel, did not rely on power alone in its efforts to secure expansion. It adjusted its policies to the centrality of the international norm of self-determination. Jakarta was committed to this principle, at least in part, as it legitimized Jakarta's own political project of independence. Faced with a challenge to the legitimacy to its actions and the possible costs it carried, Jakarta responded by using a settlement project. The settlement project was driven initially by the traditional reasons of the "push factor," as institutionalized by the transmigration program, and the effort to exert social control. Indonesia also used the transmigration project to make a modernization claim for the territory by portraying East Timor as a backward territory that needed imported farmers to elevate it from its extremely under-developed state.

East Timor's fate was indeed decided by the implementation of the right of self-determination in the 1999 referendum. Why, therefore, did Indonesia not try to affect that referendum's outcome through the settlement project in a more direct way, as Morocco did? Unlike Morocco, Indonesia did not antici-pate that a referendum would determine the final sovereignty question in the region. Once a referendum was set, the government had little time to deploy settlers in large numbers. Moreover, Indonesia used other methods that were readily available. The UN refugee commission team in East Timor estimated that 40,000–60,000 people were "internally displaced" into camps, where they were subjected to propaganda broadcasts urging them to vote for integration with Indonesia (Friend 2003, 440). As East Timor was preparing for the 1999 referendum, there were still 21,000 Indonesian soldiers deployed in the ter-ritory (441). Indonesia also encouraged local militias, partially based on the settler population, to threaten and attack pro-independence supporters (444). Militia violence was intended to affect the referendum in three ways. First, by creating the impression that the East Timorese themselves were divided over the question of independence. This served Jakarta as it framed the conflict for outside observers not as one of self-determination for a colonized people but rather as a civil war between two factions that envisioned a different future for their territory. Second, Indonesia believed that violence could delay the refer-endum. Third, Indonesia thought that violence could erode the political base of support for independence (Tanter 2001, 192–193). Yet, neither settlement nor violence helped Jakarta secure its sovereignty over the region. In 1999 Indonesia gave up control over the region, and by 2002 East Timor became an independent state.

Finally, the heavy reliance on the transmigration program is a reminder that settlement projects can be understood not simply as spatial and demographic political projects, as largely described in this volume, but also, at the same time, as traditional state-run development projects. This is evident not only in the Indonesian case but also in the Israeli case, as development agencies such as the Jewish National Fund and the Ministry of Housing conduct both kinds of development projects. The observable implications are similar and, at least in the Indonesian case, the stated policy also seems to have been focused on the non-politicized aspects of the settlement projects. This state of affairs poses a difficulty to the small community of scholars who study these projects, as we need to identify other indicators to ascertain the real meaning of placing settlers in contested territories.

6 Settlers and State-Building: The Kirkuk Case

Denise Natali

DISPUTED TERRITORIES ARE A BYPRODUCT OF STATE-building strategies and settlement policies. Demographic and territorial gerrymandering can cause small shifts in the status quo and at some relatively discrete point, trigger a discontinuous change in the nature of a territory. These "institutional-shaping transforming episodes"—or substantial changes in the nature and shape of the state—create settlement myths about a country and ambiguities in the minds of local populations as to ownership of the territories and their sense of belonging in them (Lustick 1993b, 29–32; Kellerman 1996, 363).[1] In the Kurdistan Region of Iraq, these ambiguities commenced with Iraqi state-building and settler policies that Arabized Iraqi identity and institutions and also Kurdish-populated territories, including the northern, oil-rich province of Kirkuk. These measures created beliefs among Kurds that Kirkuk is an integral and nonnegotiable part of the Kurdistan Region. Still, Kirkuk's founding myths coexist with changing incentive structures in the federal Iraqi state that have left its status unsettled. Kurds have engaged in their own settler policies that are contested by Iraqi Arabs and other minority groups. Power struggles over Kirkuk also have emerged between Kurdish parties. What explains these shifts, and how have they shaped opportunities for resolving this protracted territorial conflict?

This chapter examines Iraqi state-building and settlement policies that have shaped Kurdish claims to Kirkuk, and the implications for negotiating a solution to Kirkuk's administrative and territorial status. It argues that the

presence and number of settler populations play a key role in initially framing issues for disputed territories by creating demographic tipping points that
change the character of the territory and local balance of power. Settler processes also interact with domestic and international politics that reinforce or
challenge demographic changes and group territorial claims. Over time, the
disputed territory can assume a life of its own. It can become part of new and
more complex political processes, incentive structures, and disputes outside
the presence of settler populations, further complicating a political resolution.

For instance, settlement processes linked to state-led violence (policies of
expulsion, ethnicization of identity and territories, and ethnic cleansing) are
likely to create more psychologically and politically embedded claims than
those involving less violent processes where native populations are not displaced or power relations are not significantly unsettled. Settlement myths
can also change over time, based on shifts in state-building strategies, settlement policies, competing group claims, and alternative opportunity and alliance structures. Thus, it is not just the number or nature of settler populations
that matter in shaping claims and negotiating a disputed territory but the
domestic and regional politics in which settlement claims are rooted.

This chapter will examine changes in the trajectory of the Kirkuk problem by analyzing the institutional-shaping, transforming episodes that have
helped to create myths about and claims to Kirkuk by Kurdish elites since the
Iraqi state-formation period. These episodes include different phases of Iraqi
state-building that altered the nature and shape of the Iraqi state, the Kurdistan Region, and the province of Kirkuk. The final section will examine how
political transformations in Iraq since 2003 have led to new framing processes
and opportunities and obstacles to negotiating Kirkuk.

Examining the demographic and morphological variability of state boundaries in Iraq has important policymaking implications. It will enable those
interested in resolving the Kirkuk problem to understand when and how the
perceived permanence of Kirkuk as a natural connection to the Iraqi state
came into question, the changing perceptions of Kirkuk in different political
contexts, and the inter-communal relations in Kirkuk tied to these territorial
transformations. Patterns of behavior can then be determined, reactions and
actions to sensitive issues detected, and policy measures designed to address
the changing nature of the Kirkuk conflict over time. Moreover, the analysis can clarify the expectations we might realistically entertain regarding the
negotiation of the contemporary Kirkuk problem.

Inventing Kirkuk

The Kirkuk problem is an elite-engineered political outcome and not a natural part of Iraqi history and identity (Lustick 1993b). Kirkuk's perceived permanence as an integral part of Iraq came into question as the boundaries of the defunct Ottoman Empire and territories of the new Iraqi state were being negotiated (See Map 6.1).[2] During this tumultuous post–World War I period, the status of Mosul Vilayet, which included the administrative units of Kirkuk, Suleymaniya, and Erbil, remained unclear, either as a potential Kurdish state or part of Iraq (Khorshid, 2005, 53; Mohammed 2005, 22–25; Talabany 2004, 9–10). The "struggle for Mosul Vilayet" also became part of the power plays among regional states, foreign governments, and local groups that attempted to secure control of the region's territories, populations, and petroleum resources. Even after the Treaty of Sèvres (1923) determined the borders of the new Iraqi state and overruled the suggestion of Kurdish statehood, Mosul Vilayet remained a contested region among Kurds, Arabs, and Turks (Olson 1992; Danielson 1995; "Administration Report of Kirkuk Division" 1920, 1).[3]

While some Kurds regarded Kirkuk as an integral part of a potential Kurdish state during this early Iraqi state-formation period, most others did not. Rather, Kurdish political demands were based on recognition of Kurdish rights in the new Iraqi state, the role of Islam, the nature of the Iraqi system, and the relationship of Iraq to the larger Arab union. Kurdish claims to Kirkuk also were relatively absent due to the nature of the late Ottoman and early Iraq states. Administratively, the Ottoman policy was a tolerant one that did not ethnicize the composition of Kirkuk city or political positions. Representation in the Kirkuk administration was based on population majorities and not ethnic group quotas (Natali 2008, 434–435). Even with the Ottoman Porte's centralizing tendencies and Midhat Pasha's administrative reforms in Baghdad (1869–1872), authority structures in the province were unclear, permitting different power centers and communities to coexist at the local level.

Communal relations were also defined by a relatively balanced distribution of power between the two main ethnic groups in the city: Kurds and Turcoman. Except for high-level appointments from Istanbul, local positions in Kirkuk, including the post of *serok ṣarewan* (mayor), were reserved for representatives of the Ottoman state, mainly Kurds from the Talabani family and some Turcoman, but not Arabs. Two-thirds of the members of the Kirkuk governorate in the Baghdad parliament were Kurds, and the

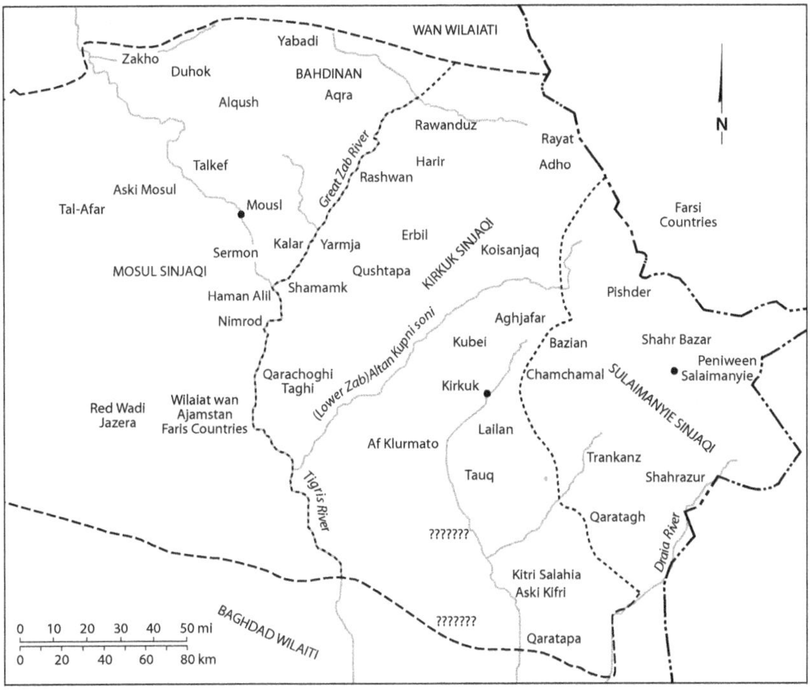

MAP 6.1 Kirkuk during the late Ottoman period (c. 1850)
SOURCE: KRG Ministry of Extra-Regional Affairs 2007.

other one-third were Turcoman (Natali 2008, 434; Talabany 2004, 10, 21; Khorshid 2005, 42).[4]

Further, Kurds did not make claims to Kirkuk as an exclusive Kurdish territory because their sense of nationalism was inchoate and not highly ethnicized. During the early state period, Kurds were deeply fragmented and their interests as tribal, local, and religious communities took precedence over a unified national identity or agenda. Although some tribes from Kirkuk called for "Kurdistan for the Kurds," others such as the Talabani refused to support Shaykh Mahmoud Barzinji's nationalist uprising in Suleymaniya province and instead supported the Iraqi government ("Administration Report of Kirkuk Division" 1920, 4). Additionally, during the early state formation period, the diverse populations that defined Kirkuk—Arabs, Kurds, Turcoman (Shi'a Qizilbash), and Christians—lived together as Kirkukis and supported neither an Iraqi state nor a Kurdish one.[5] When the 1921 referendum was implemented in Iraq, for instance, some Kurds supported Faysal as king while most Kirkukis refused to participate and argued for separation as an independent province (Mohammed 2005, 28, 76; Talabany 2004, 11, 15; Khadduri 1969, 3).[6]

Indeed, with the creation of the modern Iraqi state, the trajectory of Iraq, the Kurdistan Region, and Kirkuk province started to alter. As part of their state-building efforts British and Iraqi elites started to Arabize the political apparatus and repress opposition groups, including some Kurdish nationalist communities. They gave Sunni Arabs, a group that represented about 17 percent of the population, high-level positions in the government and the military. Further, after the discovery of petroleum in Kirkuk in 1927, the Iraqi government encouraged Arab population movements to Kirkuk province and elevated Sunni Arabs to key positions in the local administration. It settled Arab tribes (al-Ubaid and al-Jiburi) in Kirkuk, appointed Sunni Arabs as governor of the province, and engaged in territorial and administrative gerrymandering (Natali 2008, 435; Ministry of Extra Regional Affairs [MERA] 2007). By 1947, the territorial shape and size of Kirkuk had decreased from eight to four districts ("Aqlim Kurdistan Iraq" 2006, 9–16; Talabany 2004, 10).

Still, Kurdish claims to Kirkuk were not highly salient because Iraqi settler policies did not significantly alter the perceived nature and identity of the province or the city. Most Kurds continued to regard Kirkuk as an integral part of the Iraqi state. Small groups of Arab settlers were transferred to the Hawija district, an area in western Kirkuk known for livestock raising, and were virtually absent from the city center and urban power structures (Talabany 2004).[7] Settler communities were also differentiated from other Arab and Christian families that migrated naturally to Kirkuk during this period for employment, particularly in Iraq's developing oil industry. Some became civil servants, while others were stationed as part of the Iraqi Army's Second Division in Kirkuk. Even then, Arab settlers were not a majority representation in the city, which still had only two Arab families: the Tikriti and the Hadidi (Talabany 2006).

Limited Kurdish claims to Kirkuk also reflected the nature of the political space during the early state-formation period, which was not highly or clearly ethnicized. Rather, it was based on an ideologically ambiguous sense of Iraqi nationalism shaped by different currents: *qawmiyya* and *wataniyya* Arab nationalism, monarchists—those loyal to the British Crown (taba'i nationalism)—and an emergent Kurdish nationalism (Natali 2005, 35–36).[8] Even during Nuri Said's premiership, when the Iraqi government started to Arabize high-level positions, the Iraqi government did not ethnicize the state or Kurd-ish-populated territories enough to disrupt the demographic balance of power or sense of belonging in Kirkuk province. According to the 1957 Iraqi census, which identified groups by mother tongue, the ethnic composition of Kirkuk remained relatively diverse and included a combination of Kurds (48%), Arabs (28.2%), Turcoman (21.4%), and Kurds (and Christians) (1.3%) (Talabany 2007).

New Demographic Tipping Points

The trajectory of the Iraqi state, Kirkuk, and Kurdish claims started to change, however, after Iraqi independence in 1958 and the emergence of *qawmiyya* Arab nationalism and Ba'athism as a dominant political ideology and notion of Iraqi citizenship. The violent overthrow of General Abd-al Qasim as Iraqi prime minister (1958–1963) and his replacement by successive Sunni Arab nationalist leaders reshaped alliance structures, norms, and power relations in the state (Dumper 1992, 44). It also led to the increasing Arabization of Iraqi identity, territories, resources, and institutions. Kirkuk became the cen-ter of the state's territorial expansionist and Arabization programs, mainly due to its large petroleum resources and strategic location in the northern territories. To influence local politics, centralize state wealth, and legitimize Baghdad's claim to sovereignty, the Iraqi government started to settle large numbers of Arabs in Kirkuk. This resettlement policy was not part of any ideologically informed movement defined by historical or religiously based meanings. Despite Ba'athist rule that became predominant after 1968, the rationale behind the Iraqi government's settlement processes was an artificial one. Baghdad simply wanted to increase the number of Arabs and decrease Kurdish and Turcoman populations in Kirkuk (Lustick 1993b, 46).

In contrast to the first settlement phase, where Baghdad had gradually and discreetly relocated small groups of Sunni Arab tribes to remote agricultural areas, the second wave of Arab settlers, which commenced after 1963, recon-figured demographics, the balance of power, land ownership, and the local administration in Kirkuk. The Iraqi government repopulated entire districts of Kirkuk with settlers from outside the region. During the first six months of their early rule in 1963, Ba'athist officials evacuated the residents from forty-two Kurdish villages in Kirkuk (Dubuz) and replaced them with Sunni Arabs. The Iraqi government also co-opted and resettled Sunni Arab tribes from the al-Jazeera desert, such as the al-Hadidi, who abandoned their nomadic life and settled in rural areas of Kirkuk. Other tribes such as the al-Shammar, al-Tai, al-Jebouri, and al-Abeed were transferred to Kurdish-populated districts. Similarly, the Turcoman Shi'a village of Bashir in Kirkuk city was transformed into a locality for Sunni Arabs from Hawija. Sunni and Shi'a Arabs were also mixed in Kurdish villages.[9] Moreover, the Iraqi government reconfigured the territorial shape of Kirkuk once again, having transferred four districts from Kirkuk and attached them to other provinces in the Kurdistan Region and Iraq (MERA 2007, 11).[10]

Consequently, from 1957–1977, the demographic composition of Kirkuk had altered so significantly that Kurdish populations decreased from 48 percent to 38 percent of the total population of the province, while Turcoman populations declined from 21 to 14 percent of the population. During this same period Arab populations increased from 28 to 44 percent of the total population (MERA 2007, 9–10). By the late 1970s, about 20 percent of the total population in Kirkuk comprised Arab tribes, 70 percent of which originated from central and southern Iraq ("Aqlim Kurdistan Iraq" 2006, 64). Additionally, as the Iraqi state resettled populations it further Arabized territories by changing the names of localities from Kurdish to Arabic. Kirkuk became al-Ta'mim, alongside the nationalization of the Iraqi Petroleum Company in 1972.

Demographic tipping points also involved changes in the character of Kirkuk (See Table 6.1). Second wave resettlement processes were highly politicized and reconfigured the socioeconomic nature of the province. Settlers were mainly Shi'a Arabs from professional cadres (teachers, doctors, engineers), who were forced or co-opted by Baghdad to leave their homes in southern Iraq and resettle in the Kirkuk city center and its environs. Most notable were settlers that arrived after 1981, who were called the Deh Hezaris (Ten Thousand) in reference to the amount of Iraqi Dinars (ID) the central government paid each family to transfer to Kirkuk.[11] In contrast to the first group of settlers, the second wave represented a distinctly privileged stratum and was made a more permanent part of Kirkuk city. They received jobs, benefits, and land from the Iraqi government. Those employed in the North Petroleum Company (NPC) also received government housing, which reinforced emergent boundaries between Arab settlers and "authentic Kirkukis" including Kurds and Turcoman.[12]

TABLE 6.1 Number of workers in the Northern Oil Company in Kirkuk, 1958–2003

Year	Arabs	Kurds	Turcoman	Christians	English	Total
1958	40	850	370	900	70	2,230
1960	55	1,350	500	1,100	65	3,070
1963	100	1,150	700	1,400	60	3,410
1965	170	1,000	800	1,350	55	3,375
1968	300	875	850	1,000	50	3,075
1972	900	700	900	1,000		3,500
1978	2,700	500	1,200	850		5,250
1982	4,500	400	1,500	800		7,200
1988	5,200	300	1,700	750		7,950
1995	6,600	260	1,800	700		9,360
2000	7,200	119	1,920	600		9,839
2003	7,300	610	2,100	500		10,510

SOURCE: KRG Ministry of Extra-Regional Affairs 2007.

Mythicizing and Re-Mythicizing Kirkuk

The growing presence of settler communities, the manner in which they assumed lands, and the demographic tipping points they created affected local perceptions of the role of Kirkuk in the Kurdish nationalist agenda. The accumulation of these changes over time, alongside an exclusionary Arab nationalist state-building project, alienated most Kurds from the Iraqi state and reshaped their vision of the territorial component of the Kurdistan Region (Abowd 1999, 35; Lustick 1993b, 32). It was not just the displacement of Kurds and Turcoman from Kirkuk that mattered but also the strategic implications of the displacements. For Kurds, the Arabization of Kirkuk became associated with its de-Kurdification, and the removal of Kurdish history, populations, identity, and resources from the province (See Maps 6.2 and 6.3, pp. 122–23).

What emerged was a highly salient sense of Kurdish ethnonationalism defined by victimization and uncompromising notions of entitlement to Kirkuk (Natali 2005, xviii–xxx, 48–64; Abowd 1999, 36). Kurdish elites expressed this sense of entitlement by reframing settlement myths and nationalist claims to Kirkuk. Whereas Kurdish territorial claims during the late Ottoman and early state-building period were largely based on ties to Ottoman lands or demands for Mosul Vilayet as part of a potential Kurdish

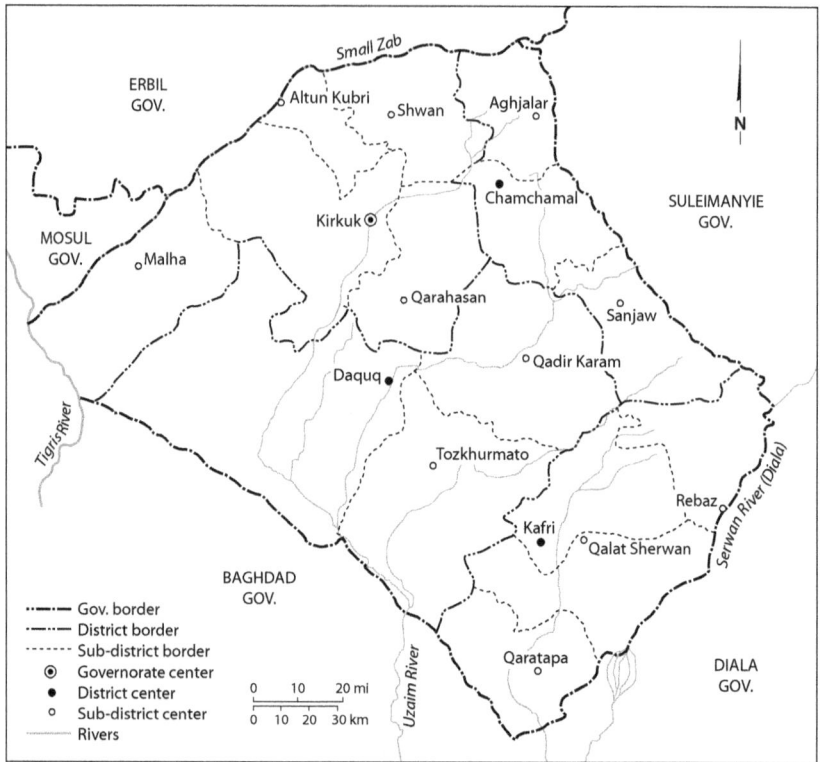

MAP 6.2 Administrative units in Kirkuk, 1947
SOURCE: KRG Ministry of Extra-Regional Affairs 2007.

state, by the mid-1970s they had centered on Kirkuk as an integral part of a Kurdistan Region. Even though Iraqi Vice-President Saddam Hussein negotiated the March 1970 Autonomy Agreement with Kurdish leader Mullah Mustafa Barzani that recognized an "Autonomous Kurdish Region," Barzani eventually rejected the agreement because it excluded Kirkuk from Kurdish territories.

The inability to cross the threshold of Kirkuk also obstructed nine months of negotiations between Kurdish leaders and Baghdad after the 1990 Gulf War. Kurdish officials broke off discussions because by late 1991 they had alternative incentives not to negotiate with Saddam: international humanitarian and security assistance in the form of a safe haven and no-fly zone promised to protect parts of the Kurdistan Region apart from the rest of Iraq. External patronage and recognition helped to semi-legitimize the Kurdistan Region

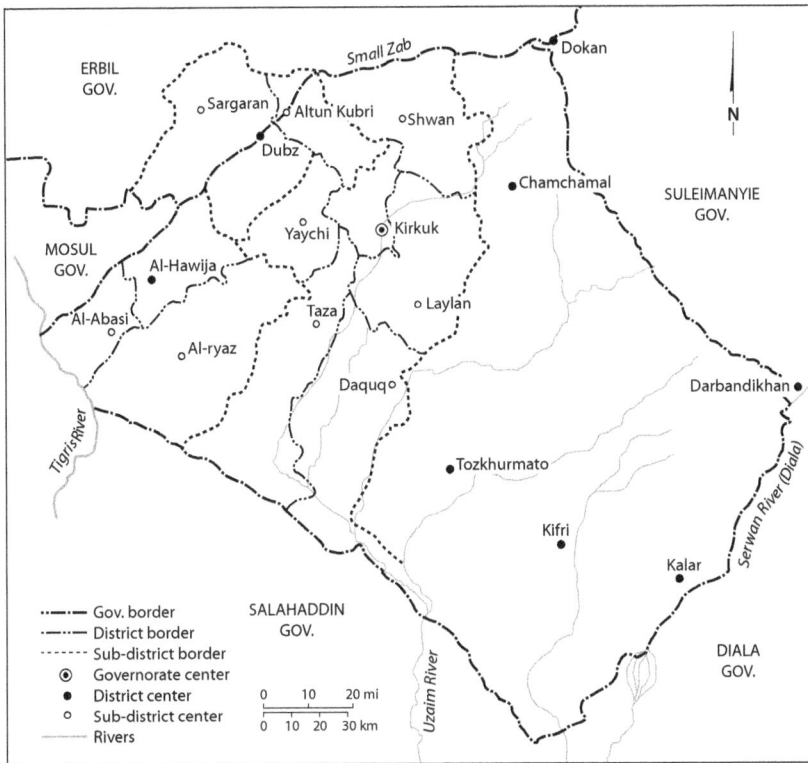

MAP 6.3 Administrative units in Kirkuk, 1977
SOURCE: KRG Ministry of Extra-Regional Affairs 2007.
NOTE: The areas in eastern Kirkuk, including Chamchamal, Khormatu, Kifry, and Kalar, designate lands detached from Kirkuk and annexed to other governorates in the Kurdistan Region and Iraq.

and Kurdish nationalist claims, which were embedded in a sense of victimization by Saddam and the Ba'athist regime and demands for protection within a distinct territory now called "Free Kurdistan."

The post-1990 Gulf War context also reshaped and reinforced Kurdish claims to Kirkuk in another way. When the Iraqi army withdrew from the Kurdish north to an arbitrarily created internal boundary, the "Green Line," that line divided Iraqi Arab provinces from the "liberated" autonomous Kurdistan Region. Kirkuk and other "disputed territories" were located south of the Green Line and in Iraqi-controlled territory. This territorial division helped to create a new map image for Kurds of what an authentic and enlarged

Kurdistan Region should be.[13] The image represented a more politically ambitious nationalist agenda aimed at maximizing Kurdish autonomy and territorial control.

Kurdish territorial claims were reinforced by ongoing Iraqi government settler policies that displaced or discriminated against Kurds and Turcoman in Kirkuk. Alongside Baghdad's internal embargo against the Kurdish north, Saddam displaced an additional 120,000 Kurds to areas south of the Green Line, mainly to depressed urban centers in Suleymaniya and Erbil. In 1996 the Iraqi government implemented an "Identity Law" that required Kurds and Turcoman to sign ethnic identity correction cards, register officially as Arabs, and join the Ba'ath army or Kurdish jash (traitors), or face deportation (Talabany 2006, 12). As a result, by 2003 the percentage of Kurds in the workforce at the NPC in Kirkuk decreased from 38 percent (1958) to about 6 percent. Arab representation during this same period increased from 1 percent to nearly 70 percent (MERA 2007, 26) (also see Figure 6.1).

Despite the deep fissures that emerged over territories and national identity, Kirkuk's status did not necessarily have to become contested. Had demographic and territorial transformations occurred as a consequence of natural urbanization and migration processes then perhaps Kurdish claims to Kirkuk would not have become so highly salient and ethnicized. Had the Iraqi government made efforts to integrate Arab settlers into existing communities, then their presence as a demographic tipping point might not have become so politically salient or sensitive for Kurds. Similarly, had Iraqi elites attempted to create a sense of citizenship and political boundaries that did not discriminate against Kurds as an ethnic community, then the notion of a distinct Kurdish national identity or territories apart from Arab Iraq might also not have become embedded in Kurdish political claims. Moreover, had the Iraqi state economically developed the Kurdistan Region, including its hydrocarbon resources, or provided the region with an equal share of the country's oil wealth, then perhaps the drive to control Kirkuk's resources would not have become so integral to the nationalist agenda of the Kurdish Regional Government (KRG).

Yet Ba'athist officials did just the opposite. Settler policies became linked to the state's ethnically exclusionary state-building policies that reinforced the Kurds' sense of distinction from Arab populations. They created clear markers that differentiated settler from non-settler communities, and that overlapped political boundaries between Kurds and Arabs over time. As part

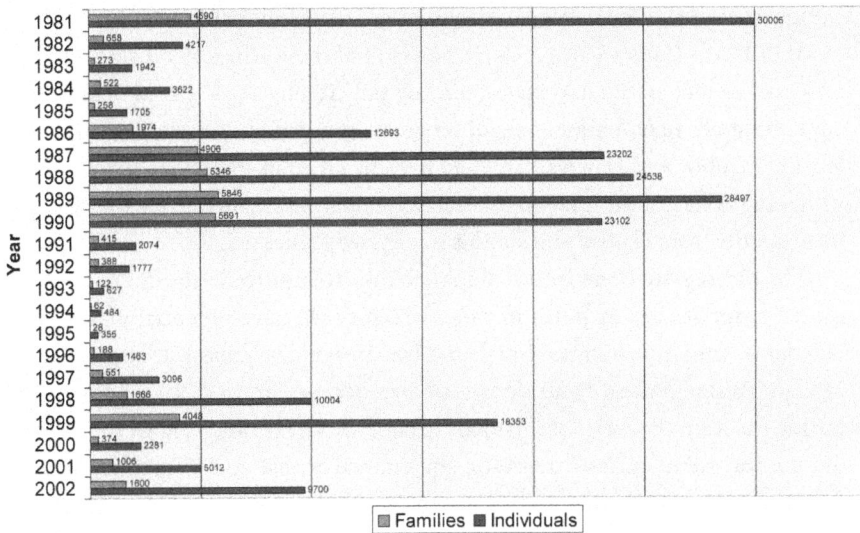

FIGURE 6.1 Arabs settled in Kirkuk, 1981–2002
SOURCE: Data collected by Arif Qorbani (independent researcher) from Ba'athist files in Kirkuk.

of their resettlement policies the Iraqi elites built collective towns for Arabs around Kirkuk in neighboring localities, prevented local populations living in Old Kirkuk from renovating their houses for fifteen years, and prohibited Arab settler populations from returning to their original lands or reselling their homes.[14] Some settled territories were also left to deteriorate and in many cases, became underdeveloped ghettos without basic services (Abowd 1999, 35). Arab settlers, in turn, were regarded by native Kirkuki populations as symbols of the authoritarian Iraqi state and its Ba'ath party apparatus. These trends were exacerbated during the Iran-Iraq War (1980–1988), when Saddam transferred more than 130,000 Arab settlers to Kirkuk, a majority of whom were unemployed and uneducated.

Second- and third-wave resettlement also occurred during state-led violence and mass population upheavals, including the exodus of over 200,000 Kurds to Iran and southern Iraq after the collapse of the 1975 Barzani Revolution. During the latter years of the Iran-Iraq War, Saddam transferred the headquarters of Iraqi Commander Ali Hassan Majid to Kirkuk city and, with it, the power of the Iraqi military and Kurdish jash. Many Kurds from Kirkuk were expelled from the city and became part of the larger Kurdish populations that were chemically gassed by the Iraqi government during the al-Anfal campaign, which destroyed hundreds of villages and killed tens of thousands of Kurds (Hiltermann 2007). As a result of these ethnically discriminatory and violent settler and state-building policies, by 1987 Kirkuk had lost approximately 10,000 kilometers of territory, comprised only three districts (Kirkuk, Dubiz, and Hawiya), and had become an Arab-majority province in which 16 percent of the total population were migrants from outside the province, mainly from central and southern Iraq (see Figure 6.2).[15]

Nor did regional and international actors attempt to delegitimize Iraq's settler processes at any point in time, which could have potentially altered outcomes. The United States, Israel, and Iran provided clandestine support to Mullah Mustafa Barzani and Kurdistan Democratic Party (KDP) peshmerga during the Iraqi civil wars of the 1960s to check Arab Ba'athism; however, they did not intervene in Iraq's domestic governance or seek to reconstitute state functions or policies. The political morass of Kirkuk, as well as other sensitive issues, was considered an internal Iraqi concern and not one in which foreign actors would engage on behalf of the Kurds or any other minority group. State sovereignty remained sacrosanct; Saddam Hussein continued to be supported by most western governments as a "moderate" Iraqi leader, even after the Anfal campaign. In fact, on the eve of the 1990 Persian Gulf War, some Western leaders continued to negotiate with Saddam (Hiltermann 2007) despite knowledge of the chemical gassing of the Kurds.

Reframing Kirkuk in a Federal Iraqi State

Even though the Kirkuk issue seemed indelibly tied to fixed Kurdish priorities, debates and claims about its status shifted once again after the overthrow of Saddam Hussein and creation of a federal Iraq in 2003. Negotiating Kirkuk became part of an ambiguous political space linked to contestations over authority, revenues, and resources in a weakened Iraqi state. Part of this ambiguity was a function of the ill-conceived 2005 Iraqi Constitution, which attempted to right the wrongs of Iraq's past by weakening the central government; disfranchising Sunni Arabs; devolving powers to the provinces; giving the KRG extensive revenues, rights, and recognition; and creating group representation through ethnic and sectarian group quotas (Natali 2010). The constitution also attempted to clarify Iraq's territorial boundaries. Article 140, which replaced Article 58 of the Law of Administration for the State of Iraq for the Transitional Period (TAL), addressed the status of Kirkuk as part of a

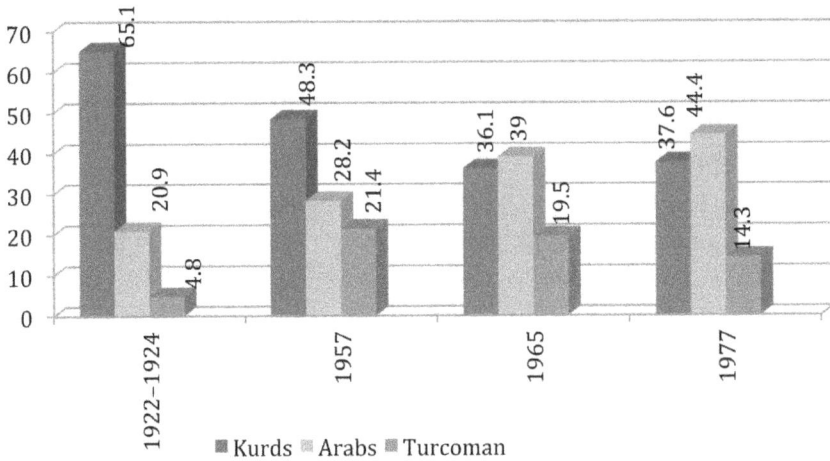

FIGURE 6.2 Changing demographic composition of Kirkuk governorate, 1922–1977
SOURCE: KRG Ministry of Extra-Regional Affairs, 2007.

larger, government-mandated process of settling all of Iraq's disputed territorial boundaries within an established time frame and through a special Iraqi parliamentary committee.

The legal codification of Kirkuk's status assumed political and symbolic value for the Kurds because, for the first time in Iraq's modern history, it placed the issue of territorial borders on the state's official political agenda as part of constitutional processes. Article 140 now framed the KRG's political discourse and territorial claims to disputed territories. Constitutionally, "normalizing Kirkuk" meant (1) conducting a census, (2) conducting a referendum by December 2007 to decide whether Kirkuk should remain an administrative component of the Iraqi government or of the KRG, (3) returning settler Arabs to their original lands, (4) resettling expelled Kurds back to Kirkuk, and (5) returning the administrative units in Kirkuk to their pre-1976 status.[16] Attempts to institutionalize territorial boundary issues were also subsumed into the larger U.S-led effort to stabilize post-Saddam Iraq, which brought third-party actors into the negotiation process. The United Nations Assistance Mission to Iraq (UNAMI), for instance, attempted to balance different communal claims to the disputed territories by proposing a potential "Special Status" for Kirkuk within the Iraqi state and in conjunction with the Iraqi constitution.

New opportunity structures in the weak federal Iraqi state have also encouraged the KRG to address the Kirkuk issue through extra-constitutional means. For most Kurdish officials, normalization processes have meant reversing decades of Arabization policies, not only in Kirkuk but in other disputed lands as well, as a means of returning the territorial status quo to its pre-Ba'athist period. A key part of this effort has involved sensitizing local populations to the issue and convincing them that Kirkuk unquestionably belongs to the Kurdistan Region. For instance, after 2005, Kurdish officials launched an intensive media and informational campaign in the Kurdistan Region based on the normalization process, Article 140, and the history and culture of Kirkuk. To reinforce their territorial claims, they instrumentalized the Kurds' history of violence and victimization. A key effort was to remythicize and remarket Kirkuk as the "Bleeding Heart of Kurdistan" and the "Jerusalem of Kurdistan."[17]

Further, rather than making claims to Kirkuk as a distinctly Kurdish territory, Kurdish officials started publicly referring to Kirkuk as a "Kurdistani city" in which peoples of different ethnic and religious groups could live together on a shared territory called Kurdistan. This effort was part of the KRG's larger attempt to reframe Kurdish identity from an ethnic to a territorial notion of "Kurdistani" citizenship as a means of co-opting and incorporating non-Kurdish communities in the disputed territories into an expansive Kurdistan territory. It involved differentiating between Arab settler populations and *authentic* Kirkukis, which included Arabs, Turcoman, and Kurds as Kurdistani citizens.[18] The theme was that Kirkukis could live together as different ethnic and religious groups in one political unit, and under the jurisdiction of the KRG.

Despite this KRG-engineered public discourse, most Kurdish officials and local populations have maintained a narrow and ethnically exclusionary sense of ownership to Kirkuk. Rather than trying to incorporate Arabs into Kirkuk and particularly the city center, KRG officials and their party apparatus started to "Kurdify" what the Iraqi government had "Arabized." The KRG engaged in its own territorial gerrymandering, demographic changes, and settler policies that attempted to erase the notional Green Line, which the Kurds considered the "Saddam Line," from the public imagination. From 2003 to 2014 Kurdish officials took advantage of the weak and dysfunctional Iraqi government and the political and security vacuum in the disputed territories. Over time, Kurdish peshmerga forces gradually pushed deeper into the disputed areas and assumed squatters' rights and de facto control over lands they regarded as essentially Kurdish, including Kirkuk.[19] In doing so, the peshmerga created a new "front line" between the Kurdistan Region and the rest of Iraq.

"Repossessing" and Kurdifying Kirkuk and other disputed territories has also involved creating "new facts on the ground" in order to ascertain Kurdish majority populations, reaffirm Kurdish ethnic identity, and control key resources. Since 2003, KRG officials have redistributed lands in Kirkuk to Kurds expelled by the former regime, resettled—at times forcibly—more than one hundred thousand Kurds to the Kirkuk region, transferred Arabs to their original homes, and channeled funds to Kurdish party supporters and communities as a means of securing political party patronage networks (International Crisis Group, 2006). These policies were replicated in other disputed areas, mainly the Ninewah plains, where Barzani's KDP forces have pushed out some Assyrian and Yezidi communities from their homes, prevented them from voting in local elections, and have assumed de facto control of territories and oil fields (Assyrian International News Agency, 2005).

Indeed, the departure of Arab communities and Kurdification of Kirkuk was not entirely conducted through force or conflict. In the absence of an ideological commitment to Kirkuk and title deeds to their lands, some settler communities, mainly from rural areas, returned to their original homes voluntarily after the "liberation of Kirkuk" in 2003 and temporary occupation of the city by Kurdish peshmerga. Other Arab settlers departed with the incentive of generous financial payments from the Iraqi government (20 million ID) and a plot of land in southern or central Iraq as part of the normalization process.

Still others have tacitly accepted or support KRG control of Kirkuk as a better option than Iraqi government control. This acceptance has emerged over time and as part of changing national and local politics and incentive structures. For instance, as a result of the Sunni Arab boycott of Iraqi elections in 2005 and military cooperation between Kurdish peshmerga and U.S. security forces, Kurdish parties won majorities on key provincial councils in disputed areas of Kirkuk, Mosul, and Diyala, which continued until 2009. In Kirkuk, Kurdish parties gained about 55 percent of the vote in the province, while 41 percent was shared between Iraqi Arab and Turcoman groups. Kurds also gained a majority representation in administrative positions, heading thirty-seven of the sixty-two offices in the city and holding twenty-six of the forty-one seats on the Kirkuk Provincial Council (Mohammed 2005, 243–243; Natali 2008, 437).[20]

As the KRG gained influence in Kirkuk's local administration and politics, it appeased, co-opted, and asserted control over non-Kurdish communities, as well as its party constituencies. Although the Iraqi government retained official jurisdiction over Kirkuk and continued to pay salaries of local civil servants, the KRG started to provide social welfare services, security, electricity, and government food rations to Kurdish-populated territories. In some areas Kurdish party officials collaborated with provincial leaders, while in others they acted unilaterally to enhance party patronage networks (Kane 2011, 11). During this period, Kurdish officials also made Kurdish the dominant language of provincial council meetings and reserved jobs and privileges for Kurdish party cadres—much the way their Ba'athist predecessors had done as a means of controlling populations and the identity of the province. To further influence minority groups, the KDP and the Patriotic Union of Kurdistan (PUK) handpicked particular individuals from Turcoman, Yezidi, and Assyrian communities for high-level political positions in the KRG and local councils, even though these individuals were not considered to be real representatives by their communities. By 2014 the Kurds had not only gained a majority presence in certain areas of Kirkuk but also control over services, security, and administration.

Despite Kurdish appeasement and co-optation efforts, the territorial status of Kirkuk remains disputed between Kurds and non-Kurdish communities. Part of this dispute is tied to the ambiguous language of the Iraqi constitution. It not only failed to clearly delineate the authorities of the federal government, provincial administrations, and KRG but also left terms and references of the disputed territories abstruse. For instance, while indicating that Kurdish territories could extend beyond the three governorates of Erbil, Dohuk, and Suleymaniya, the constitution does not clarify which parts of the disputed territories are included in a potentially enlarged Kurdistan Region. Constitutional ambiguity, alongside the KRG's maximalist nationalist agenda and settler policies, has enabled or encouraged Iraqi Arabs and minority groups to reinforce their own myths and claims to Kirkuk and other disputed territories. Just as KRG officials have attempted to counter decades of Arabization policies, Iraqi Arabs and some minority groups in Kirkuk have reacted to the Kurdish parties' control of the disputed territories and attempts to weaken the Iraqi state (Şwani 2007, 2). While Kurds emphasize Kirkuk as the heart of Kurdistan, Arab, Assyrian, and some Turcoman populations remain committed to the territorial integrity of Iraq and its boundaries inclusive of Kirkuk.

Even if some Sunni Arab communities seek their own region within the Iraqi state, they continue to regard Kirkuk as "the milk of the mother of Iraq"—a territory that is inherently Iraqi and nonnegotiable. Some oppose the notion of disputed territories altogether, and use the term "occupied territories" to refer to the Kurdish peshmerga's de facto control of the lands they consider to be essentially Iraqi. Some Kurdish officials, in turn, argue that the territories are no longer disputed, and refer to them as Kurdish lands outside the Kurdistan Region (Kane 2011, 7–9).

Assuming a Life of Its Own

Despite competing efforts by Baghdad and Erbil to solely control the disputed territories, the Kirkuk issue has passed a political tipping point and taken on a life of its own. In the weakened and decentralized Iraqi state, it has become part of a more complex and changing political context, whereby different groups are contesting state authority and access to revenues and resources. Territorial disputes have become more deeply embedded in local and regional politics, which overlap with the center-periphery dynamic that has shaped these disputes since the state formation period. Whereas Kirkuk was traditionally a problem to be negotiated directly between the Kurds and the Iraqi government, since 2003 it has become a multi-tiered issue involving regional states, particularly Turkey, local populations, non-state actors, and different stakeholders with competing political and economic interests.

For instance, after 2008, as the KRG's relations with Turkey started to ameliorate, Kurdish officials reframed the Kirkuk discourse to appease Turkish interests as well as to enhance party patronage networks and gain local support from non-Kurdish communities, particularly Turcoman populations. In a full-page newspaper article called "The Kirkuk question: What to do with Kurds and Turcoman?" a leading Kurdish party official emphasized the distinct historical place and cultural identity of the Turcoman in Kirkuk city. Noting the Kurdish character of Kirkuk, he suggested that the Turcoman language be given equal status with Kurdish and Arabic in the province, and affirmed that the Turcoman living in the Kurdistan Region have rights protected by the constitution (Mustafa 2008, 3).

By 2011 KRG political priorities and the politics of controlling Kirkuk had shifted once again. Kurdish elites were no longer focused on Ankara's sensitivities to Turcoman populations, particularly since then Prime Minister

Recep Tayyip Erdoğan had shown little interest in most of the Kirkuk Turco-man, due to their Shi'a affiliations and his own priorities in building a Sunni Muslim sphere of influence in Iraq. Rather, Kirkuk had become part of the KRG's expanding economic and energy sector agenda, which included infra-structure development and dozens of contracts signed with international oil companies (IOCs) in the Kurdistan Region and disputed territories. By strate-gically situating American IOCs—including Exxon Mobil and Hunt Oil—in key oil fields in disputed areas, and integrating Ankara into its commercial and energy deals, the KRG aimed to leverage its hydrocarbon interests in Baghdad and internationally, reinforce its claims to the disputed areas, and develop an autonomous revenue source that could support an independent Kurdish state. Passing a national hydrocarbons law and revenue-sharing law became paramount for KRG officials, and not necessarily resolving Article 140.

Certainly, Kurdish officials continued to publicly affirm that Kirkuk was a nationalist priority and should be incorporated into the Kurdistan Region. References to Article 140 are an essential part of any official discourse regard-ing the future of the Kurdistan Region, particularly during election periods and as a means of assuaging highly nationalist and demanding constituen-cies. When the opportunity to control Kirkuk emerged again in June 2014, immediately after the Islamic State of Iraq and al-Sham (ISIS) onslaught into the disputed territories and the Iraqi Security Forces' (ISF's) withdrawal, the Kurdish peshmerga did not hesitate to fill the security vacuum and seize the territories and oil resources and assets. This "retaking of Kirkuk" has had important symbolic value for Iraqi Kurds because, in contrast to 2003, when Kurdish peshmerga withdrew from the city to appease coalition partners, the KRG has affirmed that it has no intention of willingly returning any part of the territory back to the Iraqi government or ever letting Arabs rule Kirkuk again.

Yet the extent to which Kurds can pursue maximalist claims to Kirkuk depends not only on their relations and leverage with Baghdad. Rather, nego-tiating Kirkuk is now influenced by the political dynamics, porous borders, ungoverned spaces, and changing alliance structures in the weakened and volatile post-Saddam Iraqi state. Whereas Arab settler communities were previously representative of the Iraqi government and not part of political or ideological movements, after 2005 they became tied to competing Iraqi oppo-sition groups such as Saddam's Fedayyin, the Muqtada al-Sadr brigade, and

Arab nationalist militants from Hawija. The sectarian nature of Iraqi politics has also reshaped Kirkuk dynamics, giving non-state actors and regional states opportunities to penetrate the territories. In May 2008, for instance, the Mahdi Army, led by Shi'a cleric Muqtada al-Sadr and his Badr Organization, deployed forces to Kirkuk and offered monetary support to Arab Shi'a families and Shi'as migrating to the city because of unrest in southern and central Iraq. In their vehement opposition to the KRG's maximalist nationalist agenda and commitment to Kirkuk as an integral part of the Iraqi state, these groups have obstructed any effort to delineate the boundaries of Kirkuk.

Moreover, since the ISIS takeover of Mosul and large swaths of Iraqi and Syrian territories, the disputed territories have become ISIS battlefields. The Kurds are challenged not only to stabilize Kirkuk but also to secure and defend a new 1,000-kilometer border with ISIS and militant Sunni Arab nationalist groups. Although the KRG has gained international support and weapons to fight ISIS, it still has no backing by any Iraqi group to retain sole jurisdiction over Kirkuk and the disputed territories, including their oil resources. Intra-communal and intra-party tensions have heightened alongside the international effort to counter ISIS. Kurdish peshmerga have used coalition airstrikes to not only get rid of ISIS safe havens but also to engage in further territorial and demographic engineering, largely at Sunni Arabs' expense. KRG peshmerga forces have prevented Sunni Arabs from returning to their lands, confined many to security zones, and have taken over some Sunni Arab homes (Human Rights Watch 2015).

Security threats and anti-ISIS dynamics have undermined the KRG's ability to control non-Kurdish communities in the territories. Although the KRG Ministry of Peshmerga Affairs has created minority militias under its auspices—either through coercion or co-optation—some minority group members, including Assyrians and Turcoman, have threatened to take arms against the KRG should it unilaterally attach Kirkuk to the Kurdistan Region. These minorities are also calling for their own autonomous territories, either within or apart from the Kurdistan Region. The potential emergence of a strong Sunni Arab region or Sunni National Guard that borders the Kurdistan Region further hinders any attempt by the KRG to assert unilateral jurisdiction over Kirkuk and its revenues as part of the Kurdistan Region—at least without sustained conflict.

Determining the status of Kirkuk and making claims to it are also entrenched in local Kurdish power struggles. These dynamics have become part of the Kurdish parties' attempts to shift the local balance of power with the support of regional states and non-state actors, and assert control over revenues and resources, particularly hydrocarbons. The effort to control Kirkuk has been particularly important for the PUK, whose support base inside the Kurdistan Region has declined over the past several years, with the illness of former Iraqi President and PUK leader Jelal Talabani, the rise of the opposition Change Movement, and the concentration of Barzani-KDP power in the KRG. Controlling Kirkuk not only assures PUK's political significance in what Kurds consider a key Kurdish nationalist territory and a Talabani stronghold but also represents a means to check Barzani's power in the Kurdistan Region. By 2014 the PUK had secured half the seats on the Kirkuk provincial council (versus only two seats for KDP) and a leadership position under the PUK governor, Dr. Najmaldin Kerim.

These results have political significance for the balance of power inside the Kurdistan Region, KRG-Baghdad relations, and Kurdish claims to Kirkuk. They indicate that any attempt to incorporate Kirkuk into the Kurdistan Region would reduce Barzani and his KDP to a political minority. They also beg the key question: given the PUK's influence and majority status in Kirkuk and the Kurds' deep nationalist and territorial claims, why have Kurdish leaders, including Governor Kerim, continued to negotiate with Baghdad, even after the KRG peshmerga assumed de facto control over Kirkuk city and some of its key oil assets?

Instead of using Kurdish land claims to further antagonize Baghdad, as some hardliner KDP leaders have done, Kerim and PUK officials have attempted to balance Kurdish nationalist interests with their relationship with the Iraqi government and the diverse populations in Kirkuk. In fact, when the ISF withdrew from Kirkuk and Kurdish peshmerga seized full control of the city, Kerim continued to assuage the concerns of Arab and Turcoman populations while maintaining open communication and cooperation with Baghdad. Rather than threatening secession or unilaterally declaring Kirkuk to be part of the Kurdistan Region, Kerim argued that Kirkuk requires a "special status," to be determined by Kirkuk populations through a referendum. This balancing act has continued throughout the anti-ISIS campaign. As coalition airstrikes and foreign military assistance have largely benefited KDP-controlled peshmerga, PUK peshmerga forces have aligned with the ISF, Shi'a militia, Iranian Qods forces, and Kurdistan Worker's Party (PKK) peshmerga to counter the ISIS threat in Kirkuk, as well as in other localities.

Distinctions have also emerged between Kirkuki Kurds and KRG Kurds. Kirkukis have reacted to neglect by not only Baghdad but also Erbil. Kurdish Kirkukis—many of whom are Anfal survivors—may prefer to be attached to a Kurdistan Region than to a dysfunctional Iraqi government, but they also oppose the monopolization of power by the Kurdish parties and peshmerga in Kirkuk and the gross discrepancies in wealth between their province and the three governorates in the Kurdistan Region (Dohuk, Erbil, and Suleymaniya). These development gaps, the presence of diverse communities, and ongoing security threats have created different priorities for Kurds living inside the Kurdistan Region and those in Kirkuk. The immediate demands of most Kirkukis are not necessarily implementing Article 140 but rather securing the city, repatriating refugees, and providing services, education, employment, and effective administration. Their debate over Kirkuk's future is not only a choice between Baghdad and Erbil but a decision on the nature of Kirkuk's autonomy, provincial security, petrodollar allocations, economic development, and relationship to the Iraqi government and Erbil (Natali 2008, 439).

The increasingly complex nature of the Kirkuk issue in the weak, federal Iraqi state suggests that rather than clarifying Kirkuk's status, Erbil and Baghdad have much to gain by maintaining its political ambiguity (Natali 2010). For Kurdish officials, a non-negotiated Kirkuk can remain a symbol of their nationalist struggle, and a source of political and economic leverage with Baghdad and other Iraqi populations, without fully undermining the KRG's domestic priorities and regional relations. That is, alongside settlement myths, Kirkuk's status is a function of the geopolitical realities, economic dependencies, and security vulnerabilities of the landlocked Kurdistan Region. With Kurdish populations of their own to manage and a commitment to Iraq's territorial integrity, neither Turkey, Iran, nor Syria supports an Iraqi Kurdish state—at least not one that can be inclusive of Kirkuk. Rather than back Kurdish claims to Kirkuk, since 2003 regional governments have taken advantage of the weakened Iraqi state and autonomous Kurdistan Region by extending their influence in Kirkuk. Erdoğan has negotiated hydrocarbons agreements with Barzani in the Kurdistan Region, Kirkuk, and other disputed territories. Iranian-backed Shi'a militias remain stationed in parts of Kirkuk, alongside PUK and ISF forces, maintaining an Iraqi and Shi'a presence in the province that challenges Kurdish nationalist interests.

Moreover, Kurdish claims to Kirkuk coexist with the KRG's dependence on the Iraqi government, and increasingly on Turkey and Iran. Despite over a decade of hydrocarbons development and efforts to become economically independent, the Kurdistan region continues to rely heavily on Baghdad for the vast majority of its revenues. The very survivability of the region requires ensuring Kurdish influence in Baghdad, appeasing Sunni Arab and Turcoman communities, keeping borders with Ankara and Tehran open and secure, and gaining access to much-needed revenues and transit routes for regional energy resources. These political and economic realities not only check the potential for KRG secession from Iraq but limit the possibility of the KRG's unilateral and non-contested annexation of Kirkuk.

Conclusion

This detailed study reveals that the Kirkuk issue is a changing one tied to shifts in state-building strategies and settlement polices. Ethnic settlement has been a constitutive feature of the Iraqi state-building project and has encouraged the ethnicization of Kirkuk and Iraqi borders. Settler populations have played a key role in this process by creating demographic tipping points that fundamentally altered the balance of power and sense of communal belonging. While no specific number can be attached to this tipping point, it can be identified as part of a violent, politicalized, and ethnically exclusionary environment in which the Kurdish majorities became minority populations, and the real and perceived balance of power was assumed by Arab communities.

Over time, settlement myths can assume different meanings as new incentive structures and political challenges emerge. For instance, as KRG officials became increasingly focused on developing their own oil sector and legitimizing their region to external patrons in the federal Iraqi state, clarifying the status of Kirkuk has become less a KRG priority than ascertaining resource control and revenue generation. The KRG's overriding needs to secure borders against ISIS and other terrorist groups, develop and export the region's natural resources, and pay IOCs will continue to require concessions with Baghdad, Ankara, and Tehran, all of whom are interested in economic opportunities and asserting influence in the Kurdistan Region but are unsupportive of an overly autonomous KRG. In this context, Kurdish officials are challenged to balance the historical legacies of Kirkuk with their political, security, and financial demands. The KRG's attempts to secure unilateral access to oil fields in Kirkuk and other disputed territories will likely remain a highly contentious issue between Baghdad and Erbil, as well as among Kurds, Sunni Arab communities, and other Iraqi populations.

Additionally, the "de-Arabization" of Kirkuk and ongoing arguments over its status indicate that the role of settlers in shaping territorial disputes has limited explanatory value over time. Even after most settlers departed and the Kirkuk city center was Kurdified, Kurdish claims continued to center on delineating the territorial boundaries of the Kurdistan Region, which included Kirkuk. These claims also transformed in nature to accommodate the shifting political and economic conditions of post-Saddam Iraq. The historical legacies that have shaped the mindset of most Kurds—violence, ethnic cleansing, and displacement—now coexist with issues such as counterterrorism, economic development, the rule of law, and petroleum exports. These contemporary issues have become part of the KRG's larger effort to secure international recognition and the survivability of its region. They underline that although the Kirkuk problem has assumed a life of its own, it is still malleable in an increasingly complex and unstable region.

Ongoing arguments about the status of Kirkuk, even among Kurdish populations, further underline the continued uncertainty about territorial ownership and clarification of borders. That is, while the Kirkuk problem is psychologically embedded in the minds of most Kurds, it has not necessarily become a commonsense notion for all Kirkukis that Kirkuk must be incorporated into the Kurdistan Region. Even though some Kurdish elites insist that Kirkuk will never be returned to Iraq voluntarily, there is no certainty that the KRG can permanently and unilaterally secure and maintain control over Kirkuk and the disputed territories—at least without conflict and instability. What has not emerged is the presumption among all Kurds that their relationship to Kirkuk has ceased to be problematic (Lustick 1993b, 34, 44).

Absence of such a presumption has implications for negotiating Kirkuk. Ambiguity and disagreement can open the possibilities for compromise on the jurisdiction and ownership of Kirkuk by creating greater alternatives outside the "either Baghdad or Erbil" option. Building upon decentralization trends in Iraq since 2003, local populations in Kirkuk may have the option to remain as a special status province, outside both the KRG and Baghdad, although one in which international supervision and third-party management may be necessary.

Greater complexity in the Kirkuk issue also requires a more nuanced and managed approach to negotiation that extends beyond the issue of repatriating settler populations and resettling internally displaced persons (IDPs) to their original homes. The multi-level nature of the Kirkuk problem means that negotiations will involve economic incentives, security issues, discussions on cross-border trade, and the spoils and sharing of future petroleum revenues in Iraq and the Kurdistan Region. Its increasing complexity requires greater and ongoing international and regional involvement that can help to reshape the problem and lead to its long-term management.

Notes

The views expressed represent those of the author and do not reflect the official policy or position of the National Defense University, the U.S. Department of Defense, or the U.S. government.

1. Settlement myth is a specific type of myth, shaped by ideology that gives specific meanings to settlement activity. It includes the socially negotiated meanings of settlements, recurrent practices, and the material products and outcomes of the settlement process which enable future settlement practices.

2. Kirkuk was the center of the Vilayet of Sharezur and in 1879 was annexed as a *sanjaq* to Mosul Vilayet. It was situated along an important trade route, and it served as a garrison town between Istanbul and Baghdad. The Persian and Ottoman governments tried to assure its administrative control by supporting, respectively, Shi'a and Sunni populations in the province.

3. The Treaty of Lausanne (1921) suggested a state of Kurdistan that would comprise parts of the Kurdish-populated regions of Turkey and Iraq but not include Iran or Syria. It was replaced by the Treaty of Sévres (1923), which made no mention of Kurdish statehood.

4. Author interview with Arif Qorbani, independent researcher and former director of the Kirkuk city television station, October 15, 2006, in Erbil.

5. The Shi'a Turcoman Qizilbash communities arrived in Kirkuk in the late 17th century under the Safavid Dynasty and have remained in the city center ever since. Sunni Turcoman, accounting for about 2.5 percent of the total population of Iraq, arrived as part of the Ottoman administration and lived in districts such as Kirkuk city, Tuz Khurmatu, Kifry, and Qaratapa. Chaldeans are the oldest community in the city, located in the citadel.

6. During the referendum, some Kirkukis held a series of meetings in their homes to discourage local support for Faysal, accusing him of being a Yezidi. On July 23, 1918, the Mufti of Kirkuk issued a fatwa stating that those who supported Faysal would be accused of being bad Muslims.

7. Most Kurdish populations were located in the north and eastern sections of Kirkuk; Arab communities (mainly Jebouris and Bedouins) lived in the western region of Hawija; and some Turcoman villages were south of Kirkuk: Dahut, Tasa,

and Tuz Khurmatu. Author interview with Nouri Talabany, member of the Kurdistan National Assembly, October 7, 2007, in Erbil.

8. *Qawmiyya* Arab nationalism emphasizes the revival of the Arab nation and does not recognize the authenticity of non-Arab identities. In contrast, *wataniyya* nationalism focuses on an Iraqi identity based on linguistic and cultural ties between groups living in the same geographical area and recognizes the localist identities of non-Arab groups. It is important to note that *wataniyya* nationalism has undergone changes in the states in which it has emerged.

9. Author interview with Arif Qorbani, former director of the Kirkuk television station, October 15, 2009.

10. Kifry district was attached to Diyala governorate, Tuz Khurmatu was attached to Tikrit (Salahaddin), and Kalar and Chamchamal districts were annexed to Suleymaniya governorate.

11. Shi'a Arab settlers originated from Kerbala, Diwana, and Basra. Author interview with displaced Kirkukis living in a collective camp outside Erbil, June 19, 2009.

12. The Iraqi government gave settlers who were government employers a raise in salary after they were transferred to Kirkuk. It also offered Arabs settlers in Kirkuk city a title deed to the land but offered no legal documentation to settlers in rural areas.

13. Disputed territories include Sinjar, Tel Afar, Zammar, Sheikhan, east Mosul, Makhmur, Tuz Khurmatu, Kifry, Khanaqin, and Mandali.

14. Author interview with Serbest Kirkuki, head of the Kurdish Cultural Center, August 31, 1996, in London.

15. Half came from the central provinces of Baghdad, Salahaddin, Zikar, and Diyala. Ten percent originated from southern Iraq, and the remainder were from Mosul (12%), and the Kurdistan region (16%). The central government also sent villagers neighboring Kirkuk to collective towns: Benislawa and Darlatu in Erbil and Shoresh and Chamchamal in Suleymaniya.

16. Since 2003, according to local sources, about 90 percent of Kurds originally from rural areas in Kirkuk governorate had a more rapid return rate than Kurds from Kirkuk city center, where the recovery of property and lands was more complex. Almost 100 percent of the Turcoman IDPs returned to different districts in Kirkuk in 2003 (Talabany 2007).

17. See, for instance, "Hezbey Kurdistaniyekan ley Kirkuk key bekemterkhem dezanin? Kurd yan hakumati Iraq," *Awena*, December 18, 2007, p. 3. Five political parties are interviewed and asked to discuss their opinions on how to resolve the Kirkuk problem. All of them focused on implementing Article 140 of the Iraqi constitution.

18. It is important to note that while the Kurdish elites are marketing their Kurdistani identity, since September 2001 they have responded to Islamization trends in Iraq and the region by creating new myths linked to the origins of Kurdish identity. KRG elites have attempted to differentiate Kurds from Arabs and Sunni Muslims through the Latinization and purification of the Kurdish language. The "pure" Kurd

is not portrayed as a Sunni Muslim but rather as someone linked to Zoroastrianism and Yezidism.

19. The New Green Line, as redrawn by the Kurds, is about forty kilometers south of the notional Green Line. It extends from West Erbil to Highway 2 north to the Greater Zab, then around Ain Sifny to Mosul Lake. The Kurdish peshmerga has enhanced its presence and created more clearly defined military positions.

20. Although twenty-four political parties representing Arabs, Turcoman, Kurds, and Chaldo-Assyrians participated in the provincial council elections, only five parties passed the 3 percent threshold and received seats on the council, with twenty-six of the forty-one seats allocated to the Kurdish list (Kirkuk al-Mutaakhiya).

7 Settlers, Immigrants, Colonists: The Three Layers of Settler-Induced Conflict in Sri Lanka

Evangelos Liaras

SCHOLARS OF THE SRI LANKAN CONFLICT ARE ACUTELY aware of the role that disputes over "settlers" and "settlement" have played in the island's history (Fearon and Laitin 2011).[1] Until recently, however, Sri Lanka had not received much attention in the comparative literature on settler disputes, which has been largely focused on discussions of Israel/Palestine, Northern Ireland, and various white versus non-white colonial and post-colonial settings, most notably South Africa. In the wake of the defeat of the Liberation Tigers of Tamil Eelam (LTTE) in 2009, armed conflict in Sri Lanka has abated. Paradoxically, the advent of peace may actually exacerbate the settler dimension which contributed so much to Tamil-Sinhalese tensions in the past. At a first level, this chapter aims to rectify this lack of attention by the subfield to Sri Lanka's long-standing conflict by fully outlining its settler dimensions and drawing attention to the contrast between the case of the Indian Tamils and that of Sinhalese colonization of the northeast. At a second level, the chapter makes a larger argument about the need for three conceptual distinctions: a *discursive* one between populations labeled as "settlers" and those labeled as "natives," a *temporal* one between conflicts stemming from relatively recent settlements and those related to historically remote settlements, and a *situational* one between settlements resulting from opportune immigration waves and those resulting from determined colonization projects. The discursive element is important because it defines the conflict as settler related—for social scientists as well; also some conflicts contain multiple layers of settlement, and each group may accuse the other of trying to alter the demography. The temporal proximity forms part of the discourse but also affects the range of possible avenues for conflict resolution. Finally, the situational context of the settlement is already well-noted in the scholarly literature as a key determinant for the evolution of conflict, with state-driven settlement projects more likely to lead to violence than more market-driven ones. Sri Lanka is an excellent case study in which to unravel this empirical tangle, as it features a rare array of settler disputes anchored in both modernity and antiquity, and touching upon the conflict, migration, and post-colonial literatures.

Sri Lanka's population of roughly twenty million is divided into four major ethnic groups (the percentages are provisional data from the 2011 census): Sinhalese (74.9%), Sri Lankan Tamils (11.2%), Indian Tamils (4.2%), and Sri Lankan Moors (9.2%). The three minority communities are all Tamil speaking, but the Moors traditionally stress their Muslim identity, have higher rates of bilingualism in Sinhala than other Tamil speakers, and have distanced themselves from the Tamil nationalist movement in Sri Lanka. Indian Tamils descend from indentured laborers recruited in South India by the British from the mid-19th to the early 20th century to work in Ceylon's plantations. They are therefore differentiated by ancestry and caste from the Sri Lankan (or Ceylon) Tamils, an older community situated primarily in the north and east of the island. The conflict between Sinhalese and Tamils has revolved around two major issue areas, language and territory. Leaving the language question aside (covered in detail by DeVotta 2004), this chapter will focus on issues of land and homeland. On the one hand, Sinhalese nationalists have argued for decades that British rule hastened a Tamilization of Lanka at the expense of the majority community. Tamil nationalists, on the other hand, protest that whereas Tamils were co-founders of the multi-ethnic state, state policies since independence have promoted Sinhalization—a process that for Sinhalese nationalists simply restores an alleged prior status quo. Tamils have decried discrimination by the Sinhalese majority, while the Sinhalese have pointed to the much larger Tamil population of South India, and the worldwide Tamil diaspora, as ominous threats. The Sri Lankan conflict has been aptly described as one between a minority community with a majority complex and a majority community with a minority complex (De Silva 1998), a parallel it shares with Northern Ireland and Cyprus (see Loizides's chapter in this volume).

Before delving further into the empirics, some definitions of terms are needed. In the following discussion I will avoid the dichotomy of natives versus settlers, preferring the terms *autochthonous* and *heterochthonous* populations. This is done for two reasons: first, because I will use different terms to refer to settler groups depending on their time and mode of arrival, and second, to minimize confusion, since settlers in internal colonization projects may be natives to the larger homeland but newcomers in the specific contested territory. When the historical precedence of settlement is disputed, autochthony and heterochthony are difficult to assess. Over time, originally heterochthonous groups become established and can advance their own claims of autochthony, a point of interest for the first distinction, the temporal one. The situational distinction refers to the material and ideational context of the heterochthonous group's arrival. Maintaining consistency with the conceptual framework presented in the introduction to this volume, people who are haphazardly injected into a territory by market forces, human trafficking, or inadvertent refugee waves will be termed *immigrants*; in contrast, and somewhat diverging from Haklai and Loizides's conceptualization, people intentionally settled as part of a determined demographic engineering campaign will be termed *colonists*. The distinction can be viewed as a spectrum based on the purposefulness and degree of state involvement, acknowledging intermediate situations where a state may have particularly welcomed certain refugees and/or immigrants due to their perceived allegiance.[2] This range is captured by Ian Lustick in his typology of ideologically driven, politically connected, and underprivileged settlers (Lustick 1985).

A settlement can be "recent" or "primordial" (meaning that it significantly predates the current framework of conflict so that family ties with the ancestral homeland, memories of specific lineage among the heterochthonous population, and records of land acquisition or appropriation have been lost). Primordial settlements may have been migratory or colonizing originally, but in the long term what is important is the reaction of the autochthonous group and the self-perception of the heterochthonous group in relation to the memory of settlement. Groups that preserve a legend of plantation to the land and are still seen by the autochthonous as outsiders will be called *settlers*; groups for which the emic and etic salience of heterochthony has diminished over time will simply constitute an ethnic group which is not part of a settler-induced conflict. I believe that this conceptualization fits well with the mundane connotations of these terms. In short-term contexts, depending on the circumstances of arrival, one is either a colonist or an immigrant. In long-term contexts, depending on the reaction of the indigenous group and the formation of identity discourses by the arriving group, colonists and/or immigrants may be viewed either as settlers or simply as another local community.[3]

In Sri Lanka each of these categories features differently into the fabric of the conflict. Sinhalese and Tamil historical narratives paint a picture of the respective "other" as a settler, in a debate that oscillates between emphasizing perennial conflict or coexistence of the two groups on the island. The injection of Tamil laborers from South India and the migration of Sri Lankan Tamils to the commercial hub of Colombo in colonial times has been a source of agitation for Sinhalese nationalists, deploring the Tamilization of traditional Sinhalese lands (National Joint Committee 2001, 11–29). Post-independence, most Indian Tamils were deprived of citizenship, and half were repatriated to India; the remaining community has developed a local identity largely reconciled with the Sinhalese-dominated state. Post-independence, the state also undertook major land development projects, settling thousands of Sinhalese farmers in the predominantly Tamil Eastern Province in the process, and triggering reaction to this perceived colonization of traditional Tamil homelands. Sri Lankan Tamil nationalism embraced secessionism for an independent or at least federal Tamil Eelam, a prospect now ever so distant after the defeat of the LTTE in a three-decade-long civil war. The fourth group, the Moors, pride themselves on their purported Arab lineage, although at least a section of the community also hails from Muslim Indian traders (Nuhman 2007). More integrated into Sinhalese society, the Moors also became engulfed by the Tamil-Sinhalese conflict, primarily because of the alignment of their political elites with the Sinhalese leadership and due to local competition for land in the Eastern Province.[4]

The Sri Lankan conflict therefore has three layers of settler disputes: the macro-historical one between Sinhalese and Tamils on the entire island, the modern one between Sinhalese natives and Indian Tamil migrants to the island, and the contemporary one in Eastern Province (and the southern outskirts of Northern Province) between Sri Lankan Tamil farmers, Sinhalese colonists, and Muslim squatters, all natives of the island. In the rest of this chapter I will empirically outline these three layers, before returning to a conclusion about the theoretical merits of treating them separately. A fundamental paradox is the violent escalation of the conflict between the autochthonous Sri Lankan Tamils and the Sinhalese colonists compared with the peaceful resolution of the conflict between the autochthonous Sinhalese and the Indian Tamil immigrants. Another curiosity is that the Muslims, who trace the most geographically distant ancestry (Arab, Gujarati, or Malay), have been the relatively least assaulted for their inherent heterochthony.

Settlers on Serendipity

Lanka is an ancient, ethnically neutral name found in the Sanskrit epic *Ramayana*. Ceylon and the older Arabic Serendib both derive from foreign renditions of Sinhala, the island's traditionally dominant language. Sinhala, like Dhivehi spoken in the Maldives, is an insular Indo-Aryan language whose vocabulary and structure is very different from the Dravidian languages of South India. But old place names and some unique phonetic and syntactical features betray Sinhala's long coexistence with Tamil, and also point to a possible past assimilation of Dravidians. The Sinhalese preserve the historical memory of their migration from northeast India in the 6th century BCE— chronicled in the epic poem *Mahavamsa*, composed in Pali, the liturgical language of Theravada Buddhism and literary predecessor of Sinhala. The Tamils have no such specific recollection of their first arrival on Lanka. Pali sources recurrently mention the "Dameda" and "Damila" (Dravidians, Tamils) as people who traded with, inhabited, and occasionally invaded the island from South India; but Pali inscriptions long antedate any Tamil inscriptions on Sri Lanka. The Tamil concentration in the Jaffna peninsula probably traces to the 10th-century invasion by the Chola Empire of south India, which destroyed the Sinhalese ancient capital Anuradhapura and established Tamil control of the north. South Indian Tamil rulers were supplanted by local Tamil dynasties under the Kingdom of Jaffna (13th–17th centuries), which rivaled the Sinhalese kingdoms of Kotte and Kandy in the south until the arrival of the Portuguese (De Silva 2005).

That was the distant past, wrapped in myth and verse. In modern times, Sinhalese and Tamil literati have engaged in an equally epic debate over the historical precedence of settlement, remindful of the brawls between Romanian and Hungarian historians over ancient Transylvania or Israeli and Arab historians over pre-modern Palestine. Arguably, all such historiographic debates are largely moot, but the way they have been ingrained into the conflict discourse, particularly when intertwined with religious doctrine, is far from irrelevant (Akenson 1992; Little 1995; A. Smith 2003). Since the

Buddhist revival movement of the late 19th century, Sinhalese nationalism has revolved around an idealization of Sri Lanka as the sacred Buddhist island (*dhammadeepa*) which the Sinhalese have fought throughout history to protect from nonbeliever outsiders (Gunawardena 1990; Bartholomeusz and De Silva 1998). According to this view, the Sri Lankan Tamils are descendants of Hindu invaders who simply preceded the European imperialists. Sinhalese nationalists are passionate about any Buddhist archaeological finds in Northern and Eastern Provinces that indicate ancient Sinhalese habitation of the so-called traditional Tamil homelands. Tamil scholarship has opposed this preaching, insisting that Tamil presence on the island at least matches and possibly predates the arrival of the Sinhalese (Rajanayagam 1994; Manogaran 2000). Reactive in nature, the spirit of Tamil rebuttals ranges from promoting the inclusion of Tamils in the national narrative to defending their exclusion from it as owners of a separate coastal homeland (Arudpraghasam 1996; Sitrampalam 2007). In turn, Sinhalese scholars have countered these claims, arguing that there is little evidence of Tamil large-scale settlement on the island before the late medieval period and that the Kingdom of Jaffna only intermittently controlled the eastern seaboard (De Silva 1987; Peiris 1991).

The argumentation quickly exhausts itself: no self-respecting Sinhalese historian can deny that Tamil has been a minority culture on the island for more than a millennium; no serious Tamil historian can deny that Sinhala has been the majority culture of the island for all its recorded history, while the Tamil character of the north and east became consolidated only later. And yet, the memory of pre-colonial statehood has been used as a precedent for Sri Lankan Tamil sovereignty, while the Buddhist scriptural tradition has served as a facile cultural depository feeding the Sinhalese siege mentality (Stokke 1998). The Jaffna Kingdom was part of the rhetoric of the Lanka Tamil Federal Party from the time of its emergence in the 1950s; when the main Tamil parties merged in 1976 to form the Tamil United Liberation Front (TULF), the Kingdom of Jaffna was incorporated in the party's founding document and electoral manifesto as the legitimation of Tamil Eelam (De Silva 1987). Similarly, the thesis of Sinhalese autochthony and Tamil heterochthony pervades Sinhalese political culture. In 1998, while personally leading a constitutional amendment process for regional devolution, President Chandrika Kumaratunga enraged Tamil politicians by stating in an interview on South African television that "they are wanting a separate state—a minority community which is not the original people of the country" (quoted in the *Sri*

Lanka Sunday Times, November 15, 1998).[5] After the government army victory against the Liberation Tigers of Tamil Eelam (LTTE), President Mahinda
Rajapakse kept peppering his speeches with inclusive language about a united
homeland of Sinhalese, Tamils, and Muslims. In practice, however, the whole
issue of further devolution has been put in the deep freeze. It remains to be
seen whether this will change after the election of Maithripala Sirisena to the
presidency, partly thanks to the Tamil vote.

Of course, the underlying historical discourse of homelands is present in
all ethno-territorial conflicts (Murphy 2002). In Sri Lanka the historical perceptions of settlement have seeped into other aspects of the conflict in two
major ways. First, they touch on the constitutional conception of the state: is it
primarily a Sinhalese homeland with some tolerated imported minorities, or
is it a multi-ethnic project in a historically diverse land? Second, they under-
pin the normative context of territoriality: do Sri Lankan Tamils have special
rights over the north and east of the island that are legitimate and inalienable
vis-à-vis the other ethnic communities? These questions have dominated all
debates on Sri Lanka's constitutional structure and possible devolution in the
last century.

Immigrants in Ceylon

The development of the plantation economy under the British went hand in
hand with the importation of indentured laborers from South India, introduc-
ing a second Tamil population on the island. Between the 1840s and the 1930s,
hundreds of thousands of Indian Tamils arrived on Sri Lanka, their numbers
eventually surpassing the priorly established Ceylon Tamils. Initially, immigrants were male and only seasonal; but as tea replaced coffee as the main
crop after the 1860s, the need arose for a year-round stable workforce and
planters encouraged whole families to settle permanently (Samarasinghe
1988, 158). The recruited laborers were dispersed all over the island, but particularly in the central highlands around Kandy, the capital of the last independent Sinhalese kingdom and the center of a rising tea economy. Largely
drawn from the untouchable castes, the Indian Tamils were not integrated
into Ceylonese Tamil society. They were additionally reviled by Sinhalese
nationalists for diluting the ethnic makeup of the hill country and allegedly
causing Sinhalese unemployment. Their situation changed little after indentured labor was banned in India in 1917. Immigration reform in the 1920s

allowed a representative of the colonial government of India to oversee the interests of plantation Tamils, but Sinhalese politicians resisted the extension of residency and voting rights to them. Indians were also excluded from land grants in the settlement schemes initiated in the 1930s. Two prominent Sinhalese politicians (and later founders of Sri Lanka's two major political parties), D. S. Senanayake and S.W.R.D. Bandaranaike, competed in championing the anti-Indian cause. In a famous parliamentary debate in 1940, Bandaranaike stated that "nothing will please me more than to see the last Indian leaving the shores of Ceylon," while Senanayake hyperbolized further: "I do not think that a greater blow to the national life of a country has been dealt, even by the Germans in Poland, than what has been done Upcountry by the enfranchisement of so many Indian labourers" (quoted in Peebles 2001, 210). The settlement of low-caste Indian Tamils in the Sinhalese heartland was a particular affront to Sinhalese nationalism, and a complaint mentioned alongside the economic ascendancy and overrepresentation of Ceylon Tamils during the British period.

In 1939 India banned emigration to Ceylon, and Nehru's official visit prompted the formation of the Ceylon Indian Congress (CIC) as a plantation Tamil trade union cum political party (Peebles 2001). The CIC gained six seats in the 1947 election, but following independence in 1948, Senanayake's government passed laws that impeded citizenship acquisition and disenfranchised Indian Tamil voters. India engaged in bitter negotiations with Sri Lanka over their status. Both Senanayake's United National Party (UNP) and Bandaranaike's Sri Lanka Freedom Party (SLFP) wanted India to accept the compulsory repatriation of most Indian Tamils, which Nehru rejected in principle. India's stance softened after Nehru's death. The 1964 Sirimavo-Shastri and 1974 Sirimavo-Gandhi pacts stipulated that out of a stateless population of 975,000, Sri Lanka would grant citizenship to 375,000, while India would confer citizenship on and repatriate the remaining 600,000. In 1981, however, after admitting half a million people, India reneged on the agreement. With the Citizenship Act of 1988, Sri Lanka finally naturalized the remaining stateless Tamils who had not applied for Indian citizenship. This marked the official recognition of the Indian Tamils as a native group on equal footing with the rest (Sahadevan 1995).

Enduring social stigma and depressing housing and health conditions, the Indian Tamils developed into Sri Lanka's most marginalized ethnic community. Compared with Indians transplanted during the same historical period to Guiana and Fiji, the plantation Tamils of Ceylon became trapped, without prospects for upward mobility.

> When the Indian Tamils were indentured as plantation labor in Sri Lanka, they had very little opportunity to break into the rest of the economy and find a foothold immediately, or even gradually. They were more or less condemned to be in their original status of entry. Even when they managed to secure some alternate employment it was at unskilled lower-paid levels, mainly in the urban sector already controlled by the elite investors. The attitude of the local population too had not by any means . . . been helpful in this regard. (Nithiyanandam and Gounder 2004, 214)

Their political mobilization also followed different lines than that of the Sri Lankan Tamils. The All Ceylon Tamil Congress (ACTC), the original Ceylon Tamil party, formed around the conservative elite of Jaffna, acquiesced in the disenfranchisement of Indians. ACTC's progressive wing consequently split and formed the Lanka Tamil Federal Party (ITAK) in 1949. ITAK favored the diminution of caste discrimination, but its nationalist agenda focused on separate status for the Northern and Eastern Provinces, thus excluding the central areas where most Indian Tamils lived (Wilson 2000). The CIC and its successor, the Ceylon Workers' Congress (CWC), dominated Indian Tamil politics for decades, under the leadership of trade unionist Savumiamoorthy Thondaman—a role inherited today by his grandson. In 1964 Thondaman switched allegiances from SLFP to UNP, which promised not to place naturalized Indian Tamils on a separate electoral register (De Silva 1986, 221–225). In the 1970s CWC temporarily joined ITAK and ACTC to form the Tamil United Liberation Front (TULF). But once TULF declared support for a separate Tamil state, CWC retreated to its alliance with UNP. The odd affair between the trade union of plantation workers and the party of Sinhalese capitalists bore fruit in the 1980s, when UNP enfranchised the Indian Tamils and then captured their votes (Sahadevan 1995, 218–232). Since then, CWC's monopoly has been challenged by new political forces (the Upcountry People's Front and the Western People's Front), but the pattern remains the same: Indian Tamil parties are readily accepted by UNP and SLFP as minor coalition partners, trading their loyalty to the Sinhalese-dominated state for political patronage.[6]

As a result of the repatriation, the Indian Tamil share of Sri Lanka's population was halved between the 1960s and the 1980s (see Table 7.1). Many of the people thus "repatriated" were born in Sri Lanka and had never set foot

TABLE 7.1 Sri Lankan Tamil and Indian Tamil population of Sri Lanka, 1946–2012

Census Year	Ceylon Tamil	Percentage	Indian Tamil	Percentage
1946	733,700	11.02%	780,600	11.73%
1953	884,700	10.93%	974,100	12.03%
1963	1,164,700	11.01%	1,123,000	10.61%
1971	1,424,000	11.22%	1,174,900	9.26%
1981	1,886,900	12.71%	818,700	5.51%
2001	732,100	4.32%	855,000	5.05%
2011	2,270,924	11.21%	842,323	4.16%

SOURCE: Sri Lanka Department of Census and Statistics.
NOTE: The low percentage of Ceylon Tamils and Sri Lankan Tamils in 2001 reflects the government's inability to carry out the census in LTTE-controlled territories.

on India before. The identities of the Indian Tamils remaining on the island were redefined during the struggle for citizenship and the armed conflict in the northeast. Since the 1970s many naturalized Indians have identified as "Sri Lankan Tamils" on the census in order to emphasize their nativeness (Sahadevan 1995, 88; Bass 2007). Adding the disenfranchisement of Indian Tamils to its long list of grievances, the LTTE welcomed them into the ranks of the insurgency. The LTTE also continued ITAK's tradition of ignoring caste divisions and preaching that their perpetuation harmed Tamil nationalism. As a result, intra-Tamil cleavages gradually shifted from caste and ancestry to region. The distinction between Sri Lankan and Indian Tamils in the northeast has become blurred, while the highlanders emphasize their Upcountry Tamil (Malaiyaka Tamil) identity (Bass 2007). After the defeat of the LTTE, the Tamil National Alliance (TNA), the new agglomeration of Ceylon Tamil parties, has dropped the demand for independence, saying it would accept a federal structure encompassing the North and East Provinces. This is simply a return to the pre-war Tamil nationalist agenda, and leaves out the bulk of the Indian Tamils who do not live in the northeast. The TNA's position serves to underline the fact that the political trajectories of the two Tamil communities on the island have parted ways.

Colonists to Eelam

The most dramatic and ongoing settler dispute in Sri Lanka revolves around the Sinhalese colonization of the dry zone. Climatically, Sri Lanka is divided into the central-southwestern wet zone, which receives ample year-round rainfall, and the northeastern dry zone, where a short winter monsoon is followed by a long drought. The island has few perennial rivers, and the largest one, the Mahaweli Ganga ("Great Sandy River") is the only one that flows from the wet to the dry zone. The wet zone is overwhelmingly Sinhalese with an Indian Tamil minority, whereas the dry zone includes a predominantly Sinhalese interior and the predominantly Tamil and Muslim northeast coast (see Maps 7.1 and 7.2 at the end of the chapter). The dry zone was the cradle of ancient Lankan civilizations, the fabled kingdoms of Anuradhapura and Polonnaruwa that constructed massive irrigation tanks, sustaining a large agricultural population (De Silva 2005). The region was gradually depopulated in the Late Middle Ages by a combination of invasions and malaria. Revitalization of the dry zone began in the British period by the colonial authorities with support from the Sinhalese bourgeoisie, for whom development in the region was a source of both financial profit and nationalistic fascination (Meyer 1992).

The colonization schemes began in the 1930s, spearheaded by D. S. Senanayake as colonial minister of agriculture, and continued when he became Ceylon's first prime minister after independence. The stated economic goal of the projects was to promote development by reclaiming jungle land, irrigating it, and distributing it to landless peasants. Some of these peasants came from the local communities, but most were Sinhalese relocated from the wet zone. The largest project in this initial phase was Gal Oya ("Rock Creek") in Eastern Province (Muggah 2008, 84–86). Gal Oya became the site of the first anti-Tamil riots in June 1956, while parliament was passing the "Sinhala only" Official Language Act. Tamil politicians protested the effects of these policies already before independence, and ITAK made colonization part of its agenda right from its inception in 1949. Sinhalese prime ministers attempted twice (in 1957 and 1965) to reach an agreement with ITAK, promising, among other things, to give Tamils greater say in settlement issues, but these pacts were repudiated under pressure from Sinhalese nationalist circles (De Silva 1986). Colonization schemes briefly stalled in the early 1970s as a leftist SLFP-led coalition focused on land reform. They resumed, however, when UNP returned to power in 1977, concurrently with the radicalization of Tamil youth and the rise of the separatist LTTE. Colonization acquired new nationalist overtones when Prime Minister J. R. Jayawardene launched the accelerated Mahaweli Development Program and made an occasion of his appearance at the opening ceremony with a procession mimicking Sinhalese kings (Moore 1985, 45). The ambitious project of dam construction and land resettlement proceeded thanks to very lenient funding from foreign donors (Levy 1989; Esman and Herring 2001; Bastian 2007; Muggah 2008, 88). In addition to agricultural production, the Mahaweli project generated hydroelectric power, contributing between a third and a half of Sri Lanka's total energy needs in the 1980s and 1990s (Mahaweli Authority of Sri Lanka 2009).

Tamil leaders recurrently protested that the settlements were designed to weaken the Tamil character of Eastern Province, also citing the creation of two Sinhalese-majority electoral constituencies—Amparai in 1959 and Seruwila in 1976 (Manogaran 1994). The standard government response was that the projects were reclaiming sparsely populated forest land that had served as an ecological buffer zone between the two ethnic groups but was now necessary for national development and the subsistence of the Sri Lankan people. K. M. De Silva, the most prominent Sinhalese historian of modern Sri Lanka, unabashedly defended this position in his writings: "Resources of land and water are scarce in all the dry zone regions and the preservation of an uninhabited no-man's land in the face of unprecedented population pressure is as unreasonable as it is inequitable" (De Silva 1987, 38).

The cumulative demographic impact of colonization schemes since the 1930s is reflected in government sources and cannot be denied by any number doctoring. Approximately 1.1 million people were resettled in the entire course of these projects—including in the non-ethnically contested central areas (Yiftachel and Ghanem 2004). Various government initiatives in the last thirty years have claimed to address ethnic imbalances in settlement projects, but the reality remains that the main beneficiaries of the land policies have been Sinhalese peasants. A comparison of figures from the 1946 and the 1981 census reveals the threefold increase in the proportion of Eastern Province's Sinhalese population (see Table 7.2). Estimates from the special enumeration of 2007 illustrate the population displacement caused by the civil war: the flight of Sinhalese from Batticaloa, the swelling of the Muslim population of Trincomalee due to the arrival of refugees from the north, and the consolidation of Ampara into a predominantly Muslim and Sinhalese district— from what was a predominantly Muslim and Tamil district in the early 20th

TABLE 7.2 Ethnic demographics of Eastern Province districts in 1946, 1981, 2007, and 2012

1946	Tamils	Muslims	Sinhalese	Total
Trincomalee	33,795 (44.5%)	23,219 (30.6%)	11,606 (15.3%)	75,926
Batticaloa	102,264 (50.3%)	85,505 (42.2%)	11,850 (5.8%)	203,186
Eastern Province	136,059 (48.8%)	109,024 (39.1%)	23,456 (8.4%)	279,112
1981				
Trincomalee	93,132 (36.4%)	75,039 (29.3%)	85,503 (33.4%)	255,948
Batticaloa	237,787 (72%)	78,829 (23.9%)	11,255 (3.4%)	330,333
Ampara	79,237 (20.4%)	161,568 (41.5%)	146,943 (37.8%)	388,970
Eastern Province	410,156 (42.1%)	315,436 (32.3%)	243,701 (25%)	975,251
2007				
Trincomalee	96,142 (28.8%)	152,019 (45.5%)	84,766 (25.4%)	334,363
Batticaloa	381,984 (74.1%)	129,045 (25%)	2,397 (0.5%)	515,857
Ampara	109,188 (18.4%)	268,630 (44%)	228,938 (37.5%)	610,719
Eastern Province	590,132 (40.4%)	549,857 (37.6%)	316,101 (21.6%)	1,460,939
2012				
Trincomalee	122,080 (32.3%)	152,854 (40.4%)	101,991 (27%)	378,182
Batticaloa	382,300 (72.8%)	133,844 (25.5%)	6,127 (1.2%)	525,142
Ampara	112,915 (17.4%)	282,484 (43.6%)	251,018 (38.7%)	648,057
Eastern Province	617,295 (39.8%)	569,182 (36.7%)	359,136 (23.1%)	1,551,381

SOURCE: Sri Lanka Department of Census and Statistics.

NOTE: The very small number of Indian Tamils is included in the "Tamils" category; Ampara district was carved out of southern Batticaloa district in 1961.

century. Data from the 2012 census indicate a slow but definite postwar rise in the share of Sinhalese population throughout the province. This may partly reflect the return of refugees and partly a new inflow of Sinhalese workers and entrepreneurs, as rampant tourist development spreads to the formerly unsafe eastern coastal areas.[7]

The social circumstances of Sinhalese settlers have dictated their loyalty to the Sri Lankan state apparatus from the start. As Mick Moore noted in his classic study of Sri Lankan peasantry, the settlers were originally drawn from underprivileged populations, who easily fell prey to the patronage networks of Sinhalese government officials sent to administer the settlement areas.

> The settlers are initially uprooted from their home areas. Although not necessarily among the poorest, they are people who owned little or no land at home.

They thus include relatively few people who are socially and politically compe-
tent to deal with politicians and administrative agencies on equal terms. . . . In
the colonies it is public-sector agencies which allocate irrigation water, credit,
and fertiliser; purchase much of the crop; and decide whether the subdividing
or the mortgaging of allotments is to be formally accepted or informally tolerated. Colonists cannot help but appear dependent on government; they are in
truth very dependent. (Moore 1985, 198)

Norman Uphoff, who frequented Gal Oya as a USAID advisor in the 1980s,
made a bleaker assessment of settler backgrounds:

Few settlers had come fully voluntarily. Village headmen had often been told
to send a certain number of households to Gal Oya to settle, and they took this
opportunity to get rid of the most troublesome members of their communities. The government even gave some prisoners early release from jail on the
condition that they would relocate to Gal Oya with their families. (Uphoff,
quoted in Esman and Herring 2001, 116)

From the 1980s on, as the LTTE insurgency securitized everyday life, the
Sinhalese settlers and local Tamil farmers had built a more complex patron-
client relationship with the military and the rebels respectively. The LTTE
targeted settlers and favored Tamil peasants in their property disputes with
the former; conversely, the government tolerated and even encouraged squatting by the settlers, whose presence strengthened government control of contested zones (Korf 2005; Muggah 2008, 125–127; Somasundaram 2010). When
Tamil farmers fled government offensives, local Muslims often benefited by
grabbing their land. Land competition and the Muslims' lack of support for
Tamil separatism made them the object of Tamil indignation, a situation
astutely exploited by the Sri Lankan security forces (McGilvray 2008, 312–
329). In 1990 the LTTE expelled Muslims from Northern Province, flooding
the neighboring districts of Puttalam and Trincomalee with refugees. But
in Ampara district, where Muslims constitute a plurality, the expansion of
Sinhalese settlements has also caused Muslim reaction. After the death of its
founder M.H.M. Ashraff in 2000, the main Moorish political party, the Sri
Lankan Muslim Congress (SLMC), suffered a split between Ashraff's widow
and the deputy leader Rauf Hakeem over the question of government policies
in Eastern Province. Ms. Ferial Ashraff chose to maintain an alliance with
SLFP, while Hakeem joined a coalition with UNP in 2001.

The expulsion of Muslims from Northern Province was only a part of the massive human dislocation caused by the civil war and compounded by LTTE massacres and the creation of High Security Zones by the Sri Lankan armed forces. Up to one million internally displaced persons (IDPs) had fled their homes by the 1990s, in addition to the refugees escaping to India and western countries. With international help, the government set up welfare centers and relocation villages, but most IDPs lived outside them, squatting on any available land, and did not want to be resettled in their places of origin. The resettlement process has been chaotic, plagued by overlapping authority of government agencies (Muggah 2008, 93–100, 137–185). To this man-made catastrophe was added the natural disaster of the 2004 tsunami, which heavily affected the Eastern Province. Although international actors initially saw the humanitarian crisis as an opportunity for reconciliation, the influx of aid became yet another topic of contention, with the Sri Lankan government accusing foreign NGOs of funneling money to the Tamil Tigers (McGilvray and Gamburd 2010; Holt 2011).

Sinhalese colonization has not been limited to Eastern Province, but it was most successful there. Initial Mahaweli plans extended to the southern portions of Northern Province (Weli Oya in Sinhala/Manal Aru in Tamil), which were technically not part of the Mahaweli river drainage basin. Encroaching on the rebel heartland, these settlements were even more vigorously targeted by the LTTE. In the late 1980s the government established a system of border villages (*mayim gammana*) peopled with farmers from communities along the Vavuniya-Anuradhapura district boundary. The Village Protection Officers (*gammaraksha niladhari*), recruited from among these communities by the Home Guard (today the Department of Civil Defense), are Sri Lanka's version of settler militarization.[8] Constant clashes with the rebels and LTTE retributions against civilians discouraged further colonization in the north.

Their continuing dependence on the state apparatus explains the settlers' overall low level of political mobilization. Buddhist fundamentalist groups have traditionally supported the colonization schemes, both through ideological propaganda and welfare programs; but this has been a guided, not a grassroots, religious movement (Peebles 1990). Nor have settlers consistently rallied around any one political force, their votes being usually split between UNP and SLFP. In the early 2000s the North East Sinhalese Association, affiliated with the ultra-leftist, nationalist People's Liberation Front (JVP: Janatha Vimukthi Peramuna), was an organization which lobbied for settler interests;

it became effectively defunct after the assassination of key members by the LTTE. In the 2004 parliamentary election, when the ultra-right-wing Buddhist nationalist National Heritage Party (JHU: Jathika Hela Urumaya) made a strong showing, it drew most of its support from the Colombo area, not the settlements. The Sinhalese of Eastern Province frequently expressed feelings of insecurity as a regional minority subject to Tamil hostility and atrocities committed by the insurgents (International Crisis Group 2008). Succinctly put, "the result [of the settlement policy] has been the maintenance of Sinhalese Buddhist colonies at the price of massacres by Tamil separatist guerrillas" (Peebles 1990, 52).

The Sinhalese colonization of Eastern Province poses complicated normative questions. On the one hand, the Sinhalese leadership has hardly bothered to veil its ultimate demographic engineering goals, which were evident and documented in public statements even before the outbreak of the civil war. On the other hand, the Sri Lankan government has also framed its land policy as developmental, an exercise of its exclusive rights over its sovereign territory. Due to the lack of meaningful regional devolution, Sri Lankan Tamils can raise no domestic legal barrier to these projects, and as Loizides points out elsewhere in this volume, norms and legal frameworks of protection for the territorial rights of minorities in non-federalized states are very weak.[9] In addition, the question of Tamil traditional territoriality is politically controversial in Sri Lanka, and much more so for Eastern Province, where it clashes both with the aspirations of the local Muslim minority and with the overall normative objections of the Sinhalese majority to the historical origins of Tamil settlement in Sri Lanka.

Throughout the civil war, Tamil separatist demands focused on the creation of a combined Northeastern Province, and Sinhalese colonization was seen as a calculated government strategy of severing the east from Tamil Eelam (Wilson 2003; also see Figure 7.2 at the end of the chapter). The 1987 Indo-Sri Lankan Accord envisioned a temporary joining of the two provinces, subject to a referendum to be held in Eastern Province, which could be postponed at the Sri Lankan president's discretion.[10] The two provinces were indeed merged in 1988, but the referendum in Eastern Province never took place. The failure of subsequent peace talks essentially came down to the Sri Lankan government's unwillingness to concede control of a united northeast to the rebels (Ghosh 2003; Sisk 2009). The devolution debate inherently stumbled on an ethnic commitment problem (Fearon 1998; Fearon and Laitin

2011): on the one hand, if given control of a federalized northeast, Tamil rebels were not able to credibly commit that they would not later seek secession from a stronger position or that they would not ethnically cleanse the Sinhalese settlers; on the other hand, if the state remained centralized, the government could not credibly commit that it would halt colonization or respect any concept of Tamil ethno-territoriality. Through a decision of the Sri Lankan Supreme Court, the merging of the two provinces was declared void in 2006.

Settlers, Immigrants, and Colonists in Sri Lanka

Yiftachel and Ghanem (2004) described Sri Lanka as an ethnocratic regime because, among other things, of its land policies. Robert Muggah (2008) confirms this judgment: "Under the pretext of development, counterinsurgency and disaster response, the state engaged in what amounted to demographic engineering" (68). Mesmerized by the prospects of increasing agricultural production, relieving population pressures in the south, reenacting ancient hydraulic civilizations (Sorensen 1996, 61–85), and weakening separatism, the Sinhalese leadership undermined ethnic relations and state stability through the colonization of the east. On another front, Sri Lanka's citizenship policy ostracized the Indian Tamils for four decades on grounds of their not being sons of the soil. What is striking is how these two disputes took different paths: the first contributing to the outbreak of civil war, the second fizzling out with a peaceful compromise.

David Laitin (2009) has argued that immigrant communities are less likely to initiate civil conflicts because they lack a strong collective identity and have the option of returning to their country of origin. His hypothesis holds true for the Indian Tamils, but not exactly for the reasons stated. First of all, the Indian Tamils do possess a collective identity and it even features a territorial (Upcountry) aspect. Despite suffering worse discrimination than their autochthonous counterparts, while also possessing a degree of geographic concentration and being politically mobilized, the Upcountry Tamils did not rise up in arms, even when the Tamil insurgency sprang up in the north and east of the island in the late 1970s. Much feared by the Sinhalese political leadership, the possibility of the Indian Tamils joining forces with the Sri Lankan Tamils almost came to fruition in 1972–1976 with the creation of TULF. What ultimately condemned this alliance was the Indian Tamils' lack of an autochthonous territorial identity, an ideology of exclusive entitlement to a part of the island, which, as mentioned in the first section, assumed such a central role in the Sri Lankan Tamil nationalist movement (Samarasinghe 1988). Indian Tamils were also acutely aware of their vulnerable position: living at the bottom of the ethnically stratified economy of the Sinhalese central highlands, the majority of Upcountry Tamils were both socially and geographically cut off from the Jaffna Tamil elites. Sri Lankan Tamil nationalists included the disenfranchisement of Indian Tamils in their list of grievances mostly for instrumental purposes. With their push for Tamil Eelam, ITAK's leadership abandoned the possibility of campaigning on a platform of equal civil and linguistic rights for all Tamils throughout the island. As things played out, the Tamil insurgency was not orchestrated by the downtrodden laborers of the plantations but by the educated middle-class youth of the Jaffna peninsula. Indian Tamils living in the north and some Indian Tamil refugees fleeing pogroms in the south joined the movement, but the bulk of the Upcountry Tamil population stayed out of the fray.

Nor was it an easy option for Indian Tamils to return to India, a country many had never seen and one which resisted their forced repatriation. Between 1949 and 1951, when the deadline set by the Indian and Pakistani Residents Act expired, 824,430 Indian Tamils applied for Ceylonese citizenship, while by 1953 only 182,292 opted for Indian citizenship (Sahadevan 1995, 128–134). In the following decades, India issued passports but was slow to implement actual repatriation, and eventually stopped registering people against their will. Repatriation to India seemed like an easy option only to the Sinhalese nationalists, who viewed Indian Tamils as settlers brought in by the British—a triangular situation in that the settling authority was different from the settled people's kin state. India also respected the distinction and played a different role as a kin state toward each of the two Tamil communities on the island. Far from disinterested in the plight of stateless Tamils, India was reluctant to take extreme measures on their behalf, compared to the active support it provided to the Tamil insurgents before its disastrous intervention. There was never a show of military force to compel Sri Lanka's cooperation on the stateless question similar to Operation Poomalai in 1987 which relieved the siege of Jaffna and forced Sri Lanka to accede to the Indo-Sri Lankan Accord (Bose 2002).

Why did the Sinhalese elites, at the very height of the conflict with the Sri Lankan Tamils, accommodate rather than target and expel all the Indian Tamils who had been so vilified as an alien element? Once it was clear that

Indian Tamils were not joining the insurgency en masse and did not harbor territorial claims in their areas of concentration, they were perceived as less of a security threat. Insisting on expelling them in the face of India's refusal would only push to the brink relations with Sri Lanka's colossal neighbor; keeping them on the island would serve as a symbolic demonstration of tolerance toward Tamils and sustain a useful reservoir of votes. These points could not escape the attention of the then ruling UNP leadership, which had a long record of cooperation with Tamil political leaders in general and the Indian Tamil CWC in particular. The survival of Indian Tamils as a community on Sri Lanka proves that settler disputes can be resolved even under highly challenging circumstances if the right political calculus is in place.

The Indian Tamils' socioeconomic position, lack of territorial ideology, and weak kin state support resulted from their conditions of arrival on the island. These made them stand apart from the Sri Lankan Tamils and seek a political accommodation with the Sinhalese-dominated state. The material and ideational aspects of the Indian Tamils' settlement contrast starkly with those of Sinhalese colonists. Even though the latter also came from disadvantaged backgrounds and did not necessarily all ascribe to the tenets of a Buddhist crusade, Sinhalese farmers moving into the dry zone were part of a state-driven project. But unlike Jewish settlers in the Palestinian Territories, they remained the pawns, never becoming the drivers of state policy.

Discourse, Time, and Circumstance in the Study of Settlement Conflict

The varied historical origins of Sri Lanka's settlement disputes and the links between the ancient and the contemporary should by now be clear. Yet, situating Sri Lanka within the literature on settler-induced conflict is complicated by the fact that the field has not been very systematic about making such distinctions. This is lamentable considering that forced settlement has been ubiquitous in human history and that many contemporary conflicts feature some kind of settlement aspect. Settlement disputes "pile up" in some cases (Palestine, Cyprus, Kosovo, Sri Lanka) with current settlement adding to grievance discourses about older settlements, which may have taken place a few or many generations ago.

Of course, not every case of historical settlement is linked with a modern conflict, since in many instances populations merged or the autochthonous were entirely absorbed or eradicated. But even among the universe of modern cases, there is a great diversity of historical circumstances—as Oded Haklai and Neophytos Loizides point out in the introduction to this volume, "settlement endeavors can take many shapes and forms." There are cases where colonization took place in the distant past but its memory carried on as the autochthonous groups persisted (e.g., the plantation of Ulster, the Ottoman conquest of the Balkans, the Russians in the Caucasus and Crimea); cases where colonization was more or less continuous over a long period and then halted (South Africa, Russians in Central Asia) or even reversed with the expulsion of settlers or their descendants (French Algeria, the Dutch East Indies, the Germans of Silesia and Bohemia); cases with recent state-driven colonization projects (Italy in South Tyrol, China in Tibet and Xinjiang, Russia in the Baltic States, Sri Lanka in its Eastern Province, Israel in the Palestinian Territories, Turkey in Northern Cyprus, Morocco in Western Sahara); and even cases of counter-settlement (colonial Rhodesia and post-colonial Zimbabwe, Kirkuk). Finally, there are cases where immigrants (Indians in Guyana and Fiji, Indian Tamils in Sri Lanka, Chinese in Malaysia and Indonesia) or refugees (Pontian Greeks in Greek Macedonia, Muhajirs in Sindh, Mizrahi Jews in Israel) have been viewed as settlers by an autochthonous group.

In an effort to contribute to greater clarity in the analysis of settler disputes, I propose three theoretical distinctions. The first one is the *discursive*, by which I mean the act of "branding" a population as "settlers" or "natives" in the rhetoric of the conflict. This is an emic aspect of many ethnic disputes, whose appearance we would do well to examine and explain as a dependent variable. To take Sri Lanka as an example, many researchers would probably dismiss the case of the Indian Tamils on etic grounds, describing it as a conflict over immigrants, not settlers. And yet, there are clear parallels in how Sinhalese nationalists viewed Indian Tamils as "encroaching" on the Buddhist heartland and how Tamil nationalists have viewed Sinhalese as colonists in their "Tamil Eelam." Another important discursive aspect is the use of "economic development" as a rhetorical frame for settler schemes, a frame rigorously employed by the Sri Lankan government for its colonization projects (see, e.g., the chapters on East Timor and the Italian fascist regime and its policy of *bonifica* in this volume).

The second and third theoretical distinctions are the *temporal* (distant vs. recent) and the *situational* (purposeful colonization vs. inadvertent migration) dimensions. The two-by-two matrix in Figure 7.1 attempts to map out

Colonization   Migration

	Colonization	Migration
Distant	A	C
Recent	B	D

FIGURE 7.1 A two-dimensional categorization of the origins of settlement disputes

how these concepts relate to the study of settler disputes and specifically to the case of Sri Lanka. Cases in the first quadrant (A) constitute a large subsection of ethnic conflicts in modern times, whenever conquest of one people by another was involved, but they are structurally different from cases in the second quadrant in that the dispute cannot be practically addressed through legal processes in that it involves deeper problems of historical normative justice. The second quadrant (B) is the category that the settler literature usually focuses on—the problem is that the literature often confounds (A) and (B) in structured comparisons. The fourth quadrant (D) is normally under the purview of migration studies, unless the state is attracting immigrants in order to consciously alter its ethnic composition. The third quadrant (C) is relevant to the settler literature because many of these situations have evolved into settler-type conflicts as the migrants developed a local, separate identity, even if they had no intention of dislodging the autochthonous. Immigrants may have been brought in by an intermediary (e.g., the British), not their kin society, but the kin state may still be subsequently dragged in, as happened with India in Sri Lanka. And it is well possible for disputes belonging to different categories to simultaneously unravel within the same society.[11]

A common observation is that the circumstances of arrival (both the material capabilities of the heterochthonous group to settle and organize cohesively as a separate collectivity and the ideational baggage that comes with the settlement) are major predictors of the future trajectory of conflict. In Sri Lanka, the settlement of the island in ancient and medieval times (Quadrant A) formed the backdrop for the modern reinvention of past enmities; it still underlies the dispute over Tamil sovereign rights in the northeast, but it did not have as fundamental an influence on group identity as the plantation of

Ulster did in Ireland because the Tamils were separated from the Sinhalese for an extended period by sparsely populated forest land. This separation was ended in the 20th century by the controversial Sinhalese colonization schemes (B), which had strong ideological overtones and continue to poison ethnic relations. The Muslims' arrival on the island (C) was not born out of conflict nor was their relationship with the Tamils of the east conflictual until the onset of Sinhalese colonization. Nevertheless, the Muslims have been targeted by Sinhalese nationalists due to their perceived heterochthony, and recent communal riots (in the summer of 2014) send a disquieting message. The Upcountry Tamils also migrated to the island under peaceful conditions (D), but found themselves caught in the local Tamil-Sinhalese antagonism. It is worth noting that although recent colonization (B) was a major contributing factor to the outbreak of civil war in Sri Lanka, linguistic discrimination was at least as much if not more important, and distant colonization and recent and distant migration (A, D, and C) have also played a role in the conflict.

Once established on the ground and in the mind, primordial and recent settlements may look similar, and like all other conflicts, they may be decided either by military means or by successful negotiation. The force of arms can cut the Gordian knot without normative concerns—note how South African whites settled under terms that were equally or often more exploitative than those imposed by the French Algerian *colons*, but they are now celebrated as part of the country's diversity, whereas the *pieds-noirs* fled to France with their memories. But as Haklai and Loizides point out in Chapter One, removing settler populations is far less acceptable to the international community today than it was a few decades ago. In negotiation, the temporal distinction matters, shaping and constraining the tools available to international mediators. Lustick's (1993b) framework for accepting disengagement may work more easily when colonization was attempted recently, and it has not been too deeply intertwined with overall ethnic identity. Legal recourses like property return and monetary compensation are also easier to work out before the passage of time casts its shadow. The longer a settlement dispute has lingered, the more complicated the humanitarian issues (what to do with the people already settled or dislocated) and political issues (how to manage the new demographic situation, and how to prevent future conflict by stopping further settlement). Historically primordial settlements with echoes to the present, like that in Northern Ireland, can only heal through a long process of cultural reconciliation.

Unlike the case of Israel and Palestine, where the long-standing "right of return" intersects with the more immediate question of Palestinian statehood, Sri Lanka presents an arguably easier problem. Indian Tamils have been integrated for three decades now, and the defeat of the LTTE finally put secession off the table. Tamil leaders have appeared open to an administrative compromise: detaching the border areas colonized by the Sinhalese from Eastern Province, and allowing the rest of the province, which will thus revert to being overwhelmingly Tamil and Muslim, a status of extensive autonomy. This, incidentally, mimics the proposals for redrawing the boundary of the West Bank, but with the aim of facilitating ethnic federalism (Yiftachel 2001). Unfortunately as Timothy Sisk (2009) has noted, Sri Lanka does not lack ideas for conflict resolution, nor are the general outlines of a comprehensive agreement to mend ethnic relations hard to imagine. Rather, it is political will that has been short, and the rampant triumphalism on the heels of the victory against the LTTE has so far not created an atmosphere amenable to consensus and compromise (DeVotta 2011). There is some hope that the UNP, now in power, might be able to play the role of the moderate liberal party (Mitchell 2002) and engineer such a pact, thanks to having a better standing with the Tamils than the SLFP-led coalition had. When in government, however, the UNP has historically often failed to fulfill this potential. Sri Lanka's conflict-ridden past makes it all the more imperative that the international community remain engaged and encourage political initiatives that would prevent a future relapse to violence. While having brought an end to the horrors of civil war, the defeat of the LTTE has done little to remove the underlying problems of competing claims over agricultural land and homeland, low inter-communal trust, and lack of institutional safeguards—all the factors that led to the violent escalation of the Tamil-Sinhalese dispute in the first place. The opening up of the northeast to investment and infrastructural development will likely attract thousands of Sinhalese to "Tamil Eelam" in a much more dramatic fashion than the rural colonization schemes of the 20th century.

MAP 7.1 Regional population distribution in Sri Lanka, 1981
SOURCE: Sri Lanka Department of Census and Statistics.
NOTE: Clockwise from top left: Sinhalese, Sri Lankan Tamil, Indian Tamil and Sri Lankan Moor population per district according to the 1981 census; black color indicates a majority; dark gray, a plurality; medium gray, a minority of 20% or more; and light gray, a minority of 10% to 20%.

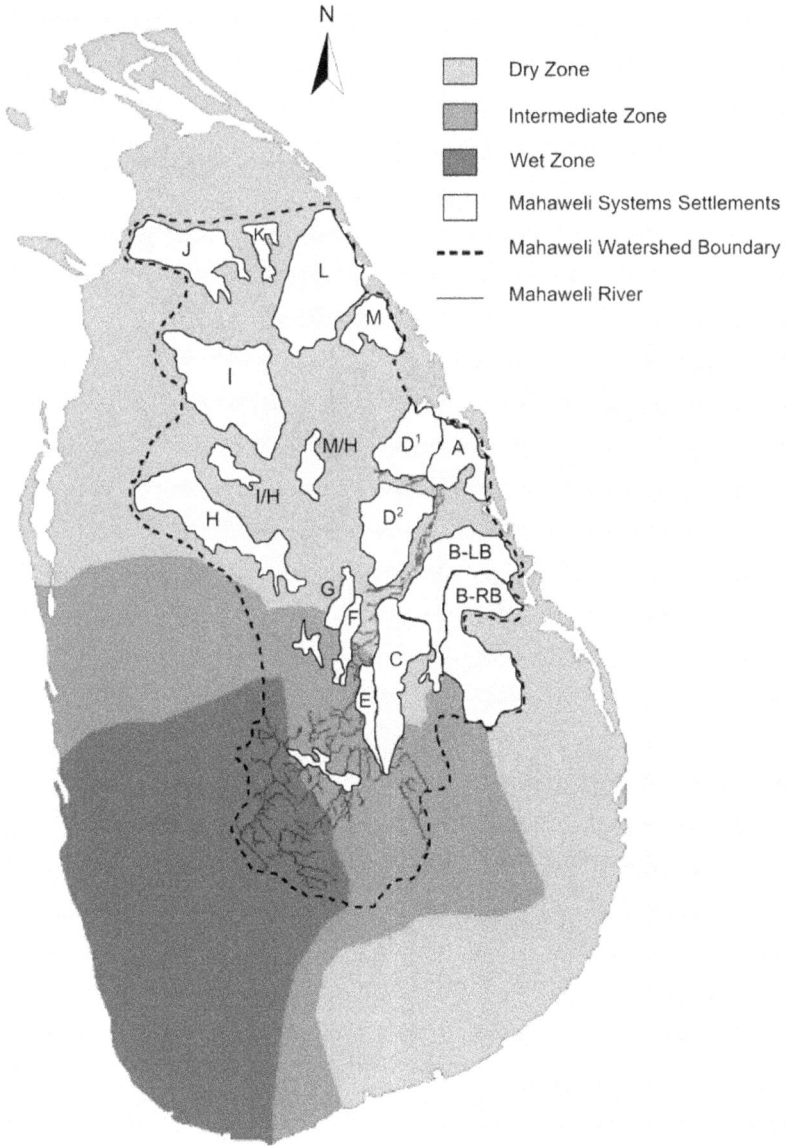

MAP 7.2 The Mahaweli Ganga Project

SOURCE: Lanka Thabrew, Vanderbilt Institute for Energy and the Environment and the ADAPT-Sri Lanka project (https://my.vanderbilt.edu/srilankaproject).

NOTE: The letters on the map indicate the various irrigation systems built over successive phases of the program.

FIGURE 7.2 Tamil propaganda cartoon protesting Sinhalese colonization as an attempt to sever the Eastern Province from Tamil Eelam
SOURCE: Courtesy of Ilankai Tamil Sangam. Accessed from http://tamilnation.co/indictment/indict003.htm. Reprinted with permission.

Notes

1. In their 2011 article on "sons-of-the-soil" conflicts, Fearon and Laitin chose to examine only "recent" migrations, focusing on the Sinhalese colonization of the northeast of the island. I will follow a broader approach here, incorporating all settler-related aspects of the Sri Lankan conflict into the discussion.

2. Usually undertaken by states, colonization may also be orchestrated by a non-state actor, as with Aliyah Bet in pre-independence Israel, or substate actors, as in the 1850s events of Bleeding Kansas.

3. An example of this situation are the French Canadians, now regarded as an autochthonous group by English Canadians and more recent immigrants, but not so by the First Nations of Quebec.

4. The Moors, or Muslims, are regionally concentrated on the eastern coast due to their migration in the 16th century from the Portuguese-controlled west. In 1915 communal riots targeted Muslim traders of South Indian descent and became a

pretext for the British to arrest the Sinhalese nationalist leadership. A smaller riot occurred in Puttalam district in 1976. During the civil war, Tamil militants targeted Muslims, accusing them of collaborating with the Sri Lankan government and squatting on Tamil land in Eastern Province. Since the end of the civil war, anti-Muslim sentiment among Sinhalese Buddhist groups has been on the rise, and anti-Muslim riots broke out in Kalutara district in the summer of 2014.

5. Kumaratunga's devolution package stumbled on the question of the Eastern Province, discussed later in the chapter.

6. CWC contested jointly with UNP in the 1989 and 1994 parliamentary elections. It switched its support to SLFP in 2000, went back to UNP in 2001, and although it elected eight deputies on the UNP ballot in 2004, it then joined the SLFP-led coalition that resumed the war against the LTTE.

7. The author experienced this firsthand as an election observer in Trincomalee district in 2010.

8. It is believed that Israeli advisors played a role in urging the Sri Lankan government to fortify settlements in strategic areas (Bose 2007, 30).

9. Notable exceptions are the International Labor Organization's 1957 and 1989 Indigenous and Tribal Peoples Conventions, which, however, have been ratified by only a small number of countries.

10. As a result of the accord, the 13th Amendment to the Constitution (Ninth Schedule, Appendix II) specified that the allotment of land in development projects "will be on the basis of national ethnic ratio," giving priority to people displaced by the project and then to landless people within the district and province. Questionably implemented so far, this provision does not, technically, protect against colonization because it refers to nationwide ratios, not the ethnic balance within each district or province.

11. Sri Lanka was the case illustrated here; consider also the two differing relationships between older and more recent Jewish immigrants in Israel and Israeli Arabs, or the differing relationships in Quebec between French Canadians, English Canadians, recent Francophone immigrants, and non-Francophone immigrants and the indigenous First Nations.

8 Settlers, Mobilization, and Displacement in Cyprus: Antinomies of Ethnic Conflict and Immigration Politics

Neophytos Loizides

THIS CHAPTER FOCUSES ON POPULATIONS WHO HAVE been settled from Turkey to Northern Cyprus after 1974. As most debates on the Cyprus issue have traditionally focused on the two "historically antagonistic" indigenous Greek and Turkish Cypriot communities, the "Anatolian settler" question has received relatively little academic attention. From an international legal perspective, the Turkish settlers were purposefully allocated properties belonging to Greek Cypriot displaced persons as result of a colonization attempt by Turkey and the Turkish Cypriot authorities aiming to transform the demographic structure of the island. Inevitably, the settler/migrant presence is seen as an obstacle to the future reunification of Cyprus and a violation of Article 49 of the Geneva Convention of 1949. Conventional wisdom assumes societies built on expulsion of indigenous groups and colonization to be inherently unstable. Yet in sociological and humanitarian terms, settlers in Cyprus, as well as in other contested territories covered in this volume, are not monolithically attached to expansionist nationalism and often have concerns and vulnerabilities comparable to those of migrant populations.

This chapter aims to uncover the antinomies of ethnic conflict and immigration politics in Cyprus and to situate the experience of Turkish settlers within the broader literature. It also examines the causes of non-politicization among Turkish settlers and identifies relevant implications for these settlers' future inclusion in a reunited Cyprus. While other contributions to this volume have demonstrated the agency of settlers in contested territories, this chapter sets the Cypriot experience apart from the current literature at the micro-macro level. As mentioned in the introduction to this volume in Chapter One, Cyprus provides a contrasting case to the settler colonial literature. For one thing, the Cypriot case demonstrates diminished agency among settlers. For another, Turkish colonization in Northern Cyprus has not aimed explicitly at the incorporation of the territory but at strengthening the position of an ethnic kin minority community that has had the intent of establishing a de facto Turkish Cypriot state in the island since 1974.

Moreover, the chapter aims to investigate whether or not colonization in Cyprus has reached a point of no return, contributing to and even consolidating partition. While the Cypriot conflict has intensified since the discovery of hydrocarbons in the island's exclusive economic zone in 2011, the election of moderate Turkish Cypriot leader Mustafa Akinci in April 2015 has renewed hopes for progress in the reunification talks. As this chapter demonstrates, there are obstacles as well as fundamental reasons for expediting mediation efforts for a negotiated settlement. On the one hand, the settler issue has been a major impediment in the negotiations, particularly for the Greek Cypriot side, as it affects questions of citizenship, electoral representation, and property return. On the other, as this chapter argues, settler voters have not opposed reunification, as demonstrated in the support for Akinci's candidacy in predominantly settler constituencies. Emphasizing the normative and sociological dimensions of the settler/immigration experience in Cyprus, this chapter argues that the point of no return in Cyprus has not been reached yet. Low levels of politicization and even growing support for a peace agreement among the settlers could enable the reunification of Cyprus, particularly if mediators proactively address native Cypriot concerns and fears with regard to future settler-related provisions. Despite four decades of partition, resolving the Cyprus problem is still feasible, but it will require a set of novel institutional arrangements aiming to balance humanitarian and justice considerations as well as creative public policy responses, particularly on the territorial aspects of a future peace settlement.

The chapter is divided into two parts. The first part highlights the typologies of settlers/migrants in contested lands and demonstrates how mobilization and politicization dynamics within the settler community in Cyprus affect prospects for peace mediation. This section aims to expand beyond its original scope Lustick's influential work on settler colonialism by demonstrating the degree of its applicability among cases of the least politicized settlers. Building on an assessment of the legal and humanitarian aspects of the settler question, the second part of the chapter draws from other conflict situations to explore potential arrangements available in the context of the Cypriot negotiations.

Peace mediations are implicitly linked to demographic questions and specifically in Cyprus to the question of settler non-mobilization. In fact, as this chapter demonstrates, the previous attempts to incorporate settler concerns partly explain non-politicization on their behalf, suggesting potential lessons for other contested settlement territories covered in this volume. Previous peace plans, including the 2002–2004 Annan Plan, have offered detailed and arguably generous provisions for the accommodation of settlers in a reunited Cyprus; therefore one might conclude that preventive peace mediations could, ceteris paribus, contribute to non-politicization of settlers in contested lands. The institutional innovations presented in the Annan Plan and other arrangements debated in the Cypriot context during the past decade have important implications for other cases emerging from ethnic cleansing, including Israel-Palestine and the former Yugoslavia (Ron 2003; Haklai 2007; Stefanovic and Loizides 2011).

Moreover, this chapter argues that settlers in Cyprus demonstrate low levels of mobilization and politicization because the socioeconomic features of settler migration often trump nationalism and settler ideology. Yet it cautions against treating a largely political question simply in immigration terms. It emphasizes creative and balanced institutional arrangements as necessary for diverting settler/migrant politics in the direction of durable peace as well as for safeguarding peace processes from counter-mobilizations of native populations, particularly formerly displaced populations. Specifically, this chapter discusses institutional arrangements tied to cross-issue linkage, asymmetrical citizenship, and the political/electoral inclusion of settler/migrants. It then concludes with a discussion of the broader implications of this study for national and ethnic conflict management.

Typologies of Settlers/Migrants

Settler societies are born out of the massive colonization of disputed territories accompanied by the expulsion and/or domination of indigenous groups and aiming at building newly minted and self-sustaining states (Pearson 2001,

5; Weitzer 1990, 24). As demonstrated in the introduction, Lustick (1985, 2005) distinguishes among three types of settlers. First, *ideologically driven* settlers commonly justify their actions in ideological terms, such as "keeping Ulster British," "building a Jewish state in Judea and Samaria" (the West Bank), and "turning Algeria into a New France." Second, *politically and economically connected* settlers enjoy disproportionate political influence in their home country and profit economically from colonization (see also Haklai 2007). Examples include commercial farmers in southern Africa and French Algeria and also people involved in the real estate and tourism industries in Cyprus who enjoy privileged access to "abandoned" Greek Cypriot land. Economic enterprises tend to de-emphasize national ideology and frequently shift their influence for or against a peace process depending on the specific incentives and disincentives. Finally, *underprivileged populations* are less interested in territorial politics and have immigrated for economic reasons, especially if they have been promised an easy life and access to "empty land."

The latter category could be compared to immigrant populations interested primarily in their personal and family advancement and much less concerned with the confrontational politics of the core state. Kymlicka (1995) and more recently Laitin (2009) have argued that international migrants are less likely to mobilize for political reasons and are almost never implicated in civil war violence, even when they face security and cultural threats in their host societies. Yet settlers cannot be accurately equated with migrants, even in cases where the primary motives are economic or broadly related to achieving a better life standard. Simply stated, viewing another population's homeland as "empty land" or attempting to enjoy unlimited economic opportunity in a contested territory has problematic ideological underpinnings about the rights of "others" in that territory (Pedersen 2005).

Settler narratives of migrating to an empty land are often inconsistent with historical realities; the settler, argues Veracini (2010, 14), "frequently hides behind the ethnic cleanser." For instance, in Australia it is not settlers that have been traditionally blamed for ethnic cleansing but "ruthless convicts" that displaced indigenous populations (Veracini 2010, 14). Furthermore, due to the dynamics of violence and conflict, settler colonialism might have a greater impact on a contested territory than immigration; as a result, core state disengagement and potential relocation could be more difficult and costly for settlers than for immigrants. Nonetheless, populations transferred to contested territories might simultaneously resemble both settlers and migrants in ways that make differentiation difficult without carefully reassessing the historical and current political aspects of each case study.

Cyprus: A Contested Partition

Cyprus became independent from British rule in 1960, but power-sharing arrangements between the Greek and Turkish Cypriots lasted for only three years. Cyprus has experienced ethnic cleansing at various times in its recent history (Hadjipavlou 2007; Yesilada and Sozen 2002) and has proportionally one of the longest instances of displacement and colonization in post–World War II Europe. In their historical narratives, Turkish Cypriots emphasize the 1963–1974 period when their community was excluded from the government, forced into enclaves, and prevented from safe access to the remaining parts of the island, including traditionally Turkish Cypriot villages and neighborhoods (Patrick 1976; Fisher 2001, 310). Meanwhile, Greek Cypriots emphasize the decades following the 1974 Turkish invasion when the island was de facto divided between Turkish army–controlled areas in the north and government-controlled areas in the south (Joseph 1997; also see Map 8.1 later in this chapter). During and after the invasion, approximately about a third of the Greek Cypriots (i.e., about 160,000 civilians) were forced by the Turkish military to flee from their own areas, while a similar proportion of Turkish Cypriots (i.e., about 45,000) living in the south chose or were coerced to abandon their houses and move to the north (Fisher 2001, 311; Attalides 1979).

Since 1974, negotiations on the Cyprus problem have focused on the right of return for displaced persons and their properties as well as the rights of new owners. In general, Greek Cypriots aim at maintaining the right of return by citing international human rights law; the principles of the European Union (EU), including the *acquis communautaire*; and the need for the settlement to be perceived as just (United Nations Security Council 2003a). Turkish Cypriots, meanwhile, wish to consolidate their demographic presence in northern Cyprus, arguing that realities on the ground, distrust, security issues, and the principle of "bizonality" dictate that the right of return should be strictly controlled (United Nations Security Council 2003a).

Individuals and governments have taken this issue to court; since the late 1990s there have been a number of legal decisions by Cypriot, UK, and European courts safeguarding the rights of displaced persons. For the most part, these decisions have also demonstrated the political and normative limitations of engaging in settlement projects in modern times. Although no legal decision has explicitly demanded the withdrawal of settlers, Turkey has been judged to be the responsible party in compensating the Greek Cypriot displaced. As highlighted in this chapter, these decisions have created important legal precedents for mediations in Cyprus as well as for other post-conflict societies. Yet these decisions have also been criticized for narrowing discussions on the legal aspects of return, sidelining other important political and sociological dimensions of the Cypriot question.

Since 1974, successive Turkish governments actively encouraged tens of thousands of mainland Turkish citizens to settle in Cyprus. Exact numbers remain a closely-guarded secret, and even members of the Turkish Cypriot negotiating team have acknowledged that they are not aware of the accurate figures.[1] Much of the confusion arises from the different types of settlers, including long-term residents naturalized by the Turkish Cypriot authorities, permanent and temporary residents, illegal workers, university students, and members of the Turkish military and their families. Although there are no reliable statistical data, Mete Hatay estimates the number of naturalized settlers to have been around 16 to 18 percent of the Turkish Cypriot electorate in 2005 (Hatay 2005, viii), while Greek Cypriot estimates suggest that settlers constitute about 50 percent of the population (Cuco 2007; Palley 2005, 67). The 2006 census in the northern part of the island found a population of 265,100 (citizens and other permanent residents). The census also found 178,031 TRNC citizens; of these, 42,572 had both parents born in Turkey. The figure for current TRNC citizens with at least one parent born in Cyprus is 132,635 (including those settlers whose non-Cypriot parents were born in the island).[2]

More importantly, these numbers have been used as a tool by politicians on both sides of the divide to foster their agendas, with head counts serving as ammunition in public debates (Tezgor 2003). Figures used to support arguments are usually exaggerated; some exceed half a million settlers, with no proper documentation provided to support facts (Charalambidou-Papapavlou 2008).

In his reports on the aborted 2001–2004 Annan Plan, the UN secretary-general gives some revealing information about the positions of the two sides and the number of settlers. During the negotiations, the Turkish Cypriot side tried to assure the Greek Cypriots that only 30,000 to 35,000 settlers had received "TRNC citizenship." The Greek Cypriots promised to change their initial position on repatriation of settlers to Turkey and to accept them as citizens provided that the Turkish Cypriot side provided a definite list of names. The Turkish Cypriot side acceded but failed to submit the list. The Turkish Cypriot leader slowly revised the number upward to 60,000 but refused to give any details, arguing that giving citizenship was part of the "exercise of sovereignty" (United Nations Security Council 2003a, 22). After the Greek Cypriots rejected the 2004 Annan Plan in a referendum, EU bodies generally refrained from taking a position on settlers in Cyprus, noting that this issue could be resolved in the bilateral negotiations. In 2011, the UN secretary-general brokered a tentative agreement between the two sides for a census, although eventually Greek and Turkish Cypriot negotiators could not agree on its implementation, suggesting the centrality of "perceived figures" for the maintenance of each side's ethnopolitical narratives. Besides numbers, a major issue in addressing the problem is politicization among populations transferred from Turkey, which also affects the prospects for a settlement in the island.

Politicization and Settlers

Although settlers constitute a significant part of the electorate, in previous (as well as the current) Turkish Cypriot assemblies, only three members among a total of fifty were natives of Turkey (Kibris 2003). As Guelke (2012) demonstrates, the division of society into settlers and natives as a legacy of colonization or conquest is a pattern to be found in many parts of the world. In the comparable cases of Israeli settlers (West Bank and Gaza), French settlers (Algeria), and Ulster Protestant settlers (Northern Ireland), there was overwhelming political activity and mobilization among settler populations seeking territorial disengagement from the core state (Lustick 1993b). Settler mobilization has arguably prevented a two-state solution in Israel-Palestine, led to the partition of Ireland, and forced massive war crimes in Algeria before French disengagement.

By way of contrast, low levels of politicization in Cyprus are generally attributed to the largely heterogeneous character of the settler population. In an interview with the author, a settler politician argued that settlers differ not only in terms of ethnic and regional background (e.g., Kurdish, Laz, and Arabic speakers) but also in terms of time and conditions of arrival in Cyprus, degree of assimilation, and political affiliation (see also Navaro-Yashin 2012, 51–61). Unlike other cases covered in this volume, post-1974 Turkish settlers did not transplant their own institutions into Northern Cyprus but faced, in the first place, a highly politicized Turkish Cypriot community. Subsequently, the several peace plans for Cyprus have also weakened the settlers' position with respect to Ankara and the Turkish Cypriot authorities and divided the community between long-term residents who will securely stay after the settlement and receive Cypriot citizenship and the rest. By extension, the most connected and established settlers are expected to gain from a negotiated settlement and therefore are less likely to mobilize against a peace settlement.

Low politicization also stems from the nature of these original settlers. As Liaras argues in this volume with regard to Sri Lanka, the original status of entry might trap settlers' prospects for upward mobility. According to Lacher and Kaymak, war veterans' and martyrs' families were given land and houses in northern Cyprus after 1974 (2005, 155). However, the overwhelming majority of settlers opted to abandon their villages in Anatolia for economic reasons and not to serve ideological purposes (although ideology and nationalism might have played a significant role in few cases). Class and status are probably the most important factors in the lack of mobilization. In most other cases of settler colonialism, settlers were economically privileged, and repatriation to the home state meant the loss of status and relative ease of life. For instance, the *pieds-noirs* in Algeria, although largely heterogeneous in composition, effectively transformed the local Muslim population into serfs (Lustick 2005). Yet in personal terms, settlers in Cyprus could gain significantly after a settlement in terms of legal land ownership, citizenship rights, and compensations. They tend, therefore, to be less committed to the ideological tenets of Turkish nationalism for instrumental reasons or, in most cases, because they simply lack the resources and incentives for mobilization.

Also important are the divisions within Turkish nationalism, clearly manifested in Northern Cyprus and making settler politicization more difficult. The Turkish army, the embassy in Nicosia, and the Turkish Cypriot authorities all control alternative resources (and funds) through which they maintain spheres of patronage and influence among underprivileged settlers. In the past, a segment of the settler vote has been controlled by the island's Turkish military and its extended network of influence and economic or social support. For the most part, these votes went to anti-deal forces who openly opposed Turkish Prime Minister Recep Tayyip Erdoğan and the moderate Islamist AKP (Justice and Development Party) in Turkey. At the same time, settlers hailing from areas in Anatolia increasingly support either AKP or pro-Kurdish parties. Religious settlers who have retained their networks in Anatolia are more likely to follow AKP, which, in 2002–2004, supported pro-unification forces on the Turkish Cypriot left. Kurdish settlers are also likely to oppose the Turkish military, particularly since many retain strong family connections with their home provinces. For instance, a settler politician in Cyprus revealed to the author in the past that a family member has served as an MP with the now outlawed pro-Kurdish Democratic Society Party (DTP) party in the province of Mardin, Turkey.

Despite low levels of politicization and violence, colonization has triggered discourses favoring indigenous Turkish and Greek Cypriot identities while often assuming discriminatory or racist overtones against settlers. The Turkish Cypriot community itself is divided on settlers; nationalist parties have traditionally supported or tolerated their arrival, while pro-unification forces have generally opposed it, seeing it as threatening to the character of the community. Nonetheless, all major Turkish Cypriot political parties have maintained a balance between domestic fears of alienation and the need to attract new settler voters. Although concerned with demographics, Turkish Cypriot leaders see settlers as important for their economy, for political and demographic parity with the Greek Cypriot side, and for their relationship with Ankara. Likewise, the presence of settlers has triggered two opposing narratives within the Greek Cypriot community: one rejecting a compromise involving large numbers of settlers (as in the Annan Plan) and the other a counter-framing favoring a negotiated compromise for humanitarian and pragmatic reasons in order to avoid new waves of uncontrolled colonization.

A number of incidents of violence have been attributed to settlers since 1974; however, there is very little evidence suggesting grassroots settler involvement in these incidents or other forms of militant extremism on their behalf. For example, the killing of two Greek Cypriot demonstrators in the buffer zone in 1996 was attributed to settlers, although all publicly available evidence indicates the direct involvement of the Turkish Cypriot police and ultranationalist groups from Turkey. A second incident involved Turkish Cypriot journalist Kutlu Adali, one of the most vocal critics of the Denktaş regime's colonization strategies. Adali was assassinated in 1996, most likely by either Turkish ultranationalists or criminal groups from Turkey whose actions he had revealed in the press. Again in this incident, Turkey has been condemned by a European Court of Human Rights (ECtHR) ruling for failing to properly investigate the incident. During the Ergenekon investigations in Turkey, information became publicly available linking suspects in Adali's assassination with members of Ergenekon, a "criminal group" plotting military coups in Turkey. The investigation revealed connections with politicians in Cyprus, including the fact that members of the group had received TRNC identity cards ("Ergenekon's Cyprus Operations" 2009).

Both Lustick (1985, 1993b) and Haklai (2007) emphasize the role of settler connections with the host state in the process of disengagement. As shown elsewhere, such reactions to withdrawal from contested territories are not unusual, and consistent with Lustick's analytical framework, Ergenekon was plotting a coup in Turkey to prevent the adoption of the Annan Plan in 2004. Plans to obstruct the peace settlement were recorded in the diary of former Navy commander Özden Örnek, published in the now defunct weekly magazine *Nokta* ("Gen. Eruygur" 2008). However, unlike settler cases elsewhere, Ergenekon-related actions seem largely disconnected from the island's settler grass roots. Additionally, evidence on Ergenekon itself seems to be dubious legally due to the politicized nature of these trials. In conclusion, during past decades there has been no major episode implicating settlers directly with political violence in Cyprus, while efforts to politicize settlers against a peace settlement have been for the most part short-lived and unsuccessful.

Legal Principles versus Pragmatic Engagements

Besides the sociological aspects surrounding settler questions, legal and political aspects are of critical importance, particularly for the Greek Cypriot side. The international community is itself divided on settler issues, often failing to resolve its own internal tensions between legal principles, human rights, and pragmatism. One school of thought advocates the centrality of justice and international law mechanisms and argues for the application of widely acknowledged standards of law documented in the resolutions of international organizations such as the United Nations and the European Court of Human Rights (Leckie 2003, 12). A particularly salient issue concerns properties illegally owned by settlers, which international legal bodies have demanded be returned to former inhabitants.[3] In the case of Cyprus, apart from UN resolutions, major decisions by the ECtHR (*Loizidou vs. Turkey*) and the European Court of Justice (ECJ) (*Apostolides vs. Orams*) have confirmed the rights of former owners to both restitution and compensation (ECJ 2009; Leckie 2003, 42). In *Apostolides vs. Orams*, the ECJ decision stipulated that British courts must enforce the judicial decisions made in the Republic of Cyprus enabling refugees to sue EU citizens over contested ownership of property in northern Cyprus (ECJ 2009). Advocates of international justice cite these decisions to argue that no matter how long ago an injustice occurred, its subsequent condemnation cannot escape international courts. These decisions also demonstrate the legal, normative, and political limitations with regard to initiating colonization and settlement projects in the context of contemporary world politics. Moreover, international legal standards should not be compromised by short-term political expediency; ignoring universal human rights standards will inevitably endanger peace processes, especially in the long term (Dicker 2011).

An alternative approach emphasizes pragmatism and the contexts behind settler-native disputes (Barkan 2000, xxxiii; Leckie 2003, 42). This approach assesses how people reconstruct their lives and prioritizes restorative justice and community rebuilding. It considers a wide range of factors, including the need for victim-offender mediation (Zehr and Mika 1998), mutually agreed-upon compromises (Loizides and Antoniades 2009), local power dynamics, and the human rights of non-indigenous groups, such as settlers and their descendants (Carens 2000, 217). A key concern is the passage of time: notably, constraints in applying international legal principles and penalizing individuals for crimes committed decades earlier by their home states. Even from a legal point of view, it could be emphasized that the ECtHR has recently adopted a political approach to similar issues by recognizing the rights of current owners, not excluding settlers. For the Court, the rehousing of potentially large numbers of men, women, and children, even with the aim of vindicating the rights of past victims, cannot be imposed as an unconditional obligation on a government (ECtHR 2010). More importantly, interpreting the European Convention on Human Rights, the Court has emphasized that "property is a material commodity which can be valued and compensated for monetary terms" (ECtHR 2010; Skoutaris 2010). Past decisions by the same Court have stated that apart from restituting properties, compensation for old owners is a legitimate option in resolving property and therefore settler-native conflicts (ECtHR 2003).

Balancing conflicting principles is often extremely difficult for courts and also for mediators and international organizations, as they could easily be charged with tolerating ethnic cleansing or, alternatively, demonstrating racism and discrimination against a potentially vulnerable population. Even using the term "settler" to describe a particular population can be contested, depending on the political context; in some cases the term has been avoided in public discourse (Andreasson 2010).[4] As a result, international institutions have dealt with settler issues in seemingly contradictory ways. In the Baltics, the European Union has encouraged the naturalization of Russian settlers and implicitly made the amendment of citizenship laws a pre-condition for EU membership (Ozolins 1999, 39). At the same time, the EU blocks trade with the Jewish settlements in the West Bank, while in 1995 the European Parliament delayed the EU-funded Panam Project in Tibet with the rationale that the "scheme aimed at feeding new Chinese settlers against the interest of the Tibetan people" (European Parliament 1995). Drawing from comparable cases, Kymlicka (2007b, 383) criticizes Article 27 of the UN International Covenant on Civil and Political Rights for failing to cover cases of colonization within a state's jurisdiction. Colonizing occupied territories violates international law, while no legal issues could be effectively raised for colonizing national minority territories, such as settling thousands of Sinhalese farmers in the predominantly Tamil Eastern province, as argued by Liaras in this volume.

A multiplicity of contextual factors could explain the varied responses to contemporary colonization, including the passage of time, whether or not the colonization/occupation is ongoing, and whether there are continuous violations of native/refugee rights. In the case of Cyprus, the Council of Europe has prepared a number of reports on the settler issue, including a 2003 recommendation by the Parliamentary Assembly advocating a population census by the European Population Committee (CAHP), calling on Turkey, "as well as its Turkish Cypriot subordinate local administration in northern Cyprus, to stop the process of colonization by Turkish settlers," and proposing the creation of a European fund to assist the *voluntary* (emphasis added) resettlement of settlers back to Turkey (Parliamentary Assembly of the Council of Europe 2003). Likewise, in 2000, the European Parliament noted in a resolution that the EU "can help resolve the problem of the controlled return of refugees and the repatriation of the settlers" (European Parliament 2000).

What makes the Cyprus case particularly informative for conflict resolution is the way in which the UN prioritized among these various considerations once the two sides allowed mediators to design, arbitrate, and finalize the Annan Plan. More broadly, the Annan Plan proposed a comprehensive set of conflict-regulating arrangements for Cyprus, including federal and consociational arrangements with significant veto rights for the minority Turkish Cypriot community (United Nations 2004).

The Turkish Cypriots were asked to return land across the designated federal border to accommodate displaced Greek Cypriots in return for limits on property restitution in their own constituent state. Meanwhile, Greek Cypriots were offered the chance to reunite the island under the European Union but with significant concessions such as naturalizing long-term settlers relocated from Turkey since 1974, compromising human rights for about half of the displaced Greek Cypriots, and maintaining Turkey's unilateral security guarantees. The Annan Plan also encompassed a novelty for international mediation tactics: in the event of failing to reach an agreement for its final form the UN secretary-general was authorized to finalize its provisions and ask for a twin referendum without the prior endorsement of the Greek or Turkish Cypriot leaderships (United Nations 2004). Surprisingly, in 2004 the Greek Cypriot leadership did not object to the fact that TRNC citizens of Turkish settler background were to vote in the referendum (Sözen and Özersay 2007).

In justifying its own proposals for the peace settlement, the UN argued that international developments since World War II had favored a negotiated agreement based on respect for individual rights. Not coincidentally, several ECtHR decisions recognized the rights of the Greek Cypriots in the northern part of the island and allocated damages at the expense of Turkey (United Nations Security Council 2003a, 23–24). Thus, Kofi Annan acknowledged that in making his suggestions, he took into account "the positions adopted recently by the United Nations and the international community in the former Yugoslavia, but also the fact that the events in Cyprus happened 30 to 40 years ago and that the displaced people (roughly half of the Turkish Cypriots and a third of the Greek Cypriots) have had to rebuild their lives and their economies during this time" (United Nations Security Council 2003a, 23–24).

In an interview during the drafting of this plan, the architect of the proposal, UN legal advisor Didier Pfirter, summarized its provisions:

> Anybody who is married to a Cypriot will automatically get citizenship. A further 45,000 people will get citizenship in a certain order of priority, and we expect that anyone who has grown up in Cyprus are the first priority category in that. Or those who stayed here for a long time should be covered by that number. Another roughly 15,000 people, it will be 10% of the Turkish Cypriot population, will get permanent residency and they will be able to

obtain citizenship after some more years, depending on how long they have already stayed in Cyprus. Students and academic staff will be allowed to stay in Cyprus in unlimited numbers. Anyone opting for return to Turkey would get substantial assistance of no less than 10,000 Euros for a family of four. That figure could be higher, it depends on what may be offered, but it wouldn't be less. (Kibris TV 2003)

In other words, the great majority of settlers received the right to remain in Cyprus either as citizens or foreign workers, with the possibility to be naturalized as Cypriots in the future. By safeguarding their presence in large numbers following a negotiated peace agreement, the Annan Plan has made anti-deal mobilization redundant, especially for long-term settlers.

On the contrary, the rights of potential Greek Cypriot returnees under Turkish Cypriot administration were significantly curtailed to preserve demographic balances. In its five versions, the Annan Plan put forward various restrictions on return for individuals under sixty-five years old, imposed lengthy time intervals for establishing residency, set limits on property restitution, and limited state and federal voting rights for potential returnees. A major stumbling block for Greek Cypriots was the sequence of concessions and the fear of non-implementation. While immediately making concessions on issues involving security, power-sharing, and more importantly settlers, Greek Cypriots were unsure about implementation of the limited rights granted to refugees and equally unsure of the actual intentions of the potential returnees, given these restrictions.

For the most part, the UN proposal included other incentives for the Greek Cypriot community; moderates in the Greek Cypriot community suggested that even the settler/migrant provisions were reasonable and argued that naturalization of long-term settlers would prevent future waves of uncontrolled colonization. Yet as Lustick argues, related policies in conflict situations are often determined by hegemonic beliefs, or what a group considers possible or impossible, natural or unnatural, problematic or inevitable (1993b, 6). In the Greek Cypriot case, provisions were broadly framed not only as unfair but also as dysfunctional, limiting the potential for a compromise.

On the one hand, the Annan Plan contributed to settler non-mobilization by largely satisfying settler group demands, primarily through the diplomatic involvement of Turkey in the negotiations. On the other hand, the plan unavoidably damaged native and Greek Cypriot refugee support for its major provisions. Could future mediations address these Greek Cypriot concerns

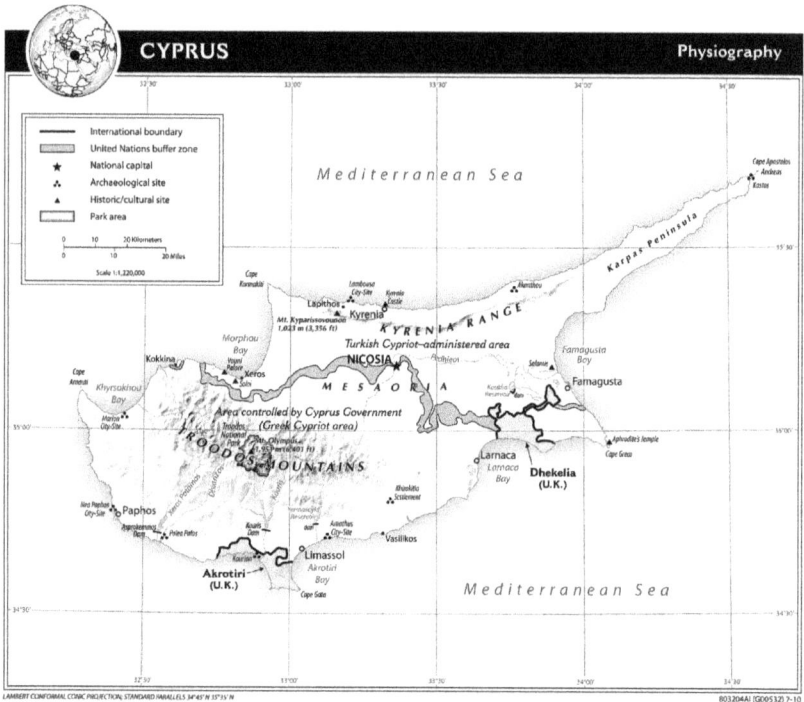

MAP 8.1 The post-1974 de facto partition of Cyprus
SOURCE: Central Intelligence Agency Library. Cyprus.

without reigniting opposition from settlers or Turkish Cypriots? This chapter discusses ways to minimize these challenges in reunification talks. Specifically, it weighs the pros and cons of linkage arrangements, asymmetrical citizenship options, and compensation schemes. These conflict resolution mechanisms are particularly relevant for environments where people desire a peace settlement but mutual trust remains low, as in Cyprus. Territorial arrangements which allow communities to live together while maintaining their identity, security, and cohesion should be prioritized in future negotiations. Aiming to link the actors' perceptions with the needs for a negotiated federal settlement, this chapter also draws from a range of comparable examples across the globe. It examines alternative arrangements and their potential advantages for settlers and the two indigenous communities of Cyprus.

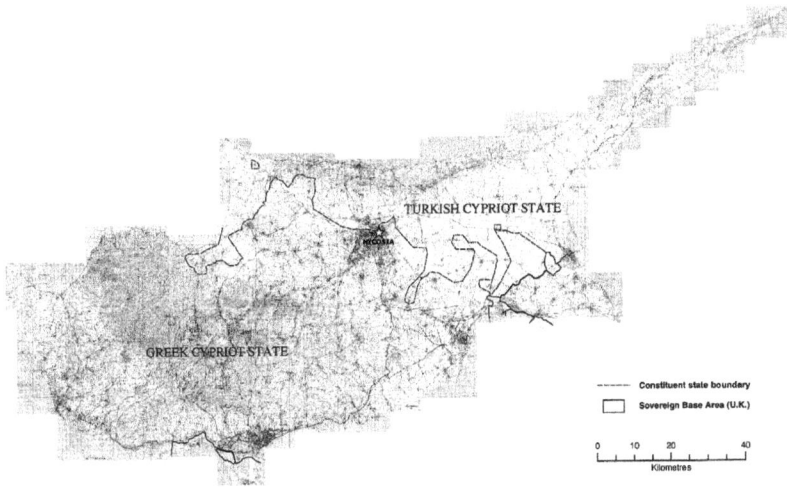

MAP 8.2 Territorial adjustments in the 2004 Annan Plan
SOURCE: United Nations.

Linkages: Settlers and Reserve Lands for the Displaced

A potential arrangement to solve the settler problem involves linking issues of major concern to Greek Cypriots, such as territory and refugee rights. Generally speaking, linkage arrangements could create win-win incentives for both sides to endorse a peace settlement. More specifically, self-adjustable linkages could relieve both communities of the fear of failing to benefit from the peace agreement.

Creative linkage strategies include naturalizing more settlers in exchange for territorial improvements for Greek Cypriots returnees. Such territorial arrangements could be made by redrawing the federal border farther north than in the Annan Plan (see Map 8.2) or by reserving lands for Greek Cypriots opting to return under Turkish Cypriot administration.

Reserved lands aim to protect a community by restricting others from purchasing land within its specified territorial boundaries. Reserved lands could be formed through land consolidation where land is reallocated by federal authorities to both former and current owners. If it also provides roads, access to water and services, and legal/undisputed titles, land consolidation could increase the value of individual properties and contribute to sustainable development, as well as to community cohesion, revival, and rebuilding.

Land consolidation introduces a language into the negotiations with which people are familiar.[5] Most non-refugee communities have gained in financial and other terms from such practices in the past decades, and land consolidation has now become an established practice. Planning for natural parks, roads, and other infrastructure could happen at the start of the negotiated agreement in order to minimize future frictions. Improved infrastructure or simply its prospect will increase the value of each individual property. Land consolidation requires prior public consultation, which could start at any stage. It is possible to imagine that most Greek Cypriots will prefer compensation, allowing for Turkish Cypriot majority land ownership. Finally, Greek Cypriots are more likely to return and feel secure if they have other Greek Cypriots as neighbors (Stefanovic and Loizides 2011). Land consolidation can also incorporate this concern by allowing predominantly Greek and Turkish Cypriot sections in each village without making the divisions too obvious or conflictual.

In addition, reserved lands for returnees in territories with majority settler populations have many potential advantages. For one thing, they could minimize Turkish and ECtHR concerns about the possible massive relocation of settlers and Turkish Cypriots. If empty agricultural land adjacent to existing villages is used, there will be few negative effects for existing communities. In addition, Greek Cypriot return under Turkish Cypriot administration will facilitate economic integration and channel public resources toward the weaker segments of the population. A little known fact in Cyprus is that in federal systems, individuals commonly pay taxes in their place of residency; therefore, Greek Cypriot returnees with higher incomes and jobs in the south could even double the tax base of the future Turkish Cypriot federal state. Reserved lands will also offer Greek Cypriots the opportunity to secure a smaller but a more stable territorial basis in each village/city of their ancestral origin; knowing that other members of their community will return as their neighbors and will provide a sense of community and security (two of the most important concerns cited by Greek Cypriot potential returnees in the 2009 Cyprus2015 survey). Finally, this arrangement is not only better from an ECtHR point of view but also from a normative perspective and, thus, is increasingly used by countries aiming to bring justice and rectify the past (Kymlicka 1995, 43).

Another linkage arrangement could tie the number of settlers to be naturalized to the number of Greek Cypriot returnees opting to return under

Turkish Cypriot administration (see also Loizides and Antoniades 2009). An agreement could postulate the return of 25,000 Greek Cypriots under Turkish Cypriot administration. If 25,001 then opt to return, the Turkish Cypriot side would increase its settler naturalization quota by two, or get equivalent credits toward another issue. This formula combines a minimum number of Greek Cypriot returns to the Turkish zone with self-adjustable linkages and incentives for the Turkish Cypriot side to accept the rest. This approach has several advantages. Greek Cypriot concessions, previously envisioned to secure a maximum refugee threshold, would not have to be made until refugees actually return. Turkish Cypriots (and Turkey) would be guaranteed majority status under all demographic scenarios, even if all Greek Cypriots decide to return. With this formula, in the unlikely event that all Greek Cypriots return, they will still make up less than 27 percent of the Turkish Cypriot constituent state (Loizides and Antoniades 2009).

Affecting current negotiations—and potential linkages—are the following dilemmas: (1) how to match difficult issues and at what phase of the negotiations; and (2) how to address the uncertainties of the ratification process, specifically the possibility of the public voting against a peace settlement that includes win-win linkages. For example, the Greek Cypriot negotiators have traditionally feared that exceeding certain thresholds in the settler figures will put ratification at risk (a legitimate fear that reduces their flexibility in the negotiations).

An unusual feature of the Cypriot negotiations is the public expectation stipulated in the 2014 joint statement of the two leaders that a twin referendum will have to take place simultaneously in both communities to have the agreement ratified. In other words, the leaders will first engage in several phases of negotiations, and if they can achieve an agreement then simultaneous referendums, as in the Annan Plan, will take place which will most likely include Turkish settlers currently holding TRNC citizenship. The Cypriot case demonstrates the limits in using direct democracy as a conflict-mitigating device in cases of unresolved conflicts such as Western Sahara, Sri Lanka, New Caledonia, Kashmir, and more recently Crimea, to name only a few. For the most part, United Nations and external mediators should consider involving the public but employ these devices only as informal consultations, to avoid questions of legality.

Another option for Cyprus and other divided societies is to add a post-referendum phase to the negotiations immediately after public ratification, further improving the settlement by addressing issues raised during the referendum campaign. Adding this third phase will increase chances for successful ratification in the referendums and allow leaders to identify and correct the plan's possible imperfections. More importantly, it will give them the mandate and flexibility to redraw the most appropriate linkages without the pressure of public opinion. Leading negotiation theorists (Raiffa 2002) have recommended this approach of securing an agreement first and then renegotiating it for improvements. In the renegotiation phase, parties could offer full confidential information to the UN about their preferences, something they might be unwilling to do earlier without a secure peace settlement (e.g., what percentage of territory should be exchanged for ten thousand more naturalized settlers). Additionally, referendums focus attention on majorities on both sides, but in this third phase, parties might prioritize considerations among vulnerable groups (e.g., ten thousand additional settlers might be unacceptable to the Greek Cypriot public but might make sense for refugees if that secures them an emotionally important territory).

On this issue, the Karpaz peninsula is particularly relevant for a potential settler-territory linkage. The territory is sparsely populated but has tremendous sentimental importance for the Greek Cypriots because of the Apostolos Andreas Monastery. In a future peace settlement, the Greek Cypriots could be offered an enclave around the village of Rizoparpaso (as in the 1992 Ghali Set of Ideas Map). If settlers exceed certain set thresholds, they will be allowed to remain in Cyprus but under the condition that the area around this enclave will expand to cover the territory proposed in the third version of the Annan Plan or even beyond, to cover other areas of historical importance for the Greek Cypriots. A final linkage proposed in this chapter is to link the level of international aid for united Cyprus to the overall numbers of settlers and returnees, thereby incentivizing both Greek and Turkish Cypriots to increase their numbers while providing the resources for social and economic integration. Such linkages have already been discussed in negotiations; refining them further will be the most appropriate direction for the future.

Asymmetrical Citizenship

As another option, one might consider providing settlers/migrants with permanent residency, including equal social and economic rights but leading only gradually to full citizenship. It is not uncommon for alien residents of

a country to be granted social and civil rights but not full political participation, with the exception of voting in municipal elections. In the case of
Cyprus, this arrangement could apply to recent settlers, thus restricting participation in power-sharing mechanisms designed to maintain a delicate compromise between the Greek and Turkish Cypriot communities. The challenge
in Cyprus is not simply to accept settlers as part of the *demos* but to accommodate natives and settlers in complex consociational arrangements, with the
concomitant danger of giving primacy to settler rights over native ones.

Admittedly, immigration literature has criticized asymmetrical citizenship arrangements for creating second-class citizens (i.e., denizens). To avoid
such unintended effects, permanent residents should enjoy full economic and
social rights and be naturalized, at the latest, within a generation. The gradual
naturalization of settlers could be a better alternative than their immediate
and unconditional naturalization as proposed in previous peace plans in
Cyprus, particularly if such naturalizations are gradually tied to comparable concessions for other vulnerable groups, such as Greek Cypriot minority
returnees.

Compensation and Incentive Mechanisms

A final possible arrangement concerns the granting of various forms of compensation to settlers willing to repatriate to Turkey. Cordell and Wolff examine this option with regard to German *resettlers* from Central and Eastern
Europe (*Aussiedler*), focusing in particular on the German government's
priority of not upsetting its new relations with post-communist Poland and
the Czech Republic (2005, 96–97). Likewise, since 2003 Germany has finan-
cially supported Namibia's land reform program aiming to secure small plots
for formerly disposed blacks, enabling at the same time the compensation of
pre-independence German settlers (Deutsche Gesellschaft für Internationale
Zusammenarbeit 2013). But it is important to note that voluntary compensation schemes in settler-related conflicts can have unintended consequences
or simply fail to work (see Jervis 1978, 174, on Rhodesia). On this issue, the
experience of international organizations in Bosnia and elsewhere suggests
that trial-and-error strategies might be needed until optimal outcomes are
reached (Dahlman and Ó Tuathail 2005). An option potentially applicable to
Cyprus is the "right to regret" allowed to Bosnian returnees who had been
living temporarily in the UK and France and who were given the option to

return with the same status if their experience with repatriation to Bosnia proved negative (Black 2001, 186–187). In the case of Cyprus, settlers could be allowed to return to Cyprus after relocating in Turkey if they changed their minds, and without losing their previous status.

Alternatively, incentives could be offered to members of the Turkish Cypriot diaspora to return to Cyprus. At the moment, the sizeable UK diaspora (some argue as many as 80,000–120,000) maintains close links with Cyprus (Østergaard-Nielsen 2003). Turkish Cypriot émigrés have suffered from exile and loss of property, and until now, they have not been offered compensation. These compensatory arrangements could maximize the options for émigrés and settlers, with potential benefits for all communities in the island.

Options similar to Greek Cypriot reserved lands could be considered for Turkish Cypriot émigrés in exchange for their properties south of the border. Reserves for Turkish Cypriot émigrés could be developed parallel to or next to or even integrated with Greek Cypriot ones (if local communities desire to do so). Arrangements for émigrés are the least likely to be resisted by the Greek Cypriots, who generally recognize the rights of Turkish Cypriots to the island. Conversely, concessions to naturalize settlers have been heavily criticized in the past in the Greek Cypriot public discourse, particularly during Demetris Christofias's presidency. This is particularly the case when such concessions are not clearly linked to equitable concessions in negotiations for the Greek Cypriots.

Conclusion

This chapter aimed at addressing the tensions between legal, humanitarian, and pragmatic considerations in the evaluation of settler questions in contested territories, looking at populations relocated against international law from Turkey to Cyprus after 1974. In contrast to other contemporary or historical cases of settler colonialism, what is particularly puzzling in Cyprus is the absence of mobilization and politicization among settlers, despite fears of relocation following a negotiated peace agreement. Moreover, the increasing presence of settlers in the island has triggered domestic insecurities and native discourses emphasizing Cypriot identities and interests. However, for the most part, both Greek and Turkish Cypriot leaders have attempted in various ways to accommodate the settler question in subsequent negotiations.

A potential contribution of the Cypriot mediations to other divided societies relates to how settler issues could be incorporated into negotiations in constructive ways to minimize confrontation on the ground and forge win-win linkages. Appropriate institutional designs along with diplomacy and leadership are critical in transforming intractable conflicts (Wolff 2010). The chapter demonstrates how the settler-indigenous division in Cyprus could become amenable to institutional innovations aiming to facilitate communities already in transition toward the right direction. Aiming to further link the actors' perceptions with the need for a negotiated federal settlement, this chapter examined a variety of possible arrangements and their potential consequences for settlers and the two communities in Cyprus.

This chapter suggests the gradual naturalization of settlers, enabled by linking concessions across various issues and making naturalization partly conditional on their collective contribution to peace. This arrangement addresses critics' concerns that legalization of settlers sets an unfortunate precedent (Chrysostomides 2000, 434). The approach proposed here is consistent with emerging international norms aiming to rectify previous injustices perpetrated by settlers or outside powers without punishing the descendants of settlers or the settlers themselves (Kymlicka 1995; Carens 2000). Unlike this chapter's proposals, previous UN plans offered insufficient incentives for the post-implementation phase and prioritized the rights of non-indigenous people over those of potential returnees. At a minimum, writing off violations of international law should involve some form of compensation toward those whose livelihoods have been significantly affected, including refugees and their descendants.

Likewise Greek Cypriot concessions on the settler issue would signal credible intentions in the negotiations. If both sides are given credible concessions and incentives for meeting each other's needs, future agreement will appear more appealing to both communities. Cypriot academics and NGO representatives have promoted the concept of reciprocity for decades in Cyprus, suggesting the basis for thinking creatively on complex issues in the Cyprus negotiations (see, e.g., Hadjipavlou-Trigeorgis and Trigeorgis 1993). The legal and political validity of such negotiation linkages could be further explored in the literature of settlers in contested territories. For example, scholars could examine which options of asymmetrical citizenship are compatible with European law and prevailing international citizenship norms. Alternatively, future scholarship could examine whether the contribution of the settlers to the implementation of peace processes could count in the naturalization process, and how it would be measured. Such contributions will help Greek

Cypriots (as well as Turkish Cypriots and other native populations in contested territories) to see settler integration in a positive light, building a more sustainable relationship in the long term.

In summary, this chapter confronted an important empirical and normative dilemma. Colonization of occupied territories such as Northern Cyprus is a violation of international norms; however, the massive and indiscriminate expulsion of settlers and their descendants is equally problematic. The challenge is particularly difficult when, after decades, settlers begin to resemble migrants in sociological terms, yet natives continue to view such populations as part of an expansionist policy of a threatening neighboring state. This chapter demonstrated that in answering this dilemma it is important to balance settlers' rights with those of native populations through creative institutional designs such as asymmetrical citizenship, development of reserved lands, and efficient compensation schemes. The major normative and political challenge for the two Cypriot communities will be to balance their own community rights to a federal homeland with the rights of others, including displaced persons and settlers/migrants. Stable ethnic relations in such a normatively complex setting require novel arrangements, particularly on issues of territory and space. These conflict resolution mechanisms are particularly relevant for environments where people desire a peace settlement but mutual trust remains low, as in Cyprus. Territorial arrangements which allow communities to live together but also to maintain their identity, security, and cohesion should be prioritized in the current negotiations.

Beyond Cyprus, this approach could be particularly relevant in disputed territories such as Western Sahara and Kirkuk, also discussed in this volume. In Western Sahara, for example, as suggested by Mundy and Zunes, there is a growing alignment between Moroccan settlers and native Sahrawis. Fearing this alignment, the Moroccan government refused in 2003 to implement its previous commitment to a referendum on the future of the territory—even though settlers now constitute the majority of Western Sahara's population. According to Mundy and Zunes, there is an increasing potential for new politics of resistance based on an alliance between native Western Saharans and Moroccan settlers, particularly those who share the ethnic Sahrawi background. Likewise, in Kirkuk, the Kurdistan Regional Government has been encouraged to implement confidence-building measures after taking over the city in June 2014 in order to assure security for the non-Kurdish populations (including settlers) and gain their trust before any referendum on the status of the province (see Natali's chapter). Thus the findings of this chapter are not unique to Cyprus, as settlers in such places as Kirkuk and Morocco might often assume the profile of a migrant population prioritizing personal economic advancement over territorial politics. Here and elsewhere, proposals and initiatives drawing and reinforcing linkages between indigenous and settler interests could foster constructive relationships in conflict-ridden societies.

Notes

1. Kudret Özersay, interviewed by the author on his academic involvement in the Cyprus mediations, September 2007.

2. For more information on the Turkish Cypriot census, see TRNC Prime Ministry (2007). TRNC refers to the self-declared Turkish Republic of Northern Cyprus, recognized internationally only by Turkey.

3. See, for instance, Scott Leckie on Security Council Resolution 361, August 30, 1974, for Cyprus (United Nations 1974) and comparisons with similar Security Council resolutions on Yugoslavia (Kosovo), Georgia (Abkhazia), Croatia, and Iraq (Kuwait) and General Assembly resolutions on Palestine-Israel (Leckie 2003, 12).

4. For instance, the UN uses the term "settler" in quotation marks in its Cyprus reports (United Nations Security Council 2003a, 5). Turkish Cypriot academics and members of the official negotiating team use the term *settlers/immigrants* (Sözen and Özersay 2007; Yesilada and Sozen 2002). In northern Cyprus, the term commonly used in public is *Türkiyeliler* (Turks of Turkey) in contrast to *Kibrisli Türk* (Turkish Cypriots). Since 1997, a settler organization has used the name KKTC Göçmenler Derneği, which means TRNC Migrant Association (see http://www.csodirectory-cyprus.eu/ana-sayfa?id=282) The term *göçmenler* may be translated as either "migrant" or "settler." At the same time, the term *settler* appears in interviews given by Nuri Çevikel, the chairman of the association, to international media (H. Smith 2003). For an extensive discussion of related terms and identity boundaries in Cyprus, see Navaro-Yashin (2006, 2012).

5. Andreas Symeou, interviewed by the author on his work on land consolidation for the Cyprus Peace Talks, May 2011.

9 Conclusion

The Political Dynamics of Settlement Projects:
The Central State–Settler-Native Triangle

Ian S. Lustick

LENIN DEFINED POLITICS AS *"KTO KOGO"*—"WHO
whom." In other words, the question of politics is always who does
what to whom—who is the subject; who the object? There is something dis-
turbingly penetrating about this assessment, but also deeply unsatisfactory.
Implicit within it is an expectation of effectiveness and control in the exertion
of power that discourages attention to the regular role played in the exercise
of power by the uncertainty of purpose and the unintended consequences of
its use.

Among other things, the studies in this volume highlight the tendency of
ambivalence of purpose and unintended consequences of action to outweigh
design and calculated implementation when it comes to the results of state-
sponsored and supported settlement projects. Each case begins with central
state leaders making a decision to employ settlers as an instrument for "right-
sizing" and/or "right-peopling" a targeted territory outside the official borders
of their state. In their introduction in Chapter One, Haklai and Loizides aptly
define "settlement" as "the organized movement of a population belonging to
one national group into a territory in order to create a permanent presence and
influence patterns of sovereignty in the settled territory." In each case covered
in this book, the decision to launch or enable the settler movement represents
a judgment based on both a desired objective—to incorporate or dominate the
targeted territory—and a theory of how that can be accomplished or facilitated
by the transfer of significant numbers of nationals from the core state.

In this concluding chapter I will compare the results of those decisions, focusing particular attention on the who-whom question. To what extent did the settlers serve as the kind of instrument imagined by the central state that sent them or facilitated their transfer into the territory? To what extent did the settlers develop interests of their own and the capability to deflect central state policies or even manipulate the state itself? In those cases where the settlers did not organize or mobilize in tension with central state policies, did their presence have the desired impact? Considering as well the British-Irish and French-Algerian cases—episodes of settlement mentioned by many of the authors but not addressed specifically in this volume—what can we learn from this kind of comparative treatment to help us understand the intractability that Haklai and Loizides suggest settlement tends to introduce into generations of conflict in and over the territories settlers come to inhabit?

A key element in the "problematique" of each of these studies is that the target territory is inhabited by "natives," or as Liaras prefers, *autochthons*, who have not chosen to be ruled by the central state or transformed by it. This forms a triangle, a kind of political ménage à trois—the central state, or at least the government representing it; the settlers the central state seeks to use to advance its purposes in the target territory; and the already present population of that territory. My discussion of the cases proceeds according to which side of this triangular relationship each chapter author identifies as the primary focus of his or her analysis.

The authors of the Israeli, Moroccan, and Italian cases focus most of their attention on the relationship between the central state and the settlers. Here Lenin's question poses itself with telling clarity. That is because, once the state has created or facilitated the emergence of a settler community, it is not at all clear that this community, imagined as an instrument of state policy, will remain the "whom" to the "who" of the state elites. Well-organized and well-resourced settler populations, supported by ideological programs and cultural attachments that connect them to powerful segments of the central state polity, can pursue highly parochial interests in addition to or camouflaged within crusades for grand political accomplishments. Opportunities for doing so, that is, for becoming the "who" in relation to the central state as "whom," will be all the more available to the extent that elites managing the central state are divided or uncertain about the purposes to be served by the settlers.

As Haklai emphasizes in his treatment of the Israeli case, the opportunities for Jewish settlers in the occupied Palestinian territories (OPT) to exert independent and even decisive influence on central state policies toward the disposition of those areas were greatly enhanced by the uncertainty and ambivalence marking high-echelon beliefs and values about what should and could be done with the territories acquired in 1967. The Labor Party, which led governing coalitions for the first decade of Israel's rule of the OPT, was itself divided. Followers of Defense Minister Moshe Dayan saw settlements as a way to prepare a path to long-term de facto annexation. Supporters of Foreign Minister and Deputy Prime Minister Yigal Allon wished to use a particular pattern of settlement to bring about permanent incorporation of part, but not all, of the areas. Doves within the Labor Party, such as Finance Minister Pinchas Sapir, opposed settlement because of the constraint it would place on trading the territories for a negotiated peace. These differences within Labor, combined with fears that the increasingly hawkish National Religious Party could force new elections by leaving its coalition with Labor, led the prime ministers of that period—Levi Eshkol, Golda Meir, and Yitzhak Rabin—to pursue what came to be known as a "decision not to decide" vis-à-vis the ultimate status of the OPT. For settlements, this meant a "muddling through" approach that gave enormous advantages to the dedicated, highly organized, and extremely well-connected settler movement under the umbrella of its ideological and organizational vanguard, Gush Emunim (Bloc of Faithful).

When the annexationist-oriented Likud Party took control of the government in 1977, its leader, Menachem Begin, found himself extraordinarily well positioned to pursue what had been the alpha and omega of his (Revisionist) movement's political program—establishment of Jewish sovereignty over as much of the "Whole Land of Israel" as possible. The settler movement that had been incubated under the indecisive but largely benevolent gaze of successive Labor Party governments was an ideal partner for implementing Begin's vision of a larger, highly nationalistic, and religiously traditionalist state. As the head of the leading party within the government, supported by coalition partners—including the National Religious Party—that favored robust expansion of settlement and pursuit of annexationist ambitions over the OPT, Begin had the desire, the financial resources, and the political capital to vastly increase settlement activity.

What he did not have were settlers. In contrast to the Labor Zionist movement, Revisionist Zionists had never built or populated settlements in outlying areas. But to move forward toward settling hundreds of thousands and even a million Jews in just the West Bank, an objective featured prominently in plans developed by his government, Begin and the ministers who were most centrally responsible for his annexationist policies—Ariel Sharon (Agriculture, Defense, and Israel Lands Administration) and David Levy (Housing and Construction)—pursued two complementary avenues. One was a partnership with Gush Emunim to establish aggressively ideological settlements in the heavily Arab central highlands of both the southern and northern bulges of the West Bank. The other was to draw very large numbers of working-class and lower-middle-class Israelis into larger urban-type settlements by offering enormous subsidies for housing much more spacious and attractive than they could ever hope to afford within Israel proper. Almost three decades after Begin's accession to power, the success of enlisting both categories of settlers into a campaign to render Israel's political separation from the West Bank impossible is reflected in the presence of nearly 600,000 Jewish settlers east of the Green Line (the 1949 armistice line that is Israel's only recognized border).

Ironically, because of the physical, economic, and legal infrastructure established for settlements by Likud governments, the immense political clout associated with the expanded interests of the "settler lobby," the settlers' high level of organization, and their strategic position in an increasingly right-wing and nationalistic Israeli political landscape, much of the numerical growth of the settler population took place under Labor Party–led governments (of Rabin and Barak) while they were, at least putatively, pursuing policies based on trying to separate Israel from the Palestinian areas. This fact, combined with the assassination of Prime Minister Yitzhak Rabin (by someone with close ideological and social ties to the settlement movement), and the enormous difficulties settler aggressiveness posed for non-Labor prime ministers who showed some flexibility toward the OPT (such as Sharon and Ehud Olmert), indicates just how much effective and independent agency the settler movement attained in Israel.

Indeed, it seems clear that post-1967 Israeli settlers were (and are) more powerful, and, for at least some state elites, more problematic, than any other settler population analyzed in this volume's seven case studies. The only other case that describes settlers as having had an important effect on state policy and on the shaping of outcomes is Morocco—but in a strikingly different direction. The King of Morocco believed that Western Sahara could be permanently incorporated into "his" state by moving hundreds of thousands of his subjects into that territory. These would be settlers, by the definition offered in this volume, not immigrants. They were sent, in an organized way, for the purpose of transforming the political status of the territory into which they were sent. Indeed, the demographic transformation of Western Sahara accomplished by this settlement enterprise, complemented by the expulsion and exclusion of tens of thousands of native Sahrawis, did dramatically change the demographic complexion of the territory. According to Mundy and Zunes, as a result of marching hundreds of thousands of Moroccan citizens southward, Moroccan settlers became at least three-fourths of the population in Western Sahara.

On the one hand, the scale of demographic transformation achieved by Morocco in Western Sahara was much bigger than was entertained by even the most optimistic planners operating with annexationist views in the Likud-administered offices of the World Zionist Organization's "Land Settlement Department" or within the high councils of settler activists. On the other hand, as is stunningly evident from the analysis Mundy and Zunes offer, the settlers evolved into a population even less straightforwardly usable as a reliable instrument of central state policy than the settler populations in the West Bank and Gaza Strip have been. Although the Moroccan settlers were not organized into the kind of mobilized, clearly directed, and highly effective political force that Jewish settlers in Israel have become, their uncertain loyalties became a critical factor in monarchical policymaking. Both powerful international norms and the regime's own commitments to honor plebiscitary expressions of popular will trapped the Moroccan government into at least pretending it would accept the outcome of a referendum as binding. Initially it put its faith in controlling voting registers, so as to dominate a referendum with votes of settlers, rather than natives. But uncertainty about whether the bulk of those who had been moved south would, in a free referendum, support royal preferences for incorporation as opposed to Polisario's goals of independence has trapped Morocco in a process of endless delay, which neither eliminates the integration of Western Sahara into Morocco from the international agenda, nor offers a way out of that territory without risking humiliating failure.

It would not be correct to think of the "agency" of the settlers in Western Sahara, if by that is meant a consciously directed and organized political force acting according to interests it has collectively defined. Again, despite differences and divisions among Israeli settlers, that kind of agency was and is clearly apparent in the Israeli case. In the Morocco–Western Sahara case, however, the agency of the settlers is expressed as a function of the uncertainty of the central state and the unevenness of its power. That state could find hundreds of thousands of Moroccans to march into the territory it wanted to absorb. With enormously expensive military investments, it could largely separate that population from Polisario guerrillas operating from sanctuaries in Algeria. But it could not, and still cannot, be confident that the uncontrolled expression of aspirations the settlers have for their lives and for the future of the territory they now inhabit will serve regime interests.

Pergher's treatment of the Italian use of settlers to establish permanent Italian rule of Libya and South Tyrol is the other contribution in this volume featuring a primary focus on the state-settler side of the state-settler-native triangle. Like Haklai for the Israeli case and Mundy and Zunes for the Moroccan, Pergher is more interested in the relationship between the state and the settlers it uses, or is used by, than with relations and interactions between the settlers and the natives or between the natives and the state. In each of these three studies, those relationships are backgrounded. The natives (Palestinians, Sahrawis, and in Pergher's treatment, primarily Libyans) do not figure directly in the story told. They are conquered, held at bay, or otherwise figured as a static, given element in each analysis, while attention is directed to the dynamics and unappreciated nuances attending the relations between the settlers and the state.

As I have noted, Haklai rightly emphasizes the agency of settlers in the OPT and the effects of their dedicated and well-organized efforts on the evolution of state policies and the constraints under which those policies are fashioned and implemented. Such agency is almost entirely absent from Pergher's account of Italian settlers sent to Libya and South Tyrol. Mundy and Zunes emphasize not so much organized agency on the part of the Moroccans used by the state to settle Western Sahara as the uncertainty about what those settlers could do if allowed to vote in a binding referendum, even in the absence of organized mobilization within the settler population. A form of this uncertainty plays a crucial role in Pergher's treatment. It is not that the Fascist state finds itself constrained by its inability to forecast the sentiments of the settlers. Both because of the short time frame of the Italian settlement experiment (brought to an end by the defeat of the Axis in World War II) and because it had no inclination to honor domestic or international norms of democratically expressed "self-determination," the Italian state never worried about settler political behavior in the way that Mundy and Zunes find to be crucial in the Moroccan–Western Sahara case.

Instead, what Pergher shows is that from the beginning the Fascist planners were highly conscious of the difficulties that would be entailed in using
settlers as an efficient instrument of their policy. Despite propaganda claims
to the contrary, they saw nothing natural in the settlement process. They had
no illusions about enthusiastic Italian settlers acting as a vehicle for the expansion of Italy into domains designated by the requirements of Italy's national
career and her imperial heritage. Their fears and anxieties are reflected in the
precautions they took to control settler behavior. Accordingly, the agency on
display in this case is not, as it was in the Israeli-OPT case, the disciplined
mobilization of dedicated settler cadres leading large voting blocs of settlers and their supporters within the core state. Nor was it the unintended
and unanticipated consequence of large numbers of settlers sent to Western
Sahara under false or at least unexamined presumptions about their political
reliability. Rather, in the Italian-Libyan case, agency appears, *in potentia* and,
to an extent, in actual evasive practices by settlers, on the level of individual
households. We see it most vividly in the careful planning of incentives and
enforcement procedures and in the calculations of the Fascist architects of
the settlement project about how to thwart what they fully expected would be
recalcitrant and passionately self-interested efforts to exploit the state's effort
for personal gain.

We see in the three cases discussed thus far that settlers do not always
develop political agency, though even without agency in its classic sense settlers can present surprising difficulties and anxieties for central states seeking
to use settlers for political, including expansionist, objectives. In this volume
the four other cases of settlement projects sponsored by central states are
Turkey-Cyprus, Indonesia–East Timor, Iraq-Kirkuk, and Sri Lanka–Tamil
and Muslim regions. In these chapters the focus of research shifts from state-
settler relations to settler-native relations (Indonesian–East Timorese, Iraqi
Arab–Kurdish) and to state-native relations (Turkey–Greek Cypriot, and Sri
Lanka–Tamil/Muslim).

The primary focus of the Indonesian and Iraqi cases is on the unexpected
impact that settlers had on the native population, though the importance of
that impact is made apparent by its contribution to the failure of the central
state's expansionist ambitions. In these cases the unintended consequences
of settlement were again more determinative of outcomes than the intended
effects. The key source of surprise here was neither the autonomous political
clout and independent objectives of the settlers (as in the Israeli case), nor

the attitudes of the settlers toward the state (as in the Moroccan case), nor recalcitrant behavior by settlers seeking to evade central state directives (as in the Italian case). Instead it was the reaction of natives to the settlers: of East Timorese and Kurds to Indonesian and Iraqi-Arab settlers.

Eiran begins his analysis of Indonesian settlement in East Timor by highlighting divisions and ambivalences among Indonesian elites with respect to the country's expansion into that territory. While the military, encouraged by Cold War alliances with the United States and Australia, advocated a forward policy, the political class was less enthusiastic, unsure about the wisdom of transplanting large numbers of Indonesian settlers to enforce Indonesian sovereignty on the portion of the island being relinquished by the Portuguese. In the event, the military faction prevailed. Jakarta subsequently adopted a strategy of settlement as its vehicle for territorial expansion. The strategy envisioned settlers as the means to develop the territory infrastructurally and economically. By thereby improving prevailing standards of living in what was described as a desperately underdeveloped land, sufficient international legitimacy and native acceptance of Indonesian rule would be attained for the permanent extension of Indonesian national state sovereignty.

That was the plan. As it turned out, settlement did not produce the kind of economic development and prosperity that attracted native support for Indonesian rule that was expected. In part for that reason, it also failed to generate international sympathy for Indonesia's efforts and legitimization for or at least acquiescence to its claims to East Timor. To the local population it seemed that virtually all the good, white collar jobs were going to settlers. As Eiran indicates, the menial jobs to which natives were confined bred stigmatization and racism in relations between settlers and the local population. Tensions arose leading to violent clashes and clumsy repressive measures by the Indonesian government. Within a few years chaos ensued, featuring a bloody end to Indonesian rule and the emergence of a UN-incubated independent state of East Timor. Although Eiran's treatment of these developments is brief, there is no question that he identifies incorrect Indonesian assessments of the economic and political impact of settlement in East Timor as a key driver in the unraveling of the entire project of Indonesian expansion into that territory.

Natali's disciplined and revealing analysis of the impact of Ba'athist-era settlement of Kirkuk by Iraqi Arabs includes a key element present in Pergher's analysis of the Italy-Libya case. In Kirkuk as well as in Libya the settlers who were induced, or more precisely, coerced, to relocate tended to resist the move and to search for opportunities to return to their regions of origin. From the elaborate restrictions placed upon them by the Saddam regime, including bans on burials outside Kirkuk, it is apparent that those in charge of the Kirkuk settlement project encountered just the sort of recalcitrance that Italian Fascist planners expected, and experienced, from settlers sent to Libya. Both in Kirkuk and in Libya settlers failed to mobilize collectively in any effective manner, but as individuals they resisted playing the role assigned to them of the heroic vehicle for national state expansion.

But the main axis of interest in Natali's treatment is not the relationship between the state and the settlers, or the question of settler agency in relation to the state or the natives. Instead her focus is on the effect of an aggressive process of Arabization, represented by Arab settlers displacing Kurds, and the unintended consequences of that campaign for sharpening nationalist trends and enlivening attachments to Kirkuk within the Kurdish political community in Northern Iraq. In a discussion similar to but more explicit than Eiran's treatment of the Indonesia–East Timor case, Natali argues that there was nothing inevitable about the emergence of a successful or even strong native (i.e., Kurdish) movement for self-determination or political independence along ethnic lines, especially a movement that placed special emphasis on Kurdish attachments to Kirkuk. In both cases it was the reaction of natives, and in Kurdistan, native politicians, to the systematic attempt to determine the political future of a territory via settlement that triggered strong counter-mobilization. In a kind of ideational backlash, Kirkuk's centrality to the national program of Kurdish political parties was established and sharpened, not by the oil riches lying underneath and immediately around it, but by outrage at the displacement of Kurds and the insult to Kurdishness associated with Saddam's settler-centered Arabization project.

Although written prior to the assertion of control by the Islamic State of Iraq and al-Sham over northwestern Iraq, in the context of that development Natali's analysis suggests an odd possibility. In 2014, effective Kurdish armed forces, the peshmerga, halted the advance of ISIS toward Kirkuk even as ISIS's threat to the city and the collapse of the Iraqi military in the area permitted effective rule of Kirkuk by Kurds. Had it not been for Saddam's settlement project, the Kurds might not have been either prepared or even inclined to control and protect Kirkuk, its population, and its oil reserves, from ISIS's brutal campaign to destroy the Middle Eastern state system. Here we see clearly how unintended consequences, and the chains of secondary and tertiary effects they produce, can make Lenin's question of "who-whom" impossible to answer without considering multiple time frames.

The two remaining cases studied in this volume are Turkey-Cyprus and the Buddhist/Sinhalese settlement of Tamil/Muslim areas (mainly an area in east central Sri Lanka known as the dry zone). The authors of these chapters focus most attention on the third side of the settler-state-native triangle—the central state's relationship to the "natives" or previously existing inhabitants of the territory targeted for settlement. In these two cases settler agency, whether at the collective or individual level, is virtually non-existent. Turkish and Sri Lankan architects of these settlement projects may have been somewhat uncertain or ambivalent about the role of settlement. They may have been in some ways surprised at the behavior or sentiments of the settlers or the effects of the settlement project as a whole. But neither such uncertainties nor such surprises feature significantly in the analyses offered by Loizides (Turkey-Cyprus) or Liaras (Sri Lanka). In these treatments the Turkish citizens settled in northern Cyprus by Turkey and the Buddhists settled in the dry zone by the authorities in Colombo *did* deliver the kind of demographic and political transformation intended by the central states who deployed them.

Liaras's treatment of the Sri Lankan case makes it clear that as a political syndrome, the dynamics associated with the central state–settler-native triangle are distinct from those in various migratory or undesigned transplantations of populations. But his analysis also shows that as a distinct kind of political syndrome, these dynamics are not confined to cases in which the target for settlement is located outside the established borders of the central state. In the Sri Lankan case, the target of settlement, the destination to which poor Buddhist peasants uprooted from the southwest of the country were sent, was within Sri Lanka itself. This large area was inhabited, densely or sparsely, by Hindu Tamils and, to a lesser extent, by Muslims—themselves citizens of Sri Lanka but not accepted as full-fledged members of the national community, defined in ethnonational and religious terms as Sinhalese and Buddhist.

Inspired by ultranationalist ambitions to implement visions of the entire island as the historic homeland of Sinhalese Buddhists, and with avid support from fundamentalist Buddhist monks, the settlement project was intended to supplant all images of the country as a "multi-ethnic project in a historically diverse land," as Liaras says in his chapter, with presumptions that the true nature of Sri Lanka was to be the "sacred Buddhist island," making it "a Sinhalese homeland with some tolerated imported minorities." Though this is not discussed in the chapter, the unsurprising and likely intended effect of the settlement project was Tamil mobilization on behalf of displaced Tamils. The violent Tamil secessionist movement that grew out of this conflict led to a prolonged and vicious civil war—one that ended in 2009 with the killing/execution of thousands of Tamils. The victory of the Sri Lankan military appears to have sealed the country's identity as the homeland and state of Sinhalese Buddhists, thereby registering a signal if costly victory for the architects of the settlement project.

Again, as in all the cases covered in this volume except for Israel, the settlers mobilized for deployment by the settlement planner in Sri Lanka were neither the originators of the idea nor ideologically motivated nor enthusiastically committed to the expansionist cause. But in Sri Lanka, as also to a somewhat less complete degree in the Turkish-Cyprus case, the central state was able to use the settlers successfully as an instrument of state policy. Here the state was "who," and the natives were "whom." The settlers were simply the instrument for wielding the power of the former against the latter.

In his analysis of the Turkey-Cyprus case Loizides emphasizes the absence of agency on the part of the settlers transferred from Turkey to Northern Cyprus. As we have seen, this aspect of settlement turns out to have not been the exception in this volume's collection of studies but the rule. Similar to Liaras's treatment of the Sri Lankan case, Loizides presents the settlers as passive instruments of the policies of Turkish elites—especially those connected to the military and, one can suppose, with Kemalist (anti-Islamist) affiliations. Although the purpose of settlement in this case was not to transform Cyprus, or even Northern Cyprus, into an integral part of the Turkish state, settlement was designed to institutionalize "bizonality" on the island. Almost forty years after the declared establishment of the Turkish Republic of Northern Cyprus, this entity has been recognized by no country other than Turkey itself. Nor have Turkish proposals been accepted for a Greek-Turkish federation of Cyprus that would regularize and make permanent most of the results of the Turkish conquest and of Turkey-sponsored population transfers and settlement.

On the other hand, Loizides's treatment makes clear that Turkey did successfully use its settlers as an instrument to transform the target of its ambitions and make it difficult if not impossible for Cyprus to return to a united and Greek or Greek-dominated nation-state. That the settlers have been an effective instrument for the attainment of this objective is apparent from his detailed and imaginative approach to the question of what compromises, cleverly arranged structure of incentives, and schedule for choice at popular, elite, and international levels could be successful in achieving a negotiated end to conflicts over the future of the island.

Although, as he writes, the settlers in this case have not been a force in their own right, it is their presence and the crucial role they play as a mechanism for the exercise of Turkish power that make these conflict resolution gymnastics necessary and that helped to doom the Annan Plan and other schemes for ending the dispute. Most of the proposals advanced by Loizides acknowledge the determinative impact of Turkey's settlement project in Cyprus by emphasizing potential concessions for Greek Cypriots from the Turkish side that would make the status of the settlers permanent and internationally recognized, and by making them citizens of Cyprus with rights to land and property acquired in connection with their move from the mainland. As in the chapter on Sri Lanka, the main focus of Loizides's treatment is on the central state–native edge of the triangle, with settlers playing the role of a passive and, for the most part, reliable instrument of central state policy.

Some Concluding Thoughts

The approach and organization of this book are designed to focus attention on settlement projects as instruments of state decisions to "right-people" a target territory and, by changing the status of that territory, "right-size" it. One likely product of the settlement enterprise is imagined to be the crystallization of the settlers as a doggedly self-interested actor likely to breed antagonism on the part of natives of the settled territory and frustration on the part of the core state. Dynamics within this triangular settler-state-native relationship are expected to render conflicts over the future of the territory much less tractable than other ethnicized or communal struggles, thereby helping to explain why they are, were, or will continue to be "protracted."

The approach grew at least partially out of the Israeli case, treated prominently here, but also out of two other cases, referred to often but not occupying the sustained attention of any of the contributors, that is, the case of Britain, Protestant settlers, and Catholic Ireland and also the case of France, European *colon* and *pied-noir* settlers, and Muslim Algeria. As I have analyzed in previous work (Lustick 1985 and 1993b), in all three of these cases—Israel, Britain, and France—the settler population did indeed organize itself to make uncompromising demands on both the natives and the central state. Indeed well-organized, disciplined, and violence-prone settler movements also showed themselves, in each of these cases, to be capable of intervening strategically, dramatically, and often decisively at the highest political and policymaking levels of the core states, always to the detriment of attempts to find common ground between the interests of core state elites and those of the native population.

The tension in this volume arises from the fact that apart from the Israeli case, settlers in the cases reported on in the other six chapters do not constitute themselves in this manner and do not collectively seek to destroy or destabilize proposals to resolve disputes over the future of the problematized territory. Hence the reader is incorrectly advised by several authors that in their cases, but not most others, one does not observe the settlers acting with self-organized and potent agency. What was expected as the norm—strong self-directed organization and influence on the part of the settlers—turned out to be the exception.

Still, we do see an important similarity across all the cases linked to the presence of settlers. In none of the cases treated in this book did the settlement project launched by the central state, and sustained with its support, act decisively as a mechanism to stabilize a new relationship between the state and the targeted territory based on "right-peopling" or "right-sizing." Rather, in each case we see that the settlement project was enough to enmesh the outlying territory into the political ambit of the central state, and enough to antagonize or alienate the native population, but not enough to remove the fate of the territory from the international agenda or from the agenda of native groups and their supporters. In other words, in all cases the targeted territory entered a state of legal and political limbo that was very much attributable to the consequences of settlement. The same was true of the British-Irish and French-Algerian relationships. Despite centuries of British sponsored and supported Protestant settlement in Ireland, the legal and political disposition of the island, in all its parts, was never, and still is not, "settled," by which I mean naturalized so that all relevant political forces act as if substantially changing its current status is not a question open to serious discussion. Nor, despite 120 years of rule and European settlement of Muslim Algeria, was France able to do that—to hegemonically establish its incorporation of the "three departments of France" south of the Mediterranean that, as it was claimed for so long, were nothing but a "prolongation of the metropole."

The question then becomes: how is the "limbo" status of a settled territory—neither a fully integrated part of the central state nor a separate territory with an agreed-upon and well-institutionalized status—brought to an end? Answering this question, for the British, French, and Israeli cases, means appreciating the implications of the fact that Britain, France, and Israel were (are) fully functioning parliamentary democracies. It also means understanding the extent to which, in these open parliamentary democracies, the scale of the threat to the central state posed by settler opposition to any change in the status of the territory that would remove it from the limbo so beneficial to the settlers was the main obstacle to change. Thus did threats of violence and organized rebellion force British governments to back away from Home Rule for all of Ireland in the 1880s, 1890s, and, most climactically, during the near outbreak of civil war in 1914. Likewise, *colon* and *pied-noir* mobilization, along with right-wing or pro-settler parties within France itself, defeated repeated attempts in the 1920s, 1930s, and 1940s to extend real citizenship rights to Algerian Muslims as a vehicle for that territory's effective integration. Repeated threats by settlers and their allies on the right and in the military to overthrow Fourth Republic governments deemed too "soft" on Algeria eventually ended in the destruction of that regime, followed by a succession of regime crises imposed upon the Fifth Republic by the same settler-centered opposition. In Israel, every government since 1977 that has been inclined to transform the "limbo" relationship Israel has had with the OPT since 1967 has been deterred or prevented from doing so by an alliance of settlers, ultranationalists, and fundamentalists. Aside from assassinating Prime Minister Rabin when he sought to move toward a Palestinian state solution, members of this alliance, including settler-organized clandestine armed groups, have murdered and intimidated both Palestinian and Jewish moderates, and organized large-scale civil disobedience and semi-violent resistance campaigns against the evacuation of settlements in both Gaza and the West Bank. As in the British and French cases, the settlers mobilized successfully enough to create the firm expectation and general fear that separating the targeted territory from the central state would require defeating them, and that would in turn entail challenges to regime stability and risks of widespread violence or even civil war.

In the French case de Gaulle faced these threats, exploited the collapse of the Fourth Republic, and repeatedly risked the integrity of the Fifth Republic in order to defeat the settlers and their allies, remove Algeria from its legal and political limbo, and make way for its independence. In Britain, Prime Minister Asquith's government, in 1914, gave up on the chance to effectively separate Britain from all of Ireland, and set the country on a course leading eventually to the division of Ireland and a status for mostly Protestant Northern Ireland that is still uncertain and not entirely stable. A key point here, distinguishing these three cases where settler agency was highly visible and effective, is that the core states were and are robust and mostly open parliamentary democracies.

The meaning of a well-institutionalized democracy is that the rules of the political game permit and even encourage large groups of citizens to organize and exert themselves on behalf of their perceived interests. When a strong state establishes a settlement movement in a non-incorporated territory where a vast majority of the population do not have such opportunities, but the settlers do, then it is almost inevitable that the settlers will not only develop powerful self-interests in the privileges that have been created for them in the targeted territory but also come to fear the natives whose interests must be ignored and whose mobilization must be suppressed if those privileges are to be protected and those fears alleviated. In such situations uprisings and violence by natives will persuade most if not all settlers that removal of their privileges would actually constitute an existential danger. The fundamental logic of the situation will lead the settlers to use their connections with allies in the center and their capacity for violence to threaten regime destabilization by breaking the rules of the political game.

Aside from Israel, and to an extent, Sri Lanka, none of the central states featured in the cases considered in this volume were open democracies, especially during the period when the settlement projects were initiated and the fundamental terms of the triangular relationships were set. Regardless of façades featuring elections and political parties, Turkey in the 1970s and 1980s, Indonesia under Suharto, Ba'athist Iraq, monarchical Morocco, and Fascist Italy, were authoritarian or, at most, semi-authoritarian systems. That does not mean that a single ruler or a small group of rulers could make all decisions without any reference to established rules or procedures. What it does mean is that the size of the political class, or "selectorate," was relatively small and that the rules governing decision making within it did not extend to large self-organized groups of citizens, such as the settlers. That in turn meant, and has meant, that no matter how well institutionalized are the rules of the game of intra-elite competition, they are not rules governing inter-group competition and so do not offer opportunities to settlers, even if well organized, to threaten serious disruption by breaking or threatening to break them. In the particular context of Sri Lanka, a pattern of vigorous competition among various Sinhalese political parties that can be coded as democratic was present. At the same time, domination of those parties by well-established elites rendered hopeless any inclination by the poor and powerless settlers to even try to wield power on their own behalf.

Turkey, in recent decades, has become substantially more democratic, with some doubt surrounding the outcome of elections. While the settlers have not organized or intervened in Turkish politics, similar to the Moroccan case, elites in Turkey, both those in favor of compromise over Cyprus and those opposed to the kinds of proposals discussed in Loizides's chapter, recognize the need to take into account the preferences and expectations of Turkish settlers on the island. The emergence of democratic elements in those two cases, even absent genuine settler agency, may explain why they do somewhat resemble the French-Algerian, British-Irish, and Israeli-Palestinian cases. In each of these five cases the problem of the disposition of the territory targeted for settlement was either resolved only after more than a century of strife or is still unresolved. By contrast, in East Timor, the Sri Lankan dry zone, Libya, and I would now argue, Kirkuk, the outcome has been determined: settler evacuation and native control in East Timor, Libya, and Kirkuk, and full integration into the central state in Sri Lanka.

Accordingly we can understand the absence of collective settler agency from these cases (apart from Israel) as linked to the absence or weakness of democracy in the core state. But this analysis also suggests an answer as to why, in all cases, the "limbo-like" status of the targeted territory lasted, or has lasted, so long. The fact that we cannot easily look inside the relatively closed world of inter-elite competition as it operates within authoritarian regimes does not mean there are no rules that govern that competition. An important but so far largely unexplored hypothesis that flows from the explanation offered so far is that a settlement project engineered from the center, and invested with the prestige of the top leadership, invests the future of that project with such importance that rivals for power stand ready to exploit proposed compromises for ending the territory's limbo status in order to promote their own interests by removing the leadership identified with those compromises—a leadership whose routines of political control *are* the regime in that state.

This theory implies that the paralysis we observe publicly and clearly in democratic sponsors of settlement exists as well, but more obscurely, in non-democratic states who engineer such projects. One pattern that lends credence to this theory is the importance, in those cases where the limbo status of settled territories has been brought to an end, of *force majeure*. The disposition of the Turkish settled zone of Northern Cyprus and of Western Sahara remain open questions, but fate of the East Timor, Libyan, Kirkuk, and Sri Lankan problems has been settled. Unlike the British and French cases, the outcomes in these four episodes were not driven by tumultuous or disciplined political processes within the central state. What mattered most were externally generated events and forces of such magnitude as to dwarf the capacities of the local actors to maneuver or impose their desires on one another: the mobilization of the international community in support of East Timor's independence, the defeat of Italy in World War II, the rise of ISIS and the collapse of the Iraqi military in the northwest of what had been Iraq, and the complete annihilation of Tamil military and political power resulting from the Sri Lankan army's victory in 2009.

The overall pattern suggests that whether the central state is democratic or not, settlement projects that do not entail the elimination of large native populations reliably produce long-term and difficult-to-resolve conflicts. In those cases involving robustly democratic central states, large-scale external events play an important and perhaps even necessary role in jolting the political system out of a traditional state of paralysis, as World War I did for Britain and World War II for France. But in these two cases, and perhaps in the Israeli case as well, real change comes (or will come) only when wider regional or global events interact with regime-threatening crises arising from the fateful triangle of central state–settler–native relations.

References

Abowd, Tom. (1999). "'The 'Land without the People': Contesting Jerusalem on the Eve of the Millennium." *Middle East Report* no. 213, pp. 34–37.

Adebajo, Adekeye. (2002). *Selling Out the Sahara: The Tragic Tale of the UN Referendum*. Occasional Papers Series. Ithaca, NY: Cornell University, Institute for African Development.

Adhiati, Adriana Sri, and Bobsien, Armin. (2001). *Indonesia's Transmigration Programme—An Update: A Report Prepared for Down to Earth*. Accessed from http://www.downtoearth-indonesia.org/sites/downtoearth-indonesia.org/files/Transmigration%20update%202001.pdf

Aditjondro, George J. (1994). *In the Shadow of Mount Ramelau: The Impact of the Occupation of East Timor*. Leiden, Netherlands: Indonesian Documentation and Information Center.

"Administration Report of Kirkuk Division." (1920). Foreign Office 371/5069, pp. 1–25. British National Archives.

Aguirre, José Ramón Diego. (1988). *Historia del Sahara español: la verdad de una traición*. Madrid: Kaydeda Ediciones.

Ahmida, Ali A. (2005). *Forgotten Voices: Power and Agency in Colonial and Postcolonial Libya*. New York: Routledge.

Akenson, Donald H. (1992). *God's Peoples: Covenant and Land in South Africa, Israel, and Ulster*. Ithaca, NY: Cornell University Press.

Amana. (2013). "Amana—the Settlement Movement." Accessed May 21, 2013, from http://www.amana.co.il/?CategoryID=101&ArticleID=166

Amnesty International. (2010a). "Morocco Must End Harassment of Sahrawi Activists," April 9. London: Amnesty International.

———. (2010b). "Morocco Urged to Investigate Deaths in Western Sahara Protest Camp," November 11. London: Amnesty International.

Andreasson, Stefan. (2010). "Confronting the Settler Legacy: Indigenisation and Transformation in South Africa and Zimbabwe." *Political Geography* 29(8), pp. 424–433.

"Aqlim Kurdistan Iraq, Al—Lijna Al Ulia Li Munahaza Ta'arib Kurdistan." (2006). *Atlasi Kirkuk*. Erbil: Mektab Aljamahir Lil taba'a.

Arudpraghasam, A. R. (1996). *The Traditional Homeland of the Tamils*. Kotte, Sri Lanka: Kanal.

Assyrian International News Agency. (2005). "Assyrians Prevented by Kurds from Voting in North Iraq," January 31. Accessed from http://www.aina.org/releases/20050131003708.htm

Attalides, Michael A. (1979). *Cyprus: Nationalism and International Politics*. New York: St. Martin's Press.

Ballinger, Pamela. (2003). *History in Exile: Memory and Identity at the Borders of the Balkans*. Princeton, NJ: Princeton University Press.

Barbier, Maurice. (1982). *Le conflit au Sahara occidental*. Paris: L'Harmattan, 1982.

Barkan, Elazar. (2000). *The Guilt of Nations: Restitution and Negotiating Historical Injustices*. London: W. W. Norton.

Barrera, Giulia. (2003). "Mussolini's Colonial Race Laws and State-Settlers Relations in AOI (1935–41)." *Journal of Modern Italian Studies* 8(3), pp. 425–443.

Bartholomeusz, Tessa J., and De Silva, Chandra R. (1998). *Buddhist Fundamentalism and Minority Identities in Sri Lanka*. Albany: State University of New York Press.

Bass, Daniel. (2007). "Making Sense of the Census in Sri Lanka." In R. Cheran, ed., *Writing Tamil Nationalism*. Colombo: ICES.

Bastian, Sunil. (2007). *The Politics of Foreign Aid in Sri Lanka*. Colombo: ICES.

Benvenisty, Meron. (1984). *The West Bank Data Project*. Washington, DC: Institute for Public Policy Research.

———. (1986). *1986 Report: Demographic, Economic, Legal, Social, and Political Developments in the West Bank*. Boulder, CO: Westview Press.

Biger, Gideon. (2008). "The Boundaries of Israel-Palestine Past, Present, and Future: A Critical Geographical View." *Israel Studies* 13(1), pp. 68–93.

Black, Richard. (2001). "Return and Reconstruction in Bosnia-Herzegovina: Missing Link, or Mistaken Priority?" *SAIS Review* 21(2), pp. 177–199.

Blackburn, Susan. (2004). *Women and the State in Modern Indonesia*. Cambridge: Cambridge University Press.

Bloom, Mia, and Licklinder, Roy. (2004). "What's All the Shouting About?" *Security Studies* 13(4), pp. 219–229.

Bose, Sumantra. (2002). "Flawed Mediation, Chaotic Implementation: The 1987 Indo-Sri Lanka Peace Agreement." In Stephen John Stedman, Donald Rothchild, and Elizabeth Cousens, eds., *Ending Civil Wars: The Implementation of Peace Agreements*. Boulder, CO: Lynne Rienner.

———. (2007). *Contested Lands: Israel-Palestine, Kashmir, Bosnia, Cyprus, and Sri Lanka*. Cambridge: Harvard University Press.

Brown, Ralph H. (1948). *Historical Geography of the United States*. New York: Harcourt, Brace.

Bruner, Stephen C. (2009). "Leopoldo Franchetti and Italian Settlement in Eritrea: Emigration, Welfare Colonialism and the Southern Question." *European History Quarterly* 39(1), pp. 71–94.

Burbank, Jane, and Cooper, Frederick. (2010). *Empires in World History: Power and the Politics of Difference*. Princeton, NJ: Princeton University Press.

Burr, William, and Evans, Michael, eds. (2001). *East Timor Revisited: Ford, Kissinger and the Indonesian Invasion: 1975–76*. National Security Archive Electronic Briefing Book No. 62. Accessed from http://www.gwu.edu/~nsarchiv/NSAEBB/NSAEBB62/index.html

Carens, Joseph H. (2000). *Culture, Citizenship, and Community: A Contextual Exploration of Justice as Evenhandedness*. New York: Oxford University Press.

Central Bureau of Statistics. (1978). *Statistical Abstract of Israel*. Jerusalem: Central Bureau of Statistics.

———. (2011). *Statistical Abstract of Israel*. Jerusalem: Central Bureau of Statistics.

———. (2013). *Statistical Abstract of Israel*. Jerusalem: Central Bureau of Statistics.

———. (2014). *Statistical Abstract of Israel*. Jerusalem: Central Bureau of Statistics.

Central Intelligence Agency Library. (2003). Timor-Leste (Map). Accessed from https://www.cia.gov/library/publications/cia-maps-publications/map-downloads/timor-leste-transport.jpg/image.jpg

Chamberlin, Ernest. (2009). *Rebellion, Defeat, and Exile: The 1959 Uprising in East Timor*. Point Lonsdale, Australia: Ernest Chamberlin.

Chapman, Thomas, and Roeder, Philip G. (2007). "Partition as a Solution to Wars of Nationalism: The Importance of Institutions." *American Political Science Review* 101(4), pp. 677–691.

Charalambidou-Papapavlou, Ireni. (2008). "Turkish Cypriots and Turkish Settlers in Cyprus." *To Sizitame*. Cyprus Broadcasting Corporation, July 28. Accessed June 16, 2009, from http://www.cybc.com.cy/index.php?option=com_content&task=view&id=729&Itemid=35

Cherkaoui, Mohamed. (2007). *Morocco and the Sahara: Social Bonds and Geopolitical Issues*. Oxford, UK: Bardwell Press.

Choate, Mark I. (2007). "Identity Politics and Political Perception in the European Settlement of Tunisia: The French Colony versus the Italian Colony." *French Colonial History* 8(1), pp. 97–109.

Chopra, Jarat. (1994). *United Nations Determination of the Western Saharan Self*. Oslo: Norwegian Institute for International Affairs.

———. (1999). *Peace-Maintenance: The Evolution of International Political Authority*. New York: Routledge.

Chrysostomides, Kypros. (2000). *The Republic of Cyprus: A Study of International Law*. The Hague: Martinus Nijhoff.

Cordell, Karl, and Wolff, Stefan. (2005). *Germany's Foreign Policy towards Poland and the Czech Republic: Ostpolitik Revisited*. London: Routledge.

Cresti, Federico. (2011). *Non desiderare la terra d'altri: la colonizzazione italiana in Libia*. Rome: Carocci.

Csergo, Zsuzsa. (2009). "The Political Integration of Minorities in New European Democracies: The Uses of Inheritance and Democratic Competition." Paper presented at the American Political Science Association Annual Conference, Toronto, Canada.

Cuco, Alfons. (1992). *The Demographic Structure of Cyprus*. Report of the Committee on Migration, Refugees and Demography, April 27. Doc. 6589. Accessed May 2009 from http://www.moa.gov.cy/MOI/pio/pio.nsf/All/20C7614D06858E9FC2256DC2 00380113/$file/cuco%20report.pdf?OpenElement

Dahlman, Carl, and Ó Tuathail, Gearóid. (2005). "The Legacy of Ethnic Cleansing: The International Community and the Returns Process in Post-Dayton Bosnia-Herzegovina." *Political Geography* 24(5), pp. 569–599.

Damis, John. (1983). *Conflict in Northwest Africa: The Western Sahara Dispute*. Stanford, CA: Hoover Institution Press.

———. (2001). "Sahrawi Demonstrations." *Middle East Report* 218, pp. 38–41.

Danielson, Eric N. (1995). "Kurdish Relations with Other Nations: Great Britain and the Origins of the Kurdish Question in Iraq (1918–1932)." *Kurdistan Times* 4, pp. 49–75.

De Silva, Kingsley M. (1986). *Managing Ethnic Tensions in Multi-Ethnic Societies: Sri Lanka 1880–1985*. Lanham, MD: University Press of America.

———. (1987). *Separatist Ideology in Sri Lanka: A Historical Appraisal for the Claim of the "Traditional Homelands" of the Tamils of Sri Lanka*. Kandy, Sri Lanka: ICES.

———. (1995). *Regional Powers and Small State Security: India and Sri Lanka*. Baltimore, MD: Johns Hopkins University Press.

———. (1998). *Reaping the Whirlwind: Ethnic Conflict, Ethnic Politics in Sri Lanka*. New Delhi and New York: Penguin Books.

———. (2005). *A History of Sri Lanka*. New Delhi and New York: Penguin Books.

Del Boca, Angelo. (1988). *Dal fascismo a Gheddafi*. Rome: Laterza.

———. (1995). "Le leggi razziali nell'impero di Mussolini." In A. del Boca, M. Legnani, and M. G. Rossi, eds., *Il regime fascista: storia e storiografia*. Rome: Laterza.

———. (1996). *I gas di Mussolini: il fascismo e la guerra d'Etiopia*. Rome: Editori Riuniti.

Deutsche Gesellschaft für Internationale Zusammenarbeit. (2013). "Support to Land Project: German Federal Ministry for Economic Cooperation and Development" (BMZ). Accessed May 21, 2013, from http://www.giz.de/themen/en/8370.htm

DeVotta, Neil. (2004). *Blowback: Linguistic Nationalism, Institutional Decay, and Ethnic Conflict in Sri Lanka*. Stanford, CA: Stanford University Press.

———. (2011). "Sri Lanka: From Turmoil to Dynasty." *Journal of Democracy* 22(2), pp. 130–144.

Di Michele, Andrea. (2003). *L'italianizzazione imperfetta: l'amministrazione pubblica dell'Alto Adige tra Italia liberale e fascismo*. Alessandria: Edizioni dell'Orso.

Dicker, Richard. (2011). "Punishing Wrongdoers Is Fundamental to Securing Lasting

Peace." *Economist Debates*. Defending the motion Richard Dicker, director of Human Rights Watch. Opposing the motion Jack Snyder, professor at Columbia University. Accessed from http://www.economist.com/debate/days/view/74

Dowty, Alan. (2012). *Israel/Palestine*. Malden, MA: Polity.

Drobless, Mattityahu. (1978). *Master Plan for the Development of the Settlement in Judea and Samaria, 1979–1983*. Jerusalem: World Zionist Organization, Department for Rural Settlement. In Hebrew.

———. (1981). *Settlement in Judea and Samaria: Strategy, Policy, and Plans*. Jerusalem: World Zionist Organization, Department for Rural Settlement, 1981. In Hebrew.

Duara, Prasenjit. (2003). *Sovereignty and Authenticity: Manchukuo and the East Asian Modern*. Lanham, MD: Rowman & Littlefield.

Dumper, Michael. (1992). "Settlement in the Old City of Jerusalem." *Journal of Palestinian Affairs* 21(4), pp. 32–53.

Dunbar, Charles. (2000). "Saharan Stasis." *Middle East Journal* 54, pp. 522–545.

Economist Intelligence Unit. (2003). *Country Profile 2003: Morocco*. London: Economist Intelligence Unit.

Eiran, Ehud. (2010). "Explaining the Settlement Project: We Know More, But What More Should We Know?" *Israel Studies Forum* 25(2), pp. 102–115.

———. (2014). "State Elite Perceptions and the Launch of the Israeli Settlement Project in the West Bank: The International-Domestic Nexus." In Miriam F. Elman, Oded Haklai, and Hendrik Spruyt, eds., *Democracy and Conflict Resolution: The Dilemmas of Israel's Peacemaking*, pp. 209–222. Syracuse, NY: Syracuse University Press.

Eisterer, Klaus, and Steininger, Rolf. (1989). *Die Option: Südtirol zwischen Faschismus und Nationalsozialismus*. Innsbruck: Haymon.

El Ouali, Abdelhamid. (2008). *Saharan Conflict: Towards Territorial Autonomy as a Right to Democratic Self-Determination*. London: Stacey International.

Elkins, Caroline, and Pedersen, Susan, eds. (2005). *Settler Colonialism in the Twentieth Century: Projects, Practices, Legacies*. New York: Routledge.

Elman, Miriam F., Haklai, Oded, and Spruyt, Hendrik, eds. (2014a). *Democracy and Conflict Resolution: The Dilemmas of Israel's Peacemaking*. Syracuse, NY: University of Syracuse Press, 2014.

———. (2014b). "Democracy and Peacemaking in Protracted Conflicts: The Israeli Case." In Miriam F. Elman, Oded Haklai, and Hendrik Spruyt, eds., *Democracy and Conflict Resolution: The Dilemmas of Israel's Peacemaking*, pp. 1–26. Syracuse, NY: University of Syracuse Press.

Elson, R. E. (2008). *The Idea of Indonesia*. Cambridge: Cambridge University Press.

Ennab, Wael R. (1994). *Population and Demographic Developments in the West Bank and the Gaza Strip until 1990*. Report for United Nations Conference on Trade and Development (UNCTD), Table 2.1, June 28. New York: United Nations.

"Ergenekon's Cyprus Operations under Spotlight." (2009). *Today's Zaman*, April 11.

Esman, Milton J., and Herring, Ronald J. (2001). *Carrots, Sticks and Ethnic Conflict: Rethinking Development Assistance*. Ann Arbor: University of Michigan Press.

European Court of Human Rights. (2003). "Chamber Judgments in the Cases of *Eugenia Michaelidou and Michael Tymvios v. Turkey* and *Demades v. Turkey*," July 31.
———. (2010). *Demopoulos and others v. Turkey*, March 1.
European Court of Justice. (2009). "Judgment of the Court of Justice in Case C-420/07: *Meletis Apostolides v. David Charles Orams & Linda Elizabeth Orams*." Press Release No 39/09, April 28. Accessed June 16, 2009, from http://curia.europa.eu/jcms/upload/docs/application/pdf/2009-04/cp090039en.pdf
European Parliament. (1995). "Resolution on Tibet." Strasbourg, May 17, B4-0768/95/RCI and 0826/95/RCI. Accessed June 16, 2009, from http://www.tpprc.org/documents/resolutions/european_parliament/17_may_1995.pdf
———. (2000). "European Parliament Resolution on Cyprus's Application for Membership of the European Union and the State of the Negotiations." Minutes of 04/10/2000 (COM(1999) 502-C5-0025/2000-1997/2171(COS)).
Fearon, James D. (1998). "Commitment Problems and the Spread of Ethnic Conflict." In David Lake and Donald Rothchild, eds., *The International Spread of Ethnic Conflict: Fear, Diffusion, and Escalation*. Princeton, NJ: Princeton University Press.
———. (2004). "Why Do Some Civil Wars Last So Much Longer than Others?" *Journal of Peace Research* 41(3), pp. 275–301.
Fearon, James D., and Laitin, David. (2011). "Sons of the Soil, Migrants, and Civil War." *World Development* 39(2), pp. 199–211.
Feige, Michael. (2009). *Settling in the Hearts: Jewish Fundamentalism in the Occupied Territories*. Detroit: Wayne State University Press.
Ferguson, Barbara G. B., and Kennedy, Tim. (1992). "North Africa at Risk as Western Sahara Peace Plan Stalls." *Washington Report on Middle East Affairs* 11(3), pp. 50–51.
Fisher, Ronald. (2001). "Cyprus: The Failure of Mediation and the Escalation of an Identity-Based Conflict to an Adversarial Impasse." *Journal of Peace Research* 38(3), pp. 307–326.
Fitzpatrick, Daniel. (2002). *Land Claims in East Timor*. Canberra: Asia Pacific Press.
Foresti, F. (1984). "Il problema linguistico nella 'politica indigena' del colonialismo fascista." *Movimento Operaio e Socialista* 7(1).
Fox, James J. (2003). "Tracing the Path, Recounting the Past: Historical Perspectives on Timor." In James J. Fox and Dionisio Babo Soares, eds., *Out of the Ashes: Destruction and Reconstruction of East Timor*, pp. 1–28. Canberra: Australian National University Press.
Franck, Thomas M. (1976). "The Stealing of the Sahara." *American Journal of International Law* 70(4), pp. 694–721.
———. (1987). "Theory and Practice of Decolonization." In Richard Lawless and Laila Monahan, eds., *War and Refugees: The Western Sahara Conflict*. New York: Pinter.
Friend, Theodore. (2003). *Indonesian Destinies*. Cambridge: Harvard University Press.
Frymer, Paul. (2014). "A Rush and a Push and the Land Is Ours: Territorial Expansion, Land Policy, and U.S. State Formation." *Perspectives on Politics* 12(1), pp. 119–144.

Fuller, Mia. (2007). *Moderns Abroad: Architecture, Cities and Italian Imperialism.* New York: Routledge.

Furnivall, John S. (1939). *Netherland's India: A Study of Plural Economy.* Cambridge: Cambridge University Press.

Galchinsky, Michael. (2004). "The Jewish Settlements in the West Bank: International Law and Israeli Jurisprudence." *Israel Studies* 9(3), pp. 115–136.

Galnor, Yitzhak. (2009). "The Zionist Debates on Partition (1919–1946)." *Israel Studies* 14(2), pp. 74–87.

"Gen. Eruygur: Fervent Coup Enthusiast." (2008). *Today's Zaman*, July 4.

Ghosh, Partha S. (2003). *Ethnicity versus Nationalism: The Devolution Discourse in Sri Lanka.* Delhi and London: Sage.

Gila, Oscar A., Zaratiegui, Ana U., and De Maturana Diéguez, Virginia L. (2011). "Western Sahara: Migration, Exile and Environment." *International Migration* 49(Suppl. 1), e146–e163.

Goddard, Stacie E. (2009). *Indivisible Territories and the Politics of Legitimacy: Jerusalem and Northern Ireland.* Cambridge: Cambridge University Press.

Good, Kenneth. (1979). "Colonialism and Settler Colonialism: A Comparison." *Australian Outlook* 33(3), pp. 339–351.

Gorenberg, Gershom. (2006). *The Accidental Empire: Israel and the Birth of the Settlements, 1967–1977.* New York: Times Books.

Gott, Richard. (2007). "The 2006 SLAS Lecture: Latin America as a White Settler Society." *Bulletin of Latin American Research* 26(2), pp. 269–289.

Goulding, Marrack. (2002). *Peacemonger.* London: John Murray.

Gramsci, Antonio. (1995). *The Southern Question* (translation and introduction by Pasquale Verdicchio). West Lafayette, IN: Bordighera.

Green, Elliott. (2012). "The Political Demography of Conflict in Modern Africa." *Civil Wars* 14(4), pp. 477–498.

Guelke, Adrian. (2012). *Politics in Deeply Divided Societies.* Cambridge, UK: Polity.

Gunawardena, R.A.L.H. (1990). "The People of the Lion: The Sinhala Identity and Ideology in History and Historiography." In Jonathan Spencer, ed., *Sri Lanka: History and the Roots of Conflict.* London: Routledge.

Hadjipavlou, Maria. (2007). "The Cyprus Conflict: Root Causes and Implications for Peacebuilding." *Journal of Peace Research* 44(3), pp. 349–365.

Hadjipavlou-Trigeorgis, Maria, and Lenos Trigeorgis. (1993). "Cyprus: An Evolutionary Approach to Conflict Resolution." *Journal of Conflict Resolution* 2, pp. 340–360.

Haklai, Oded. (2003). "Linking Ideas and Opportunities in Contentious Politics: The Israeli Nonparliamentary Opposition to the Peace Process." *Canadian Journal of Political Science* 36(4), pp. 791–812.

——— . (2007). "Religious-Nationalist Mobilization and State Penetration: Lessons from Jewish Settlers' Activism in Israel and the West Bank." *Comparative Political Studies* 40(6), pp. 713–739.

——— . (2011). *Palestinian Ethnonationalism in Israel.* Philadelphia: University of Pennsylvania Press.

———. (2013). "Regime Transition and the Emergence of Ethnic Democracies." In Jacques Bertrand and Oded Haklai, eds., *Democratization and Ethnic Democracies: Conflict or Compromise.* London: Routledge.

———. (2014). "Spoiling the Peace: State Structure and the Capacity of Hardliners to Foil Peacemaking Efforts." In Miriam F. Elman, Oded Haklai, and Hendrik Spruyt, eds., *Democracy and Conflict Resolution: The Dilemmas of Israel's Peacemaking,* pp. 67–97. Syracuse, NY: University of Syracuse Press.

Hametz, Maura E. (2005). *Making Trieste Italian, 1918–1954.* Woodbridge, UK: Boydell Press.

Harvey, E. (2003). *Women and the Nazi East: Agents and Witnesses of Germanization.* New Haven, CT: Yale University Press.

Hassner, Ron E. (2003). "To Halve and to Hold: Conflicts over Sacred Space and the Problem of Indivisibility." *Security Studies* 12(4), pp. 1–33.

———. (2006/07). "The Path to Intractability: Time and the Entrenchment of Territorial Disputes." *International Security* 31(3), pp. 107–138.

———. (2009). *War on Sacred Grounds.* Ithaca, NY: Cornell University Press.

Hatay, Mete. (2005). *Beyond Numbers: An Inquiry into the Political Integration of the Turkish "Settlers" in Northern Cyprus.* PRIO Report 4. Oslo: Peace Research Institute Oslo.

Haut Commissariat au Plan. (2005). *Population légal du Maroc.* Rabat, Royaume du Maroc: Haut Commissariat au Plan.

Hechter, Michael. (1999). *Internal Colonialism: The Celtic Fringe in Britain's National Development.* New Brunswick, NJ: Transaction.

Hietala, Thomas R. (1985). *Manifest Design: Anxious Aggrandizement in Late Jacksonian America.* Ithaca, NY: Cornell University Press.

Hiltermann, Joost. (2007). *A Poisonous Affair: America, Iraq, and the Gassing of Halabja.* New York: Cambridge University Press.

Hind, Robert J. (1984). "The Internal Colonial Concept." *Comparative Studies in Society and History* 26, pp. 543–568.

Hodges, Tony, and Pazzanita, Anthony. (1994). *Historical Dictionary of the Western Sahara.* Metuchen, NJ: Scarecrow.

Hogan-Brun, Gabrielle, Uldis, Ozolins, Meilutė, Ramonienė, and Mart, Rannut. (2008). "Language Politics and Practices in the Baltic States." *Current Issues in Language Planning* 8(4), pp. 469–631.

Holt, Sarah. (2011). *Aid, Peacebuilding and the Resurgence of War: Buying Time in Sri Lanka.* London: Palgrave Macmillan.

Horn, D. G. (1994). *Social Bodies: Science, Reproduction, and Italian Modernity.* Princeton, NJ: Princeton University Press.

Horowitz, Donald. (2000). *Ethnic Groups in Conflict.* 2nd ed. Berkeley: University of California Press.

Human Rights Watch. (1995). *Keeping It Secret: The United Nations Operations in the Western Sahara.* New York: Human Rights Watch.

———. (2004). *Claims in Conflict: Reversing Ethnic Cleansing in Northern Iraq.* Accessed from http://www.hrw.org/sites/default/files/reports/iraq0804.pdf

———. (2010). "Western Sahara: Beatings, Abuse by Moroccan Security Forces." News release, November 26. New York: Human Rights Watch.

——— . (2015). "Iraqi Kurdistan: Arabs Displaced, Cordoned Off, Detained," February 26. Accessed from http://www.hrw.org/news/2015/02/25/iraqi-kurdistan-arabs-displaced-cordoned-detained

Ibn 'Azuz Hakim, Muhammad. (1981). *Al-Siyadah Al-Maghribiyyah Fi Al-Aqalim Al-Sahrawiyyah Min Khilal Al-Wath'iq Al-Makhaziniyyah*. Casablanca: Mu'assasat Bansharah.

International Committee of the Red Cross. (1949). "Geneva Convention Relative to the Protection of Civilian Persons in Time of War."

International Crisis Group. (2006). *Iraq and the Kurds: The Brewing Battle over Kirkuk.* Middle East Report No. 56. Accessed from http://www.crisisgroup.org/~/media/Files/Middle%20East%20North%20Africa/Iraq%20Syria%20Lebanon/Iraq/56_iraq_and_the_kurds___the_brewing_battle_over_kirkuk.pdf

———. (2008). *Sri Lanka's Eastern Province.* Asia Report No. 159. Washington, DC: International Crisis Group.

Ipsen, Carl. (1996). *Dictating Demography: The Problem of Population in Fascist Italy.* New York: Cambridge University Press.

Isaacson, Walter. (1992). *Kissinger: A Biography.* New York: Touchstone.

Jenkins, David. (1997). "Alatas Cites History in East-Timor Conundrum." *Sydney Morning Herald*, September 13.

Jensen, Erik. (2005). *Western Sahara: Anatomy of a Stalemate.* Boulder, CO: Lynne Rienner.

Jervis, Robert. (1978). "Cooperation under the Security Dilemma." *World Politics* 30(2), pp. 167–214.

Johnson, Carter. (2008). "Partitioning to Peace: Sovereignty, Demography, and Ethnic Civil Wars." *International Security* 32(4), pp. 140–170.

Joseph, Joseph S. (1997). *Cyprus: Ethnic Conflict and International Politics: From Independence to the Threshold of the European Union.* New York: St. Martin's Press.

Kahin, George McTurnan. (2003). *Nationalism and Revolution in Indonesia.* Ithaca, NY: Cornell University Press.

Kane, Sean. (2011). *Iraq's Disputed Territories: A View of the Political Horizon and Implications for U.S. Policy.* Peaceworks No. 69. United States Institute of Peace. Accessed from http://www.usip.org/sites/default/files/PW69_final.pdf

Kaufmann, Chaim. (1996). "Possible and Impossible Solutions to Ethnic Conflict." *International Security* 20(4), pp. 136–175.

———. (1998). "When All Else Fails: Ethnic Population Transfers and Partitions in the Twentieth Century." *International Security* 23(2), pp. 129–156.

Kellerman, Aharon. (1996). "Settlement Myth and Settlement Activity: Interrelationships in the Zionist Land of Israel." *Transactions of the Institute of British Geographers*, New Series 21(2), pp. 363–378.

Kenny, Kevin, ed. (2004). *Ireland and the British Empire.* Oxford: Oxford University Press.

Kessler, Glenn, and Schneider, Howard. (2009). "U.S. Urges Israel to End Expansion." *Washington Post*, May 24.

Khadduri, Majid. (1969). *Republican Iraq*. Oxford: Oxford University Press.

Khorshid, Fuad H. (2005). *Kirkuk Qalb-e Kurdistan*. Suleymaniya: General Directorate for Printing and Publishing, Ministry of Culture, Kurdistan Regional Government. In Arabic.

Kibris. (2003). "Here Are the Young Persons in the Parliament." December 24.

Kibris TV. (2003). "Transcript of Didier Pfirter Interview with Suleyman Erguclu," March 20. Accessed January 19, 2005, from http://www.cyprusaction.org/projects/loizides/pfirter.php

Korf, Benedikt. (2005). "Rethinking the Greed-Grievance Nexus: Property Rights and the Political Economy of War in Sri Lanka." *Journal of Peace Research* 42(2), pp. 201–217.

Krautwurst, Udo. (2003). "What Is Settler Colonialism? An Anthropological Meditation on Frantz Fanon's "Concerning Violence." *History and Anthropology* 14(1), pp. 55–72.

Kymlicka, Will. (1995). *Multicultural Citizenship: A Liberal Theory of Minority Rights*. Oxford: Clarendon Press.

———. (2007a). *Multicultural Odysseys: Navigating the New International Politics of Diversity*. Oxford: Oxford University Press.

———. (2007b). "National Cultural Autonomy and International Minority Rights Norms." *Ethnopolitics* 6(3), pp. 379–393.

Labanca, Nicola. (2002a). *Oltremare: storia dell'espansione coloniale italiana*. Bologna: Il Mulino.

Labanca, Nicola, ed. (2002b). *Un nodo: immagini e documenti sulla repressione coloniale italiana in Libia*. Manduria: P. Lacaita.

Lacher, Hannes, and Kaymak, Erol. (2005). "Transforming Identities: Beyond the Politics of Non-Settlement in North Cyprus." *Mediterranean Politics* 10(2), pp. 147–166.

Laitin, David D. (1998). *Identity in Formation: The Russian-Speaking Populations in the Near Abroad*. Ithaca, NY: Cornell University Press.

———. (2004). "Ethnic Unmixing and Civil War." *Security Studies* 13(4), pp. 350–365.

———. (2009). "Immigrant Communities and Civil War." *International Migration Review* 43(1), pp. 35–59.

Leckie, Scott, ed. (2003). *Returning Home: Housing and Property Restitution Rights of Refugees and Displaced Persons*. Ardsley, NY: Transnational.

Levi Committee. (2012). *Report on the Legal Status of Building in Judea and Samaria*. Jerusalem: Prime Minister Office.

Levi, Yagil. (2012). "Is the IDF Becoming Theocratic?" Working Paper Series, no. 20, Research Institute for Policy, Political Economy and Society, The Open University of Israel.

Levinson, Chaim. (2013). *Tahkir: Hairgun Shebone et Hama'achazim Habilti Huki'im*

Nechsaf [Investigative report: the organization that builds the illegal outposts exposed]. *Ha'aretz,* May 11. In Hebrew.

Levy, Brian. (1989). "Foreign Aid in the Making of Economic Policy in Sri Lanka, 1977–1983." *Policy Sciences* 22(3–4), pp. 437–461.

Lill, Rudolf. (1991). *Die Option der Südtiroler 1939: Beiträge eines Neustifter Symposions.* Bozen: Athesia.

Little, David. (1995)."Belief, Ethnicity, and Nationalism." *Nationalism and Ethnic Politics* 1(2), pp. 284–301.

Lloyd, Grayson J. (2003). "The Diplomacy on East Timor: Indonesia, the United Nations and the International Community." In James J. Fox and Dionisio Babo Soares, eds., *Out of the Ashes: Destruction and Reconstruction of East Timor,* pp. 74–98. Canberra: Australian National University Press.

Loizides, Neophytos. (2011). "Contested Migration and Settler Politics in Cyprus." *Political Geography* 30(7), pp. 391–401.

Loizides, Neophytos, and Antoniades, Marcos A. (2009). "Negotiating the Right of Return." *Journal of Peace Research* 4(5), pp. 611–622.

Lustick, Ian S. (1985). *State-Building Failure in British Ireland and French Algeria.* Berkeley: University of California.

———. (1988). *For the Land and the Lord: Jewish Fundamentalism in Israel.* New York: Council of Foreign Relations.

———. (1993a). "Reinventing Jerusalem." *Foreign Policy* 93, pp. 41–59.

———. (1993b). *Unsettled States, Disputed Lands: Britain and Ireland, France and Algeria, Israel and the West Bank and Gaza.* Ithaca, NY: Cornell University Press.

———. (1997). "Has Israel Annexed East Jerusalem?" *Middle East Policy* 5(1), pp. 34–45.

———. (2005). "Settlers." Interview with Ian Lustick. By Gretchen Helfrich." *Odyssey,* Chicago Public Radio, April 13. Accessed from http://www.chicagopublicradio.org/audio_library/od_raapro5.asp

———. (2013). "What Counts Is Counting: Statistical Manipulation as a Solution to Israel's 'Demographic Problem.'" *Middle East Journal* 67(2), pp. 185–205.

Lynch, Gabrielle. (2011). *I Say to You: Ethnic Politics and the Kalenjin in Kenya.* Chicago: University of Chicago Press.

MacAndrews, Colin. (1978). "Transmigration in Indonesia: Prospects and Problems." *Asian Survey* 18(5), pp. 458–472.

Mahaweli Authority of Sri Lanka. (2009). *Statistical Handbook 2008.* Accessed from http://www.mahaweli.gov.lk

Manogaran, Chelvadurai. (1994). "Colonization as Politics." In Chelvadurai Manogaran and Bryan Pfaffenberger, eds., *The Sri Lankan Tamils: Ethnicity and Identity.* Boulder, CO: Westview Press.

———. (2000). *The Untold Story of Ancient Tamils in Sri Lanka.* Chennai, India: Kumaran.

Mazower, Mark. (2008). *Hitler's Empire: How the Nazis Ruled Europe.* New York: Penguin Press.

McGarry, John. (1998). "'Demographic Engineering': The State-Directed Movement of Ethnic Groups as a Technique of Conflict Regulation." *Ethnic and Racial Studies* 21(4), pp. 613–638.

McGilvray, Dennis B. (2008). *Crucible of Conflict: Tamil and Muslim Society on the East Coast of Sri Lanka*. Durham, NC: Duke University Press.

McGilvray, Dennis B., and Gamburd, M. R. (2010). *Tsunami Recovery in Sri Lanka: Ethnic and Regional Dimensions*. New York: Routledge.

Meyer, Eric. (1992). "From Landgrabbing to Landhunger: High Land Appropriation in the Plantation Areas of Sri Lanka during the British Period." *Modern Asian Studies* 26(2), pp. 321–361.

Migdal, Joel S. (2009). "Researching the State." In Mark I. Lichbach and Alan S. Zuckerman, eds., *Comparative Politics: Rationality, Culture and Structure,* 2nd ed., pp. 162–192. Cambridge: Cambridge University Press.

Ministry of Extra Regional Affairs. (2007). *Report on the Administrative Changes in Kirkuk and the Disputed Regions*. Erbil: Kurdistan Regional Government.

Mitchell, Thomas. (2002). *Indispensable Traitors: Liberal Parties in Settler Conflicts*. Westport, CT: Greenwood Press.

Mohammed, Simko B. (2005). *Mijoo-i serdemeh kargirî oo berweberiyekanî parêzga-i Kirkuk*. Kirkuk: Chapkhaney-i Shehid Azad Hawrami.

Moore, Mick. (1985). *The State and Peasant Politics in Sri Lanka*. New York: Cambridge University Press.

Moynihan, Daniel P., with Weaver, Suzanne. (1978). *A Dangerous Place*. Boston: Little, Brown.

Muggah, Robert (2008). *Relocation Failures in Sri Lanka: A Short History of Internal Displacement and Resettlement*. London: Zed Books.

Mundy, Jacob A. (2006). "Neutrality or Complicity? The United States and the 1975 Moroccan Takeover of the Spanish Sahara." *Journal of North African Studies* 11(3), pp. 275–306.

———. (2007). "Colonial Formations in Western Saharan National Identity." In Nabil Boudraa and Joseph Krause, eds., *North African Mosaic: A Cultural Reappraisal of Ethnic and Religious Minorities*. Newcastle: Cambridge Scholars.

———. (2011). "Western Sahara's 48 Hours of Rage." *Middle East Report* no. 257. Accessed from http://www.merip.org/mer/mer257/western-saharas-48-hours-rage

———. (2014). "Bringing the Tribe Back In? The Western Sahara Dispute, Ethno-History, and the Imagineering of Minority Conflicts in the Arab World." In Will Kymlicka and Eva Pföstl, eds., *Multiculturalism and Minority Rights in the Arab World*. New York: Oxford University Press.

Murphy, Alexander. (2002). "The Territorial Underpinnings of National Identity." *Geopolitics* 7(2), pp. 193–214.

Murphy, Jennifer M., and Omar, Sidi M. (2013). "Aesthetics of Resistance in Western Sahara." *Peace Review: A Journal of Social Justice* 25, pp. 349–358.

Mussolini, Benito. (1959). Edoardo and Duilio Susmel, eds., *Opera Omnia XXII*. Florence: La Fenice.

Mustafa, Nowsherwan. (2008). "Pirsi Kirkuk: Kurd legel Turkman çi bekat?" *Roj-nameh*, October 22.

Naor, Arye. (2001). *Eretz Yisrael Hashelema: Emunah u—Mediniyut* [Greater Israel: theology and policy]. Haifa: Haifa University Press. In Hebrew.

Natali, Denise. (2005). *The Kurds and the State: Evolving National Identity in Iraq, Turkey, and Iran*. Syracuse, NY: Syracuse University Press.

———. (2008). "The Kirkuk Conundrum." *Ethnopolitics* 7(4), pp. 433–443.

———. (2010). *The Kurdish Quasi-State: Development and Dependency in Post-Gulf War Iraq*. Syracuse, NY: Syracuse University Press.

National Joint Committee. (2001). *Report of the Sinhala Commission, Part II*. Colombo: Samayawardhana.

Navaro-Yashin, Yael. (2006). "De-Ethnicizing the Ethnography of Cyprus: Political and Social Conflict between Turkish Cypriots and Settlers from Turkey." In Yiannis Papadakis, Nicos Peristianis, and Gisela Welz, eds., *Divided Cyprus: Modernity, History, and an Island in Conflict*, pp. 84–100. Bloomington: Indiana University Press.

———. (2012). *The Make-Believe Space: Affective Geography in a Postwar Polity*. Durham, NC: Duke University Press.

Newman, David. (1985). "The Evolution of a Political Landscape: Geographical and Territorial Implications of Jewish Colonization of the West Bank." *Middle Eastern Studies* 21(2), pp. 192–205.

———. (2005). "From *Hitnachlut* to *Hitnatkut*: The Impact of Gush Emunim and the Settlement Movement on Israeli Politics and Society." *Israel Studies* 10(3), pp. 192–224.

Nithiyanandam, Nithi N., and Gounder, Rukmani. (2004). "Equals in Markets? Land Property Rights and Ethnicity in Fiji and Sri Lanka." In Stanley L. Engerman and Jacob Metzer eds., *Land Rights, Ethno-Nationality and Sovereignty in History*. New York: Routledge.

Noble, Kenneth. (1992). "New Dispute Roils Western Sahara: Who'll Vote?" *New York Times*, February 28.

Nuhman, M. A. (2007). *Sri Lankan Muslims: Ethnic Identity within Cultural Diversity*. Colombo: ICES.

Nützenadel, Alexander. (1997). *Landwirtschaft, Staat und Autarkie: Agrarpolitik im faschistischen Italien (1922–1943)*. Tübingen: Max Niemeyer.

O'Leary, Brendan. (2001). "The Elements of Right-Sizing and Right-Peopling the State." In Brendan O'Leary, Ian S. Lustick, and Thomas Callaghy, eds., *Right-Sizing the State: The Politics of Moving Borders*. Oxford: Oxford University Press.

O'Leary, Brendan, Lustick, Ian, and Callaghy, Thomas, eds. (2001). *Rightsizing the State: The Politics of Moving Borders*. New York: Oxford University Press.

Olson, Robert. (1992). "Battle for Kurdistan: The Church-Cox Correspondence Regarding the Creation of the State of Iraq, 1921–1923." *Kurdish Studies* 5(1–2), pp. 29–44.

Onea, Tudor. (2009). "Soaring Eagle: Prestige and American Empire, 1998–2003."

Thesis submitted to the Department of Political Science, Queen's University, Kingston.

Oren, Michael B. (2002). *Six Days of War: June 1967 and the Making of the Modern Middle East.* Oxford: Oxford University Press.

Østergaard-Nielsen, Eva. (2003). "The Democratic Deficit of Diaspora Politics: Turkish Cypriots in Britain and the Cyprus Issue." *Journal of Ethnic and Migration Studies* 29(4), pp. 683–700.

Ozolins, Uldis. (1999). "Between Russian and European Hegemony: Current Language Policy in the Baltic States." *Current Issues in Language & Society* 6(1), pp. 6–47.

Paisley, Fiona. (2003). "Introduction: White Settler Colonialisms and the Colonial Turn: An Australian Perspective" *Journal of Colonialism and Colonial History* 4(3, Special issue).

Palley, Claire. (2005). *An International Relations Debacle: The UN Secretary-General's Mission of Good Offices in Cyprus 1999–2004.* Oxford, UK: Hart.

Palloni, Alberto. (1979). "Internal Colonialism or Clientelistic Politics? The Case of Southern Italy." *Ethnic and Racial Studies* 2(3), pp. 360–377.

Parliament of the Commonwealth of Australia. (2000). *East Timor: Final Report of the Senate Foreign Affairs, Defence and Trade References Committee.* Canberra: Senate Printing Unit.

Parliamentary Assembly of the Council of Europe. (2003), "Recommendation 1608: Colonisation by Turkish Settlers of the Occupied Part of Cyprus." Accessed June 16, 2009, from http://assembly.coe.int/Documents/AdoptedText/TA03/EREC1608.htm

Patrick, Richard A. 1976. "Political Geography and the Cyprus Conflict, 1963–1971." Doctoral Dissertation. Department of Geography, Faculty of Environmental Studies, University of Waterloo.

Pazzanita, Anthony G. (2006). *Historical Dictionary of Western Sahara.* 3rd ed. Lanham, MD: Scarecrow Press.

Pearson, David. (2001). *The Politics of Ethnicity in Settler Societies: States of Unease.* London and New York: Palgrave Macmillan.

Pedersen, Jon, and Arneberg, Marie, eds. (1999). *Social and Economic Conditions in East Timor.* New York: International Conflict Resolution Program, School of International and Public Affairs, Columbia University, and Oslo: Fafo Institute of Applied Social Science.

Pedersen, Susan. (2005). "Settlers: Interview with Susan Pedersen." By Gretchen Helfrich, *Odyssey.* Chicago Public Radio, April 13. Accessed June 16, 2009, from http://www.chicagopublicradio.org/audio_library/od_raapro5.asp

Peebles, Patrick. (1990). "Colonization and Ethnic Conflict in the Dry Zone of Sri Lanka." *Journal of Asian Studies* 49(1), pp. 30–55.

———. (2001). *The Plantation Tamils of Ceylon.* London: Leicester University Press.

Peiris, Gerald H. (1991). "An Appraisal of the Concept of a Traditional Tamil Homeland in Sri Lanka." *Ethnic Studies Report* 9(1), pp. 13–39.

Pérez de Cuéllar, Javier. (1997). *Pilgrimage for Peace: A Secretary-General's Memoir.* New York: St. Martin's Press.

Peri, Yoram. (2006). *Generals in the Cabinet Room: How the Military Shapes Israeli Policy.* Washington, DC: United States Institute for Peace.

Podestà, Gian L. (2007). "L'émigration italienne en Afrique Orientale." *Annales de Demographie Historique* 1, pp. 59–84.

Pour, Julius. (1993). *Benny Moerdani: Profile of a Soldier Statement.* Jakarta: Yayasan Kejuangan Panglima Besar Sudiram.

Pressman, Jeremy. (2003). "Visions of Collision: What Happened at Camp David and Taba." *International Security* 28(2), pp. 5–43.

Prochaska, David. (1990). *Making Algeria French: Colonialism in Bône, 1870–1920.* New York: Cambridge University Press.

Quarante, Oliver. (2012). "Résistance obstinée des Sahraouis." *Le Monde Diplomatique*, no. 695, p. 18.

Quine, Maria-Sophia. (1996). *Population Politics in Twentieth-Century Europe: Fascist Dictatorships and Liberal Democracies.* New York: Routledge.

Raiffa, Howard, with John Richardson and David Metcalfe. (2002). *Negotiation Analysis: The Science and Art of Collaborative Decision Making.* Cambridge: Belknap Press of Harvard University Press.

Rajanayagam, Dagmar-Hellman. (1994). "Tamils and the Meaning of History." In Chelvadurai Manogaran and Bryan Pfaffenberger, eds., *The Sri Lankan Tamils: Ethnicity and Identity.* Boulder, CO: Westview Press.

Ravid, Barak. (2014). "In Policy Shift, Australia Declares East Jerusalem Is Not Occupied." *Haaretz*, June 5.

Republic of Indonesia. (1977). *Decolonization in East Timor.* Jakarta: Department of Information.

———. (1984). *East Timor Today.* Jakarta: Department of Information.

———. (1997). *Transmigration: A New Direction for Population Growth.* Jakarta: Department of Foreign Affairs.

Reyner, Anthony. (1963). "Morocco's International Boundaries: A Factual Background." *Journal of Modern African Studies* 1(3), 313–329.

Robert F. Kennedy Center for Justice and Human Rights. (2011). *Western Sahara: Accounts of Human Rights Abuses Persist in Wake of November Unrest.* Washington, DC: Robert F. Kennedy Center for Justice and Human Rights.

Ron, James. (2003). *Frontiers and Ghettos: State Violence in Serbia and Israel.* Berkeley: University of California Press.

Sahadevan, Ponmoni. (1995). *India and Overseas Indians: The Case of Sri Lanka.* Delhi: Kalinga.

Salerno, Eric. (1979). *Genocidio in Libia.* Milan: Sugar.

Samarasinghe, S.W.R. de A. (1988). "The Indian Tamil Plantation Workers in Sri Lanka: Welfare and Integration." In K. M. De Silva, Pensri Duke, Ellen S. Goldberg, and Nathan Katz, eds., *Ethnic Conflict in Buddhist Societies: Sri Lanka, Thailand, and Burma.* London: Pinter.

Sambanis, Nicholas. (2000). "Partition as a Solution to Ethnic War: An Empirical Critique of the Theoretical Literature." *World Politics* 52(4), pp. 437–483.

Sambanis, Nicholas, and Schulhofer-Wohl, Jonah. (2009). "What's in a Line? Is Partition a Solution to Civil War?" *International Security* 34(2), pp. 82–118.

San Martín, Pablo. (2010). *Western Sahara: The Refugee Nation.* Cardiff: University of Wales Press.

Sasson, Talia. (2005). *Havat Da'at Benose Ma'achazim Bilti Murshim* [Report on unauthorized outposts]. Jerusalem: Office of the Prime Minister. In Hebrew.

Sbacchi, Alberto. (1997). *Legacy of Bitterness: Ethiopia and Fascist Italy, 1935–1941.* Lawrenceville, NJ: Red Sea Press.

Schneider, Gabriele. (2000). *Mussolini in Afrika: die faschistische Rassenpolitik in den italienischen Kolonien, 1936–41.* Cologne: SH-Verlag.

Segrè, Claudio G. (1974). *Fourth Shore: The Italian Colonization of Libya.* Chicago: University of Chicago Press.

Shafir, Gershon, and Peled, Yoav. (2002). *Being Israeli: The Dynamics of Multiple Citizenship.* Cambridge: Cambridge University Press.

Shelef, Nadav G. (2010). *Evolving Nationalism: Homeland, Identity, and Religion in Israel, 1925–2005.* Ithaca, NY: Cornell University Press.

Shelley, Toby. (2004). *Endgame in the Western Sahara: What Future for Africa's Last Colony?* London and New York: Zed.

Sherlock, Stephen. (1996). "Political Economy of the East Timor Conflict." *Asian Survey* 36(9), pp. 835–851.

Shin, Leo K. (2006). *The Making of the Chinese State: Ethnicity and Expansion on the Ming Borderlands.* Cambridge: Cambridge University Press.

Shindler, Colin. (2009). "Opposing Partition: The Zionist Predicaments after the Shoah." *Israel Studies* 14(2), pp. 88–104.

Silbey, Joel H. (2005). *Storm over Texas: Annexation Controversy and the Road to the Civil War.* Oxford: Oxford University Press.

Singh, Bilveer. (1994). *ARBI and the Security of Southeast Asia: The Role and Thinking of General Benny Moerdani.* Singapore: Singapore Institute for International Affairs.

Sisk, Timothy. (2009). *International Mediation in Civil Wars: Bargaining with Bullets.* New York: Routledge.

Sitrampalam, S. K. (2007). "Nationalism, Historiography, and Archaeology in Sri Lanka." In R. Cheran, ed., *Writing Tamil Nationalism.* Colombo: ICES.

Skoutaris, Nikos. (2010). "Building Transitional Justice Mechanisms without a Peace Settlement: A Critical Appraisal of Recent Case Law of the Strasbourg Court on the Cyprus Issue." *European Law Review* 35(5), pp. 720–734.

Sluga, Glenda. (2001). *The Problem of Trieste and the Italo-Yugoslav Border: Difference, Identity, and Sovereignty in Twentieth-Century Europe.* Albany: State University of New York Press.

Smith, Anthony D. (2003). *Chosen Peoples.* Oxford: Oxford University Press.

Smith, Anthony L. (2000). *Strategic Centrality: Indonesia's Changing Role in ASEAN.* Singapore: Institute for South Asian Studies.

Smith, Helena. (2003). "Cyprus Bids for Unity—Again." *Guardian*, September 16.

Somasundaram, Daya. (2010). "Parallel Governments: Living between Terror and Counter Terror in Northern Lanka (1982–2009)." *Journal of Asian and African Studies* 45(5), pp. 568–583.

Sorensen, Brigitte R. (1996). *Relocated Lives: Displacement and Resettlement in the Mahaweli Project, Sri Lanka.* Amsterdam: VU University Press.

Sözen, Ahmet, and Özersay, Kudret. (2007). "The Annan Plan: State Succession or Continuity." *Middle Eastern Studies* 43(1), pp. 125–141.

Sprinzak, Ehud. (1985). "The Iceberg Model of Political Extremism." In David Newman, ed., *The Impact of Gush Emunim: Politics and Settlement in the West Bank*, pp. 27–45. London: Croom Helm.

Spruyt, Hendrik. (2005). *Ending Empire: Contested Sovereignty and Territorial Partition.* Ithaca, NY: Cornell University Press.

———. (2014). "Terrritorial Concessions, Domestic Politics and the Israeli-Palestinian Conflict." In Miriam F. Elman, Oded Haklai, and Hendrik Spruyt, eds., *Democracy and Conflict Resolution: The Dilemmas of Israel's Peacemaking*, pp. 29–66. Syracuse, NY: Syracuse University Press.

Sri Lanka Department of Census and Statistics. (2012). Sri Lanka Census of Population and Housing: Population and Housing Data. Population by Ethnic Group According to Districts (Provisional). Accessed from http://www.statistics.gov.lk/pophousat/cph2011/index.php?fileName=pop42&gp=Activities&tpl=3

Stampacchia, Mauro. (2000). *Ruralizzare l'Italia!: agricoltura e bonifiche tra Mussolini e Serpieri, 1928–1943.* Milan: F. Angeli.

Stave Tvinnereim, Helga (2007). *Agro Pontino: Urbanism and Regional Development in Lazio under Benito Mussolini.* Translated by Viviann Hansen Aarones. Oslo: Solum Forlag.

Stefanovic, Djordje, and Loizides, Neophytos. (2011). "The Way Home: Peaceful Return of Victims of Ethnic Cleansing." *Human Rights Quarterly* 33(3), pp. 408–443.

Steininger, Rolf. (2003). *South Tyrol: A Minority Conflict of the Twentieth Century.* New Brunswick, NJ: Transaction.

Stokke, Kristian, (1998). "Sinhalese and Tamil Nationalism as Post-Colonial Political Projects from 'Above,' 1948–1983." *Political Geography* 17(1), pp. 83–113.

Stoler, Ann L. (2006). "On Degrees of Imperial Sovereignty." *Public Culture* 18(1), pp. 125–146.

Storm, Lise. (2008). "Testing Morocco: The Parliamentary Elections of September 2007." *Journal of North African Studies* 13(1), pp. 37–54.

Strategic Studies Institute. (2013). *War and Insurgency in the Western Sahara.* Carlisle, PA: U.S. Army War College.

Şwani, S. (2007). "Alozi-ye rowşi Kirkuk u geran bedway-i hokar u çareserekirdinda." *Awene News*, September 25.

Talabany, Nouri. (2004). *Arabization of the Kirkuk Region.* Erbil: Aras Press.

———. (2006). "Kirkuk, Past and Present." *Kurdish Globe*, February 21.

———. (2007). "Who Owns Kirkuk? The Kurdish Case." *Middle East Quarterly* 14(1), pp. 75–78.

Tanter, Richard. (2001). "East Timor and the Crisis of the Indonesian Intelligence State." In Mark Selden and Stephen R. Shalom, eds., *Bitter Flowers, Sweet Flowers: East Timor, Indonesia, and the World Community.* Lanham, MD: Rowman and Littlefield.

Taub, Gadi (2011). *The Settlers and the Struggle over the Meaning of Zionism.* New Haven, CT: Yale University Press.

Taylor-Leech, Kerry. (2009). "The Language Situation in Timor-Leste." *Current Issues in Language Planning* 10(1), pp. 1–68.

Tezgor, Gokhan. (2003). "Settlers in the North: A Complex Mosaic of Identity." *Cyprus Mail*, June 17.

Theofilopoulou, Anna. (2006). *The United Nations and Western Sahara: A Never-Ending Affair.* Special Report 166. Washington, DC: United States Institute of Peace.

Thobhani, Akbarali. (2002). *Western Sahara since 1975 under Moroccan Administration: Social, Economic and Political Transformation.* Lewiston, NY: Edwin Mellen Press.

Thu, Pyone M. (2012). "Access to Land and Livelihood in Post-Conflict Timor-Leste." *Australian Geographer* 42(2), pp. 197–214.

Tirtosudarmo, Riwanto. (2000). "Demographic Engineering and National Integration: Past and Present Experience in Indonesia." *Masayarakat Indonesia* 26(1), pp. 85–97.

———. (2001). "Demography and Security: Transmigration Policy in Indonesia." In Myron Weiner and Sharon Stanton Russell, eds., *Demography and National Security*, pp. 199–227. New York: Bergham.

Toft, Monica D. (2002). "Indivisible Territory, Geographic Concentration, and Ethnic War." *Security Studies* 12(2), pp. 82–119.

Tolomei, Ettore. (1938). "Notiziario—vita e problemi." *Archivio per l'Alto Adige* 33(2).

TRNC Prime Ministry. (2007). *TRNC General Population and Housing Unit Census.* September. State Planning Organization. Accessed from http://nufussayimi.devplan.org/Census%202006.pdf

United Nations. (1967). United Nations Security Council Resolution 242. UN Doc. S/RES/242, November 22.

———. (1974). United Nations Security Council Resolution 361. UN Doc. S/RES/361, August 30.

———. (1979). United Nations Security Council Resolution 34/37. UN Doc. S/RES/34/37, November 21.

———. (1991). United Nations Security Council Resolution 23299. UN Doc. S/RES/23299, Annex I, para. 23, 29–31, December 19.

———. (2000). United Nations Security Council Resolution 131. UN Doc. S/RES/131, February 17.

———. (2001). United Nations Security Council Resolution 613, UN Doc. S/RES/613, Annex I, para. 5, June 20.

———. (2002). United Nations Security Council Resolution 161, UN Doc. S/RES/161, February 12.

———. (2003). United Nations Security Council Resolution 565, UN Doc. S/RES/565, Annex II, para. 5, May 23.

———. (2004). *The Comprehensive Settlement of the Cyprus Problem*, March 31.

———. (2013). United Nations Security Council Resolution 2099, UN Doc. S/Res/2099, April 25.

United Nations, Cartographic Section. (2007). Map A4-010, May 4.

United Nations General Assembly. (1977). *Report of the United Nations Visiting Mission to Spanish Sahara, 1975*. GAOR, 30th Sess., Suppl. No. 23, Vol. 3, Chap. XIII, A/10023/Add. 5. New York: United Nations.

United Nations High Commissioner for Refugees. (1997). "Geneva Convention Relative to the Protection of Civilian Persons in Time of War." Accessed May 5, 2009, from http://www.unhchr.ch/html/menu3/b/92.htm

United Nations Security Council. (2000). *Report of the Secretary-General on the Situation Concerning Western Sahara*. UN Doc. S/131, February 17.

———. (2003a). *Report of the Secretary-General on His Mission of Good Offices in Cyprus*. UN Doc. S/2003/398, April 1.

———. (2003b). *Report of the Secretary-General on the Situation Concerning Western Sahara*. UN Doc. S/565, May 23.

———. (2004). *Report of the Secretary-General on his Mission of Good Offices in Cyprus*. UN Doc. S/2004/43.

U.S. Department of State, Bureau of Democracy, Human Rights, and Labor. (2000). "Western Sahara." In *1999 Country Reports on Human Rights Practices*. Washington, DC: U.S. Department of State. Accessed from http://www.state.gov/j/drl/rls/hrrpt/1999/423.htm

———. (2003). "Western Sahara." In *2002 Country Reports on Human Rights Practices*. Washington, DC: U.S. Department of State. Accessed from http://www.state.gov/g/drl/rls/hrrpt/2002/18292.htm

———. (2004). "Western Sahara." In *2003 Country Reports on Human Rights Practices*. Washington, DC: U.S. Department of State. Accessed from http://www.state.gov/g/drl/rls/hrrpt/2003/27941.htm

———. (2008). "Western Sahara." In *2007 Country Reports on Human Rights Practices*. Washington, DC: U.S. Department of State. Accessed from http://www.state.gov/g/drl/rls/hrrpt/2007/102555.htm

Veracini, Lorenzo. (2010). *Settler Colonialism (a Theoretical Overview)*. London: Palgrave Macmillan.

Verdery, Katherine. (1979). "Internal Colonialism in Austria-Hungary." *Ethnic and Racial Studies* 2(3), pp. 378–399.

Vilar, Juan B. (1977). *El Sahara español: historia de una aventura colonial*. Madrid: Sedmay Ediciones.

Visintin, Maurizio. (2004). *La grande industria in Alto Adige tra le due guerre mondiali*. Trent: Museo Storico in Trento.

Waterbury, John. (1972). *North for the Trade: The Life and Times of a Berber Merchant.* Berkeley: University of California Press.

Waxman, Dov. (2014). "Identity Matters: The Oslo Peace Process and Israeli National Identity." In Miriam F. Elman, Oded Haklai, and Hendrik Spruyt, eds., *Democracy and Conflict Resolution: The Dilemmas of Israel's Peacemaking,* pp. 133–156. Syracuse, NY: Syracuse University Press.

Weinberg, Albert K. (1935). *Manifest Destiny: A Study of Nationalist Expansionism in American History.* Baltimore: The Johns Hopkins Press.

Weiner, Myron. (1978). *Sons of the Soil.* Princeton, NJ: Princeton University Press.

Weitzer, Ronald J. (1990). *Transforming Settler States: Communal Conflict and Internal Security in Northern Ireland and Zimbabwe.* Berkeley: University of California Press.

Wilson, Alice. (2013). "On the Margins of the Arab Spring." *Social Analysis* 57(2), pp. 81–98.

Wilson, Jeyaratnam A. (2000). *Sri Lankan Tamil Nationalism: Its Origins and Development in the Nineteenth and Twentieth Centuries.* London: Hurst.

———. (2003). "Sri Lanka: Ethnic Strife and the Politics of Space." In John Coakley, ed., *The Territorial Management of Ethnic Conflict.* London: Frank Cass.

Wimmer, Andreas. (2013). *Waves of War: Nationalism, State Formation, and Ethnic Exclusion in the Modern World.* Cambridge: Cambridge University Press.

Wolfe, Patrick. (2006). "Settler Colonialism and the Elimination of the Native." *Journal of Genocide Research* 8(4), pp. 387–409.

Wolff, Stefan. (2004). "Can Forced Population Transfers Resolve Self-Determination Conflicts? A European Perspective." *Journal of Contemporary European Studies* 12(1), pp. 11–29.

———. (2010). "The Path to Ending Ethnic Conflicts." Ted Global. Accessed May 19, 2013, from http://www.ted.com/talks/stefan_wolff_the_path_to_ending_ethnic_conflicts.html

Wood, Michael. (2005). *Official History in Modern Indonesia: New Order Perceptions and Controversies.* Leiden: Brill.

World Bank. (1988). *Indonesia: The Transmigration Program in Perspective.* Washington, DC: World Bank.

Wörsdörfer, Rolf. (2004). *Krisenherd Adria 1915–1955. Konstruktion und Artikulation des Nationalen im italienisch-jugoslawischen Grenzraum.* Paderborn: Schöningh.

Yesha Council. (2013). "About Yesha Council." In Hebrew. Accessed May 21, 2013, http://myesha.org.il/?CategoryID=167

Yesilada, Birol, and Sozen, Ahmet. (2002). "Negotiating a Resolution to the Cyprus Problem: Is Potential European Membership a Blessing or a Curse?" *International Negotiation* 7(2), pp. 261–285.

Yiftachel, Oren. (2001). "'Right-Sizing' or 'Right-Shaping'? Politics, Ethnicity, and Territory in Plural States." In Brendan O' Leary, Ian Lustick, and Thomas Callaghy, eds., *Right-Sizing the State: The Politics of Moving Borders.* New York: Oxford University Press.

Yiftachel, Oren, and Ghanem, As'ad. (2004). "Understanding 'Ethnocratic' Regimes: The Politics of Seizing Contested Territories." *Political Geography* 23(6), pp. 647–676.

Young, Louise. (1997). "Rethinking Race for Manchukuo: Self and Other in the Colonial Context." In F. Dikötter, ed., *The Construction of Racial Identities in China and Japan*. Honolulu: University of Hawai'i Press.

———. (1998). *Japan's Total Empire: Manchuria and the Culture of Wartime Imperialism*. Berkeley: University of California Press.

Zehr, Howard, and Mika, Harry. (1998). "Fundamental Concepts of Restorative Justice." *Contemporary Justice Review* 1(1), pp. 47–56.

Zertal, Idith, and Eldar, Akiva. (2007). *Lords of the Land: The War over Israel's Settlements in the Occupied Territories, 1967–2007*. New York: Nation Books.

Zunes, Stephen, and Mundy, Jacob A. (2010). *Western Sahara: War, Nationalism, and Conflict Irresolution*. Syracuse, NY: Syracuse University Press.

Index

Abyssinia, 85, 88, 89
Adali, Kutlu, 176–77
Akinci, Mustafa, 169
al-Sadr, Muqtada, 133
Alatas, Ali, 101
Algeria, 4, 36, 79, 174; French settlers of, 2, 6, 10, 160, 162, 175, 203–8; Italian emigrants in, 84; Polisario guerrillas in, 48, 197; refugee camps in, 45, 46, 52–53, 66
All Ceylon Tamil Congress (ACTC), 149
Allon, Yigal, 26–27, 30, 32, 194
Amana organization, 34–35, 37
Amazigh (Berber) movement, 57–59
Amnesty International, 72n4
Andreasson, Stefan, 12
Angola, 9
Annan, Kofi, 61–62; Cyprus peace plan of, 170, 173–74, 176–81, 185, 202
Arab Peace Initiative, 38n1
Ariel, Uri, 37
Ashraff, M.H.M., 154
Asquith, Herbert Henry, 206
Australia, 9, 14, 171; East Timor and, 100, 101, 107
Austro-Hungarian Empire, 76–78

Aviner, Shlomo, 39n9

Ba'athism, 119, 123–25, 199–200
Baker, James, 62–65
Balbo, Italo, 85, 88, 89
Balkan conflicts, 6, 159, 160, 170, 187–88
Baltic Republics, 2, 12–13, 15, 179
Bandaranaike, S.W.R.D., 148
Barak, Ehud, 37, 195
Barzani, Mustafa, 122, 125, 126, 129, 134
Barzinji, Mahmoud, 117
Basri, Driss, 49
Begin, Menachem, 194–95
Belo, Carlos, 110
Berbers, 57–59, 84
bonifica (amelioration) policy, 81–82
Bush, George W., 31, 38n1

Canada, 4, 9, 166n3
Ceylon Indian Congress (CIC), 148, 149
Ceylon Workers' Congress (CWC), 149, 159, 167n6
Cherkaoui, Mohamed, 66, 74n21
China, 160; Ming Dynasty of, 4, 5; Tibet and, 11, 160, 179
Christofias, Demetris, 188

Contributors

Ehud Eiran is a Martze (Assistant Professor) in the Department of International Relations, School of Political Science at the University of Haifa, Israel. Eiran holds degrees in law and political science from Tel-Aviv, Cambridge, and Brandeis Universities. He has held research appointments at Harvard Law School, Harvard's Kennedy School, and Brandeis University and was a lecturer in the Department of Political Science at MIT. Dr. Eiran has published in scholarly and popular outlets including the *Harvard Negotiation Law Review*, the *New York Times* online, *Foreign Affairs* online, and *Newsweek*. He is interested in theoretical and practical aspects of international conflict and conflict resolution, with a particular interest in the Arab-Israeli conflict.

Oded Haklai is Associate Professor in the Department of Political Studies at Queen's University in Kingston, Ontario. He is the author of *Palestinian Ethnonationalism in Israel*, which was awarded the Shapiro Prize by the Association for Israel Studies, as well as numerous articles and chapters on the Middle East and ethnic conflict. He is also the co-editor of *Democracy and Conflict Resolution: The Dilemmas of Israel's Peacemaking* (with M. Elman and H. Spruyt) and *Democratization and Ethnic Minorities: Conflict or Accommodation* (with J. Bertand).

Evangelos Liaras is a García Pelayo Research Fellow at the Centro de Estudios Políticos y Constitucionales (CEPC) in Madrid. He holds a BA degree in history from Harvard University and MS and PhD degrees in political science from MIT, and worked as an elections observer in Sri Lanka in 2010. His doctoral dissertation on electoral engineering in multi-ethnic societies was awarded the Juan Linz Prize for Best Dissertation by the Comparative Democratization Section of the American Political Science Association.

Neophytos Loizides is a Reader in International Conflict Analysis at the University of Kent and a British Academy Mid-Career Fellow (2014–2015). He is the author of *The Politics of Majority Nationalism: Framing Peace, Stalemates and Crises,* forthcoming from Stanford University Press. He has previously held fellowships at the Belfer Center at Harvard University and the Solomon Asch Center at the University of Pennsylvania. Dr. Loizides is currently the associate editor of *Nationalism and Ethnic Politics,* and a Leverhulme Trust Research Fellow (2015–2016).

Ian S. Lustick is the Bess W. Heyman Professor in the Political Science Department of the University of Pennsylvania, specializing in comparative politics, international politics, and social science applications of agent-based modeling computer simulations. Among his scholarly works are *For the Land and the Lord: Jewish Fundamentalism in Israel* (1988); *Unsettled States, Disputed Lands: Britain and Ireland, France and Algeria, Israel and the West Bank/Gaza* (1993); *Trapped in the War on Terror* (2006); and *Exile and Return: Predicaments of Palestinians and Jews* (2005), edited with Ann Lesch.

Jacob Mundy is an Assistant Professor of Peace and Conflict Studies at Colgate University, where he also contributes to Middle East and African studies. He is the co-author with Stephen Zunes of *Western Sahara: War, Nationalism, and Conflict Irresolution* (Syracuse University Press, 2010) and the co-editor of *The Post-Conflict Environment* (University of Michigan Press, 2014). His next book, *Imaginative Geographies of Algerian Violence,* will be published by Syracuse University Press in 2015.

Denise Natali is a Senior Research Fellow at the Institute for National Strategic Studies (INSS) at the National Defense University in Washington, DC, where she specializes in the Middle East, the trans-border Kurdish issue, regional energy security, and post-conflict state-building. Dr. Natali has spent more than two decades researching and working in the Kurdish regions of Iraq, Turkey, Iran, and Syria, and has authored numerous publications on Kurdish politics, economy, and energy, including *The Kurdish Quasi-State: Development and Dependency in Post-Gulf War Iraq* (Syracuse University

Press, 2010) and *The Kurds and the State: Evolving National Identity in Iraq, Turkey, and Iran* (Syracuse University Press, 2005), which was the recipient of the 2006 Choice Award for Outstanding Academic Title (published in Turkish as *Kurtler ve Devlet: Iraq, Turkiye ve Iran'da Ulusal Kimligin Gelismesi* [Istanbul: Avesta Press, 2009]). She provides regular commentary for national and international media, is a member of the International Institute for Strategic Studies, and a columnist for Al-Monitor.

Roberta Pergher is an Assistant Professor at Indiana University. After earning her PhD in history from the University of Michigan in 2007, she was a Max Weber Fellow at the European University Institute in Florence and an Elizabeth and J. Richardson Dilworth Fellow in the School of Historical Studies at the Institute for Advanced Study in Princeton. She has published widely on Italian fascism and on settlement policy. Her co-edited volume (with Giulia Albanese), *In the Society of Fascists: Acclamation, Acquiescence, and Agency in Mussolini's Italy*, was published by Palgrave Macmillan in 2012. She is currently completing a book manuscript, *Fascist Borderlands: Nation, Empire and Italy's Settlement Program, 1922–1943*, which explores Fascist efforts at nation- and empire-building in newly conquered territories.

Stephen Zunes is a Professor of Politics and Program Director for Middle Eastern Studies at the University of San Francisco. He is the co-author with Jacob Mundy of *Western Sahara: War, Nationalism, and Conflict Irresolution*, as well as the author of other books and articles addressing North African and Middle Eastern politics, U.S. foreign policy, human rights, and strategic nonviolent action. He serves as a senior policy analyst for the Foreign Policy in Focus project of the Institute for Policy Studies, an associate editor of *Peace Review*, a contributing editor of *Tikkun*, and chair of the academic advisory committee for the International Center on Nonviolent Conflict.

The authorized representative in the EU for product safety and compliance is:
Mare Nostrum Group
B.V Doelen 72
4831 GR Breda
The Netherlands

www.ingramcontent.com/pod-product-compliance
Lightning Source LLC
Chambersburg PA
CBHW030400270326
41926CB00009B/1200